EXPERT RESUMES™ FOR

SECOND EDITION

TEACHERS AND EDUCATORS

Wendy S. Enelow and Louise M. Kursmark

jist Works®

America's Career Publisher

Expert Resumes for Teachers and Educators, Second Edition

© 2005 by Wendy S. Enelow and Louise M. Kursmark

Published by JIST Works, an imprint of JIST Publishing, Inc.
8902 Otis Avenue
Indianapolis, IN 46216-1033
Phone: 1-800-648-JIST   Fax: 1-800-JIST-FAX   E-mail: info@jist.com

Visit our Web site at **www.jist.com** for information on JIST, free job search tips, book chapters, and how to order our many products! For free information on 14,000 job titles, visit **www.careeroink.com**.

Quantity discounts are available for JIST books. Please call our Sales Department at 1-800-648-5478 for a free catalog and more information.

Acquisitions and Development Editor: Lori Cates Hand
Cover Designer: designLab, Seattle
Interior Designer and Page Layout: Trudy Coler
Proofreader: Jeanne Clark
Indexer: Henthorne House

Printed in the United States of America
10 09 08 07 06 05   9 8 7 6 5 4 3 2

Library of Congress Cataloging-in-Publication Data

Enelow, Wendy S.
    Expert resumes for teachers and educators / Wendy S. Enelow and Louise M. Kursmark.--
    2nd ed.
        p. cm.
    Includes index.
    ISBN 1-59357-126-7 (alk. paper)
    1. Teachers--Employment. 2. Educators--Employment. 3. Résumés (Employment)
        4. Cover letters. I. Kursmark, Louise. II. Title.
    LB1780.E64 2005
    808'.06665--dc22   2004029863

We have been careful to provide accurate information in this book, but it is possible that errors and omissions have been introduced. Please consider this in making any career plans or other important decisions. Trust your own judgment above all else and in all things.

Trademarks: All brand names and product names used in this book are trade names, service marks, trademarks, or registered trademarks of their respective owners.

ISBN 1-59357-126-7

TABLE OF CONTENTS

ABOUT THIS BOOK

The "business" of education and its related careers and professions is showing strong and steady growth, according to the U.S. Department of Labor's projections. Experts anticipate that this growth will continue through at least 2008.

The business of education has changed. When we talk about education professionals, we're no longer referring to just classroom teachers and principals. The specializations and subspecializations of the education profession have grown phenomenally and now include the following:

- Pre-school, elementary, secondary, special education/remedial, gifted and talented, college and university, and proprietary school teachers

- School-based counselors, therapists, psychologists, social workers, and child advocates

- Librarians, multimedia specialists, and research assistants

- School administrators, assistant principals, principals, college and university deans, and department chairpersons

- Education support professionals, including coaches, security officers, DARE officers, secretaries, clerks, and transportation staff

- Corporate training and development professionals, instructional technology designers, multimedia training developers, "stand-up" trainers, and training consultants

And the list continues. As an educator, you no longer have to look to the school system for employment opportunities. There is now a wealth of for-profit training companies, tens of thousands of companies that employ training professionals, and unlimited opportunities as a self-employed trainer and coach. There are thousands and thousands of positions with the more traditional school-based systems, colleges, and universities. What this means is that there are unlimited employment opportunities, and that's great news for you!

To take advantage of all of these opportunities, you must first develop a powerful, performance-based resume. To be a savvy and successful job seeker, you must know how to communicate your qualifications in a strong and effective written presentation. Sure, it's important to let employers know essential details, but a resume is more than just your job history and academic credentials. A winning resume is a concise yet comprehensive document that gives you a competitive edge in the job market. Creating such a powerful document is what this book is all about.

As we move through this book, we'll explore the changes in resume writing and presentation that have arisen over the past decade. Today's resumes are achievement- and success-focused, highlighting your individual skills, qualifications, and strong work experience. Whereas previously resumes were almost always printed on paper and mailed, e-mail has become the chosen method for resume distribution in many industries today. In turn, many of the traditional methods for "typing" and presenting resumes have changed dramatically. This book will instruct you in the methods for preparing resumes for e-mail, scanning, and Web site posting, as well as the traditional printed resume.

By using *Expert Resumes for Teachers and Educators* as your professional guide, you will succeed in developing a powerful and effective resume that opens doors, gets interviews, and helps you land your next great opportunity!

INTRODUCTION

According to the U.S. Department of Labor's Bureau of Labor Statistics, the education professions are projected to show relatively strong and steady growth through 2008. Some of the most interesting statistics anticipate growth for the following specializations within the field of education:

Specialization	Percentage of Growth Through 2008
School Health Professionals	36.9%
Special Education Teachers	33.7%
School Counselors, Secondary School Teachers, and College Faculty	22.6%
Administrative Support Personnel	19.9%
Pre-School, Kindergarten, and Elementary School Teachers	11.5%
Education Administrators	11.5%
Librarians and Vocational Education Instructors	11.5%

These statistics and others clearly demonstrate that there is tremendous opportunity within the education professions. Not only is the number of positions increasing year after year, salaries are also moving upward, although at a somewhat slower rate of increase than the position growth rate.

The dramatic and rapid emergence of technology throughout all aspects of our lives has also impacted the field of education with a host of new professional opportunities.

To take advantage of these opportunities, you must be an educated job seeker. That means you must know what you want in your career, where the hiring action is, what qualifications and credentials you need to attain your desired career goals, and how best to market your qualifications. It is no longer enough to be a talented teacher, librarian, administrator, or training and development professional. Now, you must be a strategic marketer, able to package and promote your experience to take advantage of this wave of employment opportunity!

There's no doubt that the employment market has changed dramatically from only a few years ago. According to the U.S. Department of Labor, you should expect to hold between 10 and 20 different jobs during your career. No longer is stability the status quo. Today, the norm is movement, onward and upward, in a fast-paced and intense employment market. And to stay on top of all the changes and opportunities, you must proactively control and manage your career.

Education Job Search Questions and Answers

Whether you're currently employed in the education field or looking to enter the profession for the first time, here's some practical advice.

How Do You Enter the Education Profession?

As with any other industry or profession, your employment experience, education, and credentials are the keys to entry and long-term success. It is difficult to obtain a position in education without some related work experience, relevant education, or credentials. Here are a few pointers:

- **If you're just starting to plan and build your career,** consider a four-year degree in an education-related discipline or completion of a teaching certification program. Once you've earned your initial degree, you'll want to keep your sights focused on an advanced degree. Education is one of many professions where master's and doctoral degrees are virtually prerequisites for long-term career advancement.

- **If you're an educator, administrator, or other school-based professional** who wants to move forward in your career to a position of greater responsibility, leadership, and compensation, focus your resume on what you have achieved thus far in your career, your specific areas of expertise, your professional credentials, and most significantly, why you are a valuable resource.

- **If you're a classroom teacher or school administrator who wants to make a move into corporate training and development,** sell your knowledge and experience in order to "connect" yourself to T&D. Highlight the programs and courses you've designed, the instructional materials you've created, the training you've provided to other educational professionals, and more. Make the case that you're not an outsider, but rather an insider who has experience in organizational needs assessment, training, program design, and presentation. Link yourself to the new industry.

- **If you're a successful businessperson, technologist, manager, administrator, or the like,** but have no teaching or educational experience, focus your resume on your professional experiences and how they relate to the field of education. Who better to teach a business-management course than a business manager? Who better to manage the finances of a school board than an experienced CFO? Search your background and highlight the "right" skills to position yourself to transition into an education-related career.

WHAT IS THE BEST RESUME STRATEGY IF YOU'RE ALREADY IN THE EDUCATION PROFESSION?

If you're already employed in the education field but are interested in moving onward and upward, remember one critical fact:

>Your resume is a marketing tool written to sell YOU!

If you're a classroom teacher, *sell* the fact that you've been instrumental in developing new course curricula and designing innovative instructional tools. If you're a school administrator, *sell* the new initiatives you've introduced to strengthen educational standards and build support throughout your local community. If you're a corporate training specialist, *sell* the fact that you conceived, developed, and led the corporation's first-ever multimedia training presentations.

When writing your resume, your challenge is to create a picture of knowledge, action, and results. In essence, you're stating "This is what I know, this is how I've used it, and this is how well I've performed." Success sells, so be sure to highlight yours. If you don't, no one else will.

WHERE ARE THE JOBS?

The jobs are everywhere—from major universities to small rural school districts; from government education lobbies to high school libraries; from the corporate giants of the world to the local instructional technology company. The jobs are in

- **Classroom teaching,** at all levels and in all types of early-childhood, primary, secondary, and advanced educational institutions, both public and private.

- **Development** of new educational and instructional systems, methodologies, and protocols.

- **Design** of new courses, new curricula, new instructional materials, and other new teaching and learning resources.

- **Administration, funding, and management** of educational programs, systems, and facilities.

- **Educational support** professions (for example, librarians, coaches, teaching aides, and school counselors).

- **Design, engineering, marketing, and support** of instructional technologies, applications, and tools.

- **Educational research, funding, and outreach** for both public and private research facilities, universities, and foundations.

- **Design and delivery** of corporate training and development programs.

In short, the jobs are everywhere.

HOW DO YOU GET THE JOBS?

To answer this question, we need to review the basic principle underlying job search:

>Job search is marketing!

You have a product to sell—yourself—and the best way to sell it is to use all appropriate *marketing channels* just as you would for any other product.

Suppose you wanted to sell televisions. What would you do? You'd market your products using newspaper, magazine, and radio advertisements. You might develop a company Web site to build your e-business, and perhaps you'd hire a field sales representative to market to major retail chains. Each of these is a different *marketing channel* through which you're attempting to reach your audience.

The same is true for job search. You must use every marketing channel that's right for you. Unfortunately, there is no single formula. What's right for you depends on your specific career objectives—type of position, type of industry, geographic restrictions, salary requirements, and more.

Following are the most valuable marketing channels for a successful job search within the education industry. We've ranked them in order from most effective to least effective.

1. **Referrals.** There is nothing better than a personal referral to a school, company, or institution, either in general or for a specific position. Referrals can open doors that, in most instances, would never be accessible any other way. If you know anyone who could possibly refer you to a specific organization, contact that person immediately and ask for assistance.

2. **Networking.** Networking is the backbone of every successful job search. Although you may consider it a task, it is essential that you network effectively with your professional colleagues and associates, past employers, past coworkers, parents of past students, neighbors, community leaders, and others who may know of opportunities that are right for you. Another good strategy is to attend meetings of professional associations in your area to make new contacts and expand your professional network. And particularly in today's nomadic job market—where you're likely to change jobs every few years—the best strategy is to keep your network "alive" even when you're *not* searching for a new position.

3. **Responses to newspaper, magazine, and periodical advertisements.** Although, as you'll read below, the ability to post job opportunities online has reduced the overall number of print advertisements, they still abound. Do not forget about this "tried and true" marketing strategy. If they've got the job and you have the qualifications, it's a perfect fit.

4. **Responses to online job postings.** One of the greatest advantages of the technology revolution is an employer's ability to post job announcements and a job seeker's ability to respond immediately via e-mail. It's a wonder! In most (but not all) instances, these are bona fide opportunities, and it's well worth your while to spend time searching for and responding to appropriate postings. However, don't make the mistake of devoting *too* much time to searching the Internet. It can consume a huge amount of your time that you should spend on other job search efforts.

   To expedite your search, here are some of the largest and most widely used online job posting sites—presented alphabetically, not necessarily in order of effectiveness or value (see the appendix for a more complete listing of job search Web sites, including several that are specifically targeted to education professionals):

www.careerbuilder.com

www.monster.com

www.dice.com

www.sixfigurejobs.com

www.flipdog.monster.com

www.wantedtechnologies.com

www.hotjobs.yahoo.com

5. **Targeted e-mail campaigns (resumes and cover letters) to recruiters.** Recruiters have jobs, and you want one. It's pretty straightforward. The only catch is to find the "right" recruiters who have the "right" jobs. Therefore, you must devote the time and effort to prepare the "right" list of recruiters. There are many resources on the Internet where you can access information about recruiters (for a fee), sort that information by industry (education, training and development, software development, and so on), and then cross-reference with position specialization (teaching, training, administration, library services, and so on). This allows you to identify just the "right" recruiters who would be interested in a candidate with your qualifications. Because these campaigns are transmitted electronically, they are easy and inexpensive to produce.

When working with recruiters, it's important to realize that they *do not* work for you! Their clients are the hiring companies that pay their fees. They are not in business to "find a job" for you, but rather to fill a specific position with a qualified candidate, either you or someone else. To maximize your chances of finding a position through a recruiter or agency, don't rely on just one or two recruiters, but distribute your resume to many that meet your specific criteria.

6. **Online resume postings.** The Net is swarming with reasonably priced (if not free) Web sites where you can post your resume. It's quick, easy, and the only *passive* thing you can do in your search. All of the other marketing channels require action on your part. With online resume postings, once you've posted, you're done. You then just wait (and hope!) for some response.

7. **Targeted e-mail and print campaigns to employers.** Just as with campaigns to recruiters (see item 5 above), you must be extremely careful to select just the right employers that would be interested in a candidate with your qualifications. The closer you stick to "where you belong" in relation to your specific experience, the better your response rate will be. If you are targeting technology companies, you can also contact these employers via e-mail. If you are looking at employers outside the technology industries, which is extremely likely for most education professionals, we believe that print campaigns (paper and envelopes mailed the old-fashioned way) are a more suitable and effective presentation—particularly if you are a management or executive candidate.

8. **In-person "cold calls" to companies and recruiters.** We consider this the least effective and most time-consuming marketing strategy for education jobs. It is extremely difficult to just walk in the door and get in front of the right person, or any person who can take hiring action. You'll be much better off focusing your time and energy on other, more productive channels.

Conclusion

Career opportunities abound within the education industries and professions today. It has never been easier to learn about and apply for jobs. Arm yourself with a powerful resume and cover letter, identify the most appropriate marketing channels, and start your search today. You're destined to reach the next rung on your career ladder.

PART I

Resume Writing, Strategy, and Formats

Resume Writing Strategies for Education Professionals

If you're reading this book, chances are you've decided to make a career move. It may be because of one of the following reasons:

- You're graduating from college or a certification program and are ready to launch your professional career.

- You've just earned your graduate degree and are ready to make a step upward in your career.

- You're ready to leave your current position and move up the ladder to a higher-paying and more responsible position.

- You've decided on a career change and will be looking at opportunities in allied professions and industries.

- You're unhappy with your current school or employer, or its management/administrative team, and have decided to pursue opportunities elsewhere.

- You've been laid off, downsized, or otherwise left your position and must find a new one.

- You've completed a contract assignment and are looking for a new "free agent" job or perhaps a permanent position.

- You're relocating to a new area and need to find a new job.

- You're returning to the work force after several years of unemployment or retirement.

- You're simply ready for a change.

No matter the reason for your current job search, a powerful resume is an essential component of your campaign. In fact, it is virtually impossible to conduct a search without a resume. It is your calling card that briefly, yet powerfully, communicates the skills, qualifications, experience, and value you bring to a prospective employer. It is the document that will open doors and generate interviews. It is the first thing people will learn about you when you forward it in response to an advertisement, and it is the thing they'll remember when they're reviewing your qualifications after an interview.

Your resume is a sales document, and you are the product! You must identify the *features (what you know* and *what you can do)* and *benefits (how you can help an employer)* of that product, and then communicate them in a concise and hard-hitting written presentation. Remind yourself over and over as you work your way through the resume process that you are writing marketing literature designed to sell a new product—*you*—into a new position.

Your resume can have tremendous power and a phenomenal impact on your job search. Don't take it lightly. Rather, devote the time, energy, and resources that are essential to developing a resume that is well-written, visually attractive, and effective in communicating *who* you are and *how* you want to be perceived.

The Most Critical Question: Resume or CV?

As an education professional, you have to ask yourself one critical question before you even begin to think about writing a single word of your resume:

> Do you need a resume or do you need a curriculum vitae (CV)?

As we've discussed, a resume is a sales and marketing tool that is designed to entice a prospective employer to call you for an interview. It is a teaser, giving just enough information to establish you as a credible candidate. A resume focuses on the highlights of your career, your most notable achievements and contributions, your educational credentials, and more. Succinctly stated, it is your own personal career advertisement. It's usually one to two pages long, but if you've been in the work force for a long time and have extensive accomplishments, it is sometimes acceptable to use three pages.

A CV, on the other hand, is a less "aggressive" document. Obviously, just as with a resume, your objective is to sell yourself into a new position. However, the sell is more subtle, using your educational credentials, professional and teaching experience, research experience, publications, task forces, committees, and more to establish yourself as a qualified candidate. CVs, by their nature, tend to be longer than most resumes, anywhere from two to three pages to as many as 10 or more. Length should *not* be a consideration when preparing a CV; rather, your focus should be on preparing a comprehensive document that includes all of your qualifications and credentials.

As you look through all of the samples in chapters 4 through 12, you will note a dramatic difference in tone and style between resumes and CVs. However, for the purpose of this book, when we refer to resumes, we are, unless otherwise noted, also referring to CVs.

If you're uncertain about whether to write a resume or a CV, the following table may guide your decision-making. However, there are no hard-and-fast rules, and resume writing is an art, not a science. Each decision is made based on the qualifications and experience of each candidate and that individual's current career goals.

Profession	CV	Resume
Classroom teacher		X
College or university professor	X	X
Educational researcher/scientist	X	X
School administrator	X	X
College or university administrator	X	X
Guidance counselor		X
School psychologist	X	X
Librarian/media specialist		X
Corporate training professional		X

In deciding which format to use, consider the following:

- What is most accepted for your profession and the organizations you're targeting?

- Which format will best represent you and your qualifications?

- What will your competitors (those also vying for the position) use?

To add to the confusion, people in traditional CV fields such as medicine, law, and academia often use the term "CV" when referring to what is in fact a resume! We suggest you review the samples in chapters 4 through 12 and research your target institutions to find out the preferred format for your specific circumstances.

Resume Strategies

Following are the nine core strategies for writing effective and successful resumes.

RESUME STRATEGY #1: WHO ARE YOU AND HOW DO YOU WANT TO BE PERCEIVED?

Now that you've decided to look for a new position, the very first step is to identify your career interests, goals, and objectives. *This task is critical,* because it is the underlying foundation for *what* you will include in your resume, *how* you will include it, and *where* you will include it. You cannot write an effective resume without knowing, at least to some degree, what type or types of positions you will be seeking.

There are two concepts to consider here:

- **Who you are:** This relates to what you have done professionally and/or academically. Are you a teacher, school administrator, librarian, or corporate trainer? Are you an instructional media designer, curriculum developer, or education grant writer? Are you a recent graduate with a degree in elementary education, or do you have a master's in education administration? Who are you?

- **How you want to be perceived:** This relates to your current career objectives. If you're a teacher looking for a position as a departmental chairperson, don't focus solely on your teaching skills. Put an equal emphasis on curricula and instructional materials you've designed, training of other educators, your public speaking and association leadership experience, and the like. If you're an administrator for a for-profit educational services company interested in a university administration position, highlight your experience in funding, program development, records management, grant writing, and other functions directly related to the administration of teaching programs and educational facilities.

The strategy, then, is to connect these two concepts by using the *who you are* information that ties directly to the *how you want to be perceived* message to determine what information to include in your resume. By following this strategy, you're painting a picture that allows a prospective employer to see you as you wish to be seen—as an individual with the qualifications for the type of position you are pursuing.

> **WARNING:** If you prepare a resume without first clearly identifying what your objectives are and how you want to be perceived, your resume will have no focus and no direction. Without the underlying knowledge of "This is what I want to be," you do not know what to highlight in your resume. In turn, the document becomes a historical overview of your career and not the sales document it is designed to be.

RESUME STRATEGY #2: Sell It to Me...Don't Tell It to Me

We've already established the fact that resume writing is sales. You are the product, and you must create a document that powerfully communicates the value of that product. One particularly effective strategy for accomplishing this is the "Sell It to Me...Don't Tell It to Me" strategy, which impacts virtually every single word you write on your resume.

If you "tell it," you are simply stating facts. If you "sell it," you promote it, advertise it, and draw attention to it. Look at the difference in impact between these examples:

Tell It Strategy: Participated in the development of a new curriculum for the English department.

Sell It Strategy: Appointed to 3-person team charged with developing a new English curriculum for 2,000+ students, and for designing and producing all supporting instructional materials.

Tell It Strategy: Responsible for $28 million annual operating budget for a 200,000-student school district.

Sell It Strategy: Managed $28 million annual operating budget for 200,000-student school district. Closed FY 03–04 10% under budget by renegotiating services contracts, repairing used equipment, and eliminating excess expenditures.

Tell It Strategy: Served as a Multimedia Specialist for students in grades 7–9.

Sell It Strategy: Designed and produced a host of multimedia presentations to enrich student learning experiences and heighten retention for an at-risk middle-school population.

What's the difference between "telling it" and "selling it"? In a nutshell...

Telling It	*Selling It*
Describes features.	Describes benefits.
Tells what and how.	Sells why the "what" and "how" are important.
Details activities.	Includes results.
Focuses on what you did.	Details how what you did benefited your employer, department, team members, students, and so on.

RESUME STRATEGY #3: USE KEYWORDS

No matter what you read or who you talk to about job search, the concept of keywords is sure to come up. Keywords (or, as they were previously known, buzzwords) are words and phrases specific to a particular industry or profession. For example, keywords for education include *accreditation, classroom teaching, course design, instructional media, peer counseling, research, scholastic standards, standardized testing, student services, textbook review,* and many, many more.

When you use these words and phrases—in your resume, in your cover letter, or during an interview—you are communicating a very specific message. For example, when you include the words *"school administration"* in your resume, your reader will most likely assume that you have experience in budgeting, staffing, teacher training, facilities management, community outreach, emergency response, reporting and documentation, and more. As you can see, people will make inferences about your skills based on the use of just one or two individual words.

Here are a few other examples:

- When you use the words **multimedia instructional technology,** people will assume you have experience with programming, CD-ROM, graphic interfacing, the Internet, and more.

- When you mention **lifelong learning,** readers and listeners will infer that you have experience in the design and delivery of educational programs for children and adults throughout all phases of the growth, development, and aging lifecycle.

- By referencing **intercollegiate athletics** in your resume, you convey that you most likely have experience in coaching, competitive athletics, game-play strategy, scheduling, equipment management, and team leadership.

- When you use the term **alumni relations,** most people will assume that you are familiar with alumni communications, fund raising, marketing, event planning, and more.

Keywords are also an integral component of the resume scanning process, whereby employers and recruiters electronically search resumes for specific terms to find candidates with the skills, qualifications, and credentials for their particular hiring needs. Although resume scanning is not nearly as prevalent in education as in other industries, particularly technology-related industries and large corporations with significant hiring activity, it is increasing in popularity because of its ease and efficiency.

In organizations where it has been implemented, electronic scanning has replaced the more traditional method of an actual person reading your resume (at least initially). Therefore, to some degree, the *only* thing that matters in this instance is that you have included the "right" keywords to match the school's, company's, or recruiter's needs. Without them, you will most certainly be passed over.

Of course, in virtually every instance your resume will be read at some point by human eyes, so it's not enough just to throw together a list of keywords and leave it at that. In fact, it's not even necessary to include a separate paragraph called a "Keyword Summary" on your resume. A better strategy is to incorporate keywords naturally into the text within the appropriate sections of your resume.

Keep in mind, too, that keywords are arbitrary; there is no defined set of keywords for a classroom teacher, university professor, corporate trainer, librarian, or educational services administrator. Employers searching to fill these positions develop a list of terms that reflect the specifics they desire in a qualified candidate. These might be a combination of professional qualifications, skills, education, length of experience, and other easily defined criteria, along with "soft skills," such as leadership, problem-solving, and communication.

> **NOTE:** Because of the complex and arbitrary nature of keyword selection, we cannot overemphasize how vital it is to be certain that *all* of the keywords that represent your experience and knowledge are included in your resume!

How can you be sure that you are including all the keywords and the right keywords? Just by describing your work experience, achievements, credentials, publications, public speaking engagements, and the like, you will naturally include most of the terms that are important in your field. To cross-check what you've written, review online or print job postings for positions that are of interest to you. Look at the precise terms used in the ads and be sure you have included them in your resume (as appropriate to your skills and qualifications).

Another great benefit of today's technology revolution is our ability to find instant information, even information as specific as keywords for the education and training industries. Refer to the appendix to find Web sites that have thousands of education keywords, some with descriptions. Remember also to scan a variety of job listings to pick up the "buzzwords" and current terminology. These are outstanding resources.

RESUME STRATEGY #4: USE THE "BIG" AND SAVE THE "LITTLE"

When deciding what to include in your resume, try to focus on the "big" things— new programs, new curricula, reduced operating costs, improved profitability, major projects, improvements in student test results, and more. Give a good, broad-based picture of what you were responsible for and how well you did it. Here's an example:

> Senior-level Administrator with full responsibility for the strategic planning, development, budgeting, and leadership of Admissions, Financial Aid, Alumni Relations, and Career Development departments for a 13,000-student university. Manage $900,000 in annual operating and administrative budgets. Direct a staff of 42.

Then, save the "little" stuff—the details—for the interview. With this strategy, you will accomplish two things: You'll keep your resume readable and of a reasonable length (while still selling your achievements), and you'll have new and interesting information to share during the interview, instead of merely repeating what is already on your resume. Using the preceding example, when discussing this experience during an interview you could elaborate on your increases in student admission and retention, improvements to the financial aid process, reductions in annual operating expenses, and increases in alumni giving.

RESUME STRATEGY #5: MAKE YOUR RESUME "INTERVIEWABLE"

One of your greatest challenges is to make your resume a useful interview tool. Once it's been determined that you meet the primary qualifications for a position (you've passed the keyword scanning test or initial review) and you are contacted for a telephone or in-person interview, your resume becomes all-important in leading and prompting your interviewer during your conversation.

Your job, then, is to make sure the resume leads the reader where you want to go and presents just the right organization, content, and appearance to stimulate a productive discussion. To improve the "interviewability" of your resume, consider these tactics:

- Make good use of Resume Strategy #4 ("Use the 'Big' and Save the 'Little'") to invite further discussion about your experiences.

- Be sure your greatest "selling points" are featured prominently, not buried within the resume.

- Conversely, don't devote lots of space and attention to areas of your background that are irrelevant or about which you feel less than positive; you'll only invite questions about things you really don't want to discuss.

- Make sure your resume is highly readable—this means including plenty of white space, using an adequate font size, and creating a logical flow from start to finish.

RESUME STRATEGY #6: ELIMINATE CONFUSION WITH STRUCTURE AND CONTEXT

Keep in mind that hiring managers will read your resume *very quickly!* You may agonize over every word and spend hours working on content and design, but the average reader will skim quickly through your masterpiece and expect to pick up important facts in just a few seconds. Try to make it as easy as possible for readers to grasp the essential facts:

- Be consistent: For example, put job titles, company names, and dates in the same place for each position.

- Make information easy to find by clearly defining different sections of your resume with large, highly visible headings.

- Define the context in which you worked (for example, the organization, your department, and the specific challenges you faced) before you start describing your activities and accomplishments.

RESUME STRATEGY #7: USE FUNCTION TO DEMONSTRATE ACHIEVEMENT

When you write a resume that focuses only on your job functions, it can be dry and uninteresting and will say very little about your unique activities and contributions. Consider the following example:

> Responsible for the design and development of all courses for grades 3–5.

Now, consider using that same function to demonstrate achievement and see what happens to the tone and energy of the sentence. It becomes alive and clearly communicates that you deliver results.

> Forged a major initiative to redesign and enhance all course curricula for grades 3–5. Partnered with public- and private-sector organizations to identify the best practices in education and program design worldwide. Delivered 11 new curricula within the first year.

You'll create a more powerful resume presentation when you translate your functions into achievements.

RESUME STRATEGY #8: REMAIN IN THE REALM OF REALITY

We've already established that resume writing is sales. And, as any good salesperson does, one feels somewhat inclined to stretch the truth just a bit. However, be forewarned that you must stay within the realm of reality. Do not push your skills and qualifications outside the bounds of what is truthful. You never want to be in a position where you have to defend something that you've written on your resume. If that's the case, you'll lose the opportunity before you ever get started.

RESUME STRATEGY #9: BE CONFIDENT

You are unique. There is only one individual with the specific combination of employment experience, qualifications, achievements, and educational credentials that you have. In turn, this positions you as a unique commodity within the competitive job search market. To succeed, you must prepare a resume that is written to sell *you*, and highlight *your* qualifications and *your* success. If you can accomplish this, you will have won the job search game by generating interest, interviews, and offers.

There Are No Resume Writing Rules

One of the greatest challenges in resume writing is that there are no rules to the game. There are certain expectations about information that you will include—principally, your employment history and your educational qualifications. Beyond that, what you include is entirely dependent on you and what you have done in your career. You have tremendous flexibility in determining how to include the information you have selected. In chapter 2, you'll find a complete listing of each possible category you might include in your resume, the type of information in each category, preferred formats for presentation, and sample text you can edit and use.

Although there are no rules, there are a few standards to live by as you write your resume. The following sections discuss these standards in detail.

CONTENT STANDARDS

Content is, of course, the text that goes into your resume. Content standards refer to the writing style you should use, items you should be sure to include, items you should avoid including, and the order and format in which you list your qualifications.

Writing Style

Always write in the first person, dropping the word "I" from the front of each sentence. This style gives your resume a more assertive and more professional tone than the passive third-person voice. Here are some examples:

First Person:

> Manage a 12-person team in the design and market commercialization of next-generation instructional technology.

Third Person:

> Mr. Jones manages a team of 12 in the design and market commercialization of next-generation instructional technology.

By using the first-person voice, you are assuming "ownership" of that statement. You did such-and-such. When you use the third-person, "someone else" did it.

Wording to Stay Away From

Try *not* to use phrases such as "responsible for" or "duties included." These words create a passive tone and style. Instead, use active verbs to describe what you did.

Compare these two ways of conveying the same information:

> Duties included the planning and daily operation of a university library servicing 20,000 undergraduate and graduate students at the University of Wisconsin. Administered $1.2 million annual budget.

Or

> Managed a $1.2 million university library servicing 20,000 undergraduate and graduate students at the University of Wisconsin. Redesigned purchasing systems, restructured physical layout, recruited and trained support staff, and increased student satisfaction ratings by 22%.

Resume Style

The traditional **chronological** resume lists work experience in reverse-chronological order (starting with your current or most recent position). The **functional** style de-emphasizes the "where" and "when" of your career and instead groups similar experience, talents, and qualifications regardless of when they occurred.

Today, however, most resumes follow neither a strictly chronological nor strictly functional format; rather, they are an effective mixture of the two styles, usually known as a "combination" or "hybrid" format.

Like the chronological format, the hybrid format includes specifics about where you worked, when you worked there, and what your job titles were. Like a functional resume, a hybrid emphasizes your most relevant qualifications—perhaps within chronological job descriptions, in an expanded summary section, in several "career highlights" bullet points at the top of your resume, or in project summaries. Most of the examples in this book are hybrids and show a wide diversity of organizational formats that you can use as inspiration for designing your own resume.

Resume Formats

Resumes, principally career summaries and job descriptions, are most often written in a paragraph format, a bulleted format, or a combination of both. Following are three job descriptions, all very similar in content, yet presented in each of the three different formats. The advantages and disadvantages of each format are also addressed.

Paragraph Format

Fourth-Grade Teacher   2001 to 2005

Inner Harbor Magnet School, Baltimore City Schools, Baltimore, Maryland

Selected from a competitive field of 800 candidates for newly created teaching position. Solely responsible for developing curricula for all essential subjects, designing instructional tools and techniques, preparing classroom lectures, and evaluating student performance. Team-teach with remedial reading and remedial math teachers.

Provide significant input into the district's committee on "Setting 4th-Grade Benchmarks" for state curriculum. Designed and implemented multisensory reading program, a holistic approach that also involves writing and spelling. Program provides reinforcement via all learning modalities and ensures retention. Provided significant input into developing the school's first science fair. Encourage student participation to help develop presentation skills through cooperative learning.

Advantages:

Requires the least amount of space on the page. Brief, succinct, and to-the-point.

Disadvantages:

Achievements get lost in the text of the second paragraph. They are not visually distinctive, nor do they stand alone to draw attention to them.

Bulleted Format

Fourth-Grade Teacher   2001 to 2005

Inner Harbor Magnet School, Baltimore City Schools, Baltimore, Maryland

- Selected from a competitive field of 800 candidates for newly created teaching position.

- Solely responsible for developing curricula for all essential subjects, designing instructional tools and techniques, preparing classroom lectures, and evaluating student performance.

- Team-teach with remedial reading and remedial math teachers.

- Provide significant input into the district's committee on "Setting 4th-Grade Benchmarks" for state curriculum.

- Designed and implemented multisensory reading program, a holistic approach that also involves writing and spelling. Program provides reinforcement via all learning modalities and ensures retention.

- Provided significant input into developing the school's first science fair. Encourage student participation to help develop presentation skills through cooperative learning.

Advantages:

Quick and easy to peruse.

Disadvantages:

Responsibilities and achievements are lumped together with everything of equal value. In turn, the achievements get lost further down the list and are not immediately recognizable.

Combination Format

Fourth-Grade Teacher   2001 to 2005

Inner Harbor Magnet School, Baltimore City Schools, Baltimore, Maryland

Selected from a competitive field of 800 candidates for newly created teaching position. Solely responsible for developing curricula for all essential subjects, designing instructional tools and techniques, preparing classroom lectures, and evaluating student performance. Team-teach with remedial reading and remedial math teachers.

- Provide significant input into the district's committee on "Setting 4th-Grade Benchmarks" for state curriculum.

- Designed and implemented multisensory reading program, a holistic approach that also involves writing and spelling. Program provides reinforcement via all learning modalities and ensures retention.

- Provided significant input into developing the school's first science fair. Encourage student participation to help develop presentation skills through cooperative learning.

Advantages:

Our recommended format. Clearly presents overall responsibilities in the introductory paragraph and then accentuates each achievement as a separate bullet.

Disadvantages:

If you don't have clearly identifiable accomplishments, this format is not effective. It also may shine a glaring light on the positions where your accomplishments were less notable.

E-mail Address and URL

Be sure to include your e-mail address prominently at the top of your resume. As we all know, e-mail has become one of the most preferred methods of communication in job search.

We advise against using your employer's e-mail address on your resume. Not only does this present a negative impression to future employers, it will become useless once you make your next career move. And because your resume may exist in cyberspace long after you've completed your current job search, you don't want to direct interested parties to an obsolete e-mail address. Instead, obtain a private e-mail address that will be yours permanently. A free e-mail address from a provider such as Yahoo!, Hotmail, or NetZero is perfectly acceptable to use on your resume.

In addition to your e-mail address, if you have a URL (Web site) where you have posted your Web resume, be sure to also display that prominently at the top of your resume. For more information on Web resumes, refer to chapter 3.

PRESENTATION STANDARDS

Presentation is the way your resume looks. It includes the fonts you use, the paper you print it on, any graphics you might include, and how many pages your resume should be.

Typestyle (or Font)

Use a typestyle (font) that is clean, conservative, and easy to read. Stay away from anything that is too fancy, glitzy, curly, and the like. Here are a few recommended typestyles:

Tahoma	Times New Roman
Arial	Bookman
Krone	Book Antiqua
Soutane	Garamond
CG Omega	Century Schoolbook
Century Gothic	Lucida Sans
Gill Sans	Verdana

Other fonts that work well for resumes include Franklin Gothic, Myriad Roman, Helvetica, Univers, Palomino, Souvenir, and Fritz.

Although it is extremely popular, Times New Roman is our least preferred type-style simply because it is overused. More than 90 percent of the resumes we see are typed in Times New Roman. Your goal is to create a competitively distinctive document, and, to achieve that, we recommend an alternative typestyle.

Your choice of typestyle should be dictated by the content, format, and length of your resume. Some fonts look better than others at smaller or larger sizes; some have "bolder" boldface type; some require more white space to make them readable. Once you've written your resume, experiment with a few different typestyles to see which one best enhances your document.

Type Size

Readability is everything! If the type size is too small, your resume will be difficult to read and difficult to skim for essential information. Interestingly, a too-large type size, particularly for senior-level professionals, can also give a negative impression by conveying a juvenile or unprofessional image.

As a general rule, select type from 10 to 12 points in size. However, there's no hard-and-fast rule, and a lot depends on the typestyle you choose. Take a look at the following examples:

Very readable in 9-point Verdana:

Won the 2003 "Teacher of the Year" award in Montgomery, Alabama. Honored for innovative contributions to the classroom, students, and community, with an auxiliary commendation for service to special-needs children.

Difficult to read in too-small 9-point Gill Sans:

Won the 2003 "Teacher of the Year" award in Montgomery, Alabama. Honored for innovative contributions to the classroom, students, and community, with an auxiliary commendation for service to special-needs children.

Concise and readable in 12-point Times New Roman:

> Training & Development Consultant specializing in the design, development, and presentation of multimedia corporate training programs for sales, marketing, and technology professionals.

A bit overwhelming in too-large 12-point Bookman Old Style:

> Training & Development Consultant specializing in the design, development, and presentation of multimedia corporate training programs for sales, marketing, and technology professionals.

Type Enhancements

Bold, *italics,* <u>underlining,</u> and CAPITALIZATION are ideal to highlight certain words, phrases, achievements, projects, numbers, and other information to which you want to draw special attention. However, do not overuse these enhancements. If your resume becomes too cluttered, nothing stands out.

> **NOTE:** Resumes intended for electronic transmission and computer scanning have specific restrictions on typestyle, type size, and type enhancements. We discuss these details in chapter 3.

Page Length

For most industries and professions, including many people in the education professions, the "one-to-two-page rule" for resume writing still holds true. Keep it short and succinct, giving just enough to entice your readers' interest. However, there are many instances when an education resume will be longer than two pages. For example:

- When you're really not writing a resume, but rather a curriculum vitae (as discussed earlier in this chapter) used by many university professors, researchers, school administrators, published authors, and others.

- You have an extensive list of publications, public-speaking engagements, volunteer experiences, and such that are relevant to the position for which you are applying.

- You have extensive educational training and numerous credentials/certifications, all of which are important to include.

- You have an extensive list of courses you've taught and it is necessary to include them all.

- You have an extensive list of "special projects" to include, such as new educational programs you've designed, curricula you've developed, instructional materials you've created, technology-based training innovations, research projects, and more.

- You have an extensive list of professional honors, awards, and commendations. This list is tremendously valuable in validating your credibility and distinguishing you from the competition.

If you create a resume that's longer than two pages, make it more reader-friendly by carefully segmenting the information into separate sections. For instance, begin with your career summary and your work experience. This will most likely take one to two pages. Then follow with research, education, credentials, honors and awards, publications, public-speaking engagements, professional affiliations, civic affiliations, technology skills, volunteer experience, foreign-language skills, and other relevant information you want to include. Put each into a separate category so that your resume is easy to peruse and your reader can quickly see the highlights. You'll read more about each of these sections in chapter 2.

Paper Color

Be conservative. White, ivory, and light gray are ideal. Other "flashier" colors are inappropriate for individuals in the education professions.

Graphics

An attractive, relevant graphic can really enhance your resume. When you look through the sample resumes in chapters 4 through 12, you'll see some excellent examples of the effective use of graphics to enhance the visual presentation of a resume. Just be sure not to get carried away…be tasteful and relatively conservative.

White Space

We'll say it again—readability is everything! If people have to struggle to read your resume, they simply won't make the effort. Therefore, be sure to leave plenty of white space. It really does make a difference.

ACCURACY AND PERFECTION

The very final step, and one of the most critical in resume writing, is the proofreading stage. It is essential that your resume be well written, visually pleasing, and free of any errors, typographical mistakes, misspellings, and the like. We recommend that you carefully proofread your resume a minimum of three times, and then have two or three other people also proofread it. Consider your resume an example of the quality of work you will produce on an organization's behalf. Is your work product going to have errors and inconsistencies? If your resume does, it communicates to a prospective employer that you are careless, and this is the "kiss of death" in a job search.

Take the time to make sure that your resume is perfect in all the little details that do, in fact, make a big difference to those who read it.

CHAPTER 2

Writing Your Resume

For many education professionals, resume writing is *not* at the top of the list of fun and exciting activities! How can it compare to developing a new instructional methodology, designing and funding a new training center, increasing your school's enrollment numbers well beyond the projections, or working one-on-one to build a child's self-esteem? In your perception, we're sure that it cannot.

However, resume writing can be an enjoyable and rewarding task. Once your resume is complete, you can look at it proudly, reminding yourself of all that you have achieved. It is a snapshot of your career and your success. When it's complete, we guarantee you'll look back with tremendous self-satisfaction as you launch and successfully manage your job search.

The very first step in finding a new position or advancing your career, resume writing can be the most daunting of all tasks in your job search. If writing is not one of your primary job functions, it might have been years since you've actually sat down and written anything other than notes to yourself. Even for those who write on a regular basis, resume writing is unique. It has its own style and a number of peculiarities, as with any specialty document.

Therefore, to make the writing process easier, more finite, and more efficient, we've consolidated it into four discrete sections:

- **Career Summary.** Think of your Career Summary as the *master plan* of your resume. It summarizes all the components of your professional skills and experience that contribute to the success of a school, a classroom, or a corporate training and development center.

- **Professional Experience.** Professional Experience is analogous to the *courses and curricula* that you might teach. It is the specifics that make up the larger master plan. Your professional experience demonstrates how you put all of your capabilities to work.

- **Education, Credentials, and Certifications.** Think of this section as your *accreditation*, the third-party validation of your qualifications, knowledge, and expertise.

- **The "Extras"** (Publications, Public Speaking, Honors and Awards, Technology Qualifications, Professional Affiliations, Civic Affiliations, Foreign Languages, Personal Information, and so on). These make up the *extra-credit* section of your resume, the added stuff that helps distinguish you from others with similar qualifications.

Step-by-Step: Writing the Perfect Resume

In the preceding section, we outlined the four core resume sections. Now, we'll detail the particulars of each section—what to include, where to include it, and how to include it.

CONTACT INFORMATION

Before we start with the four core sections, let's briefly address the very top section of your resume: your name and contact information.

Name

You'd think that writing your name would be the easiest part of writing your resume! But there are several factors you may want to consider:

- Although most people choose to use their full, formal name at the top of a resume, it has become increasingly more acceptable to use the name by which you prefer to be called.

- Bear in mind that it's to your advantage to have readers feel comfortable calling you for an interview. Their comfort level may decrease if your name is gender-neutral, difficult to pronounce, or very unusual; they don't know who they're calling (a man or a woman) or how to ask for you. Here are a few ways you can make it easier for them:

> Lynn T. Cowles (Mr.)
>
> (Ms.) Michael Murray
>
> Tzirina (Irene) Kahn
>
> Ndege "Nick" Vernon

Address

You should always include your home address on your resume. If you use a post-office box for mail, include both your mailing address and your physical residence address.

Telephone Number(s)

You should include your home telephone number. If you're at work during the day, when you can expect to receive most calls, consider including a work phone number (if it's a direct line and you can receive calls discreetly). If others answer your work phone, you can't be assured of their discretion; so for professionals such as classroom teachers who are not readily available by phone during the day, we do not recommend including a work number. You might also include a mobile phone number (refer to it as "mobile" rather than "cellular" to keep up with current terminology) or a pager number (however, this is less desirable because you must call back to speak to the person who called you). You can include a private home fax number (if it can be accessed automatically), but do not include your work fax number. *Never* include your employer's or school's toll-free number. This communicates the message that you are using your employer's resources and budget to support your own personal job search campaign. Not a wise idea!

E-mail Address

Without question, if you have a private e-mail address, include it on your resume. E-mail is now often the preferred method of communication in job search, particularly in the early stages of each contact. Do not use your employer's e-mail address, even if you access personal e-mail through your work computer. Instead, obtain a free, accessible-anywhere address from a provider such as Yahoo!, Hotmail, or NetZero.

As you look through the samples in this book, you'll see how resume writers have arranged the many bits of contact information at the top of a resume. You can use these as models for presenting your own information. The point is to make it as easy as possible for employers to contact you!

Now, let's get into the nitty-gritty of the four core content sections of your resume.

CAREER SUMMARY

The Career Summary is the section at the top of your resume that summarizes and highlights your knowledge and expertise. You may be thinking, "But shouldn't my resume start with an Objective?" Although many job seekers still use Objective statements, we believe that a Career Summary is a much more powerful introduction. The problem with Objectives is that they are either too specific (limiting you to a "Librarian position") or too vague (doesn't everyone want "a challenging opportunity with a progressive organization offering the opportunity for growth and advancement"?). In addition, they can be read as self-serving because they describe what *you* want rather than suggesting what you have to offer an employer.

In contrast, an effective Career Summary allows you to position yourself as you want to be perceived and immediately "paint a picture" of yourself in relation to your career goal. It is critical that this section focus on the specific skills, qualifications, and achievements of your career that are related to your current objectives. Your summary is *not* a historical overview of your career. Rather, it is a concise, well-written, and sharp presentation of information designed to *sell* you into your next position.

This section can have various titles, such as the following:

Career Summary	**Management Profile**
Career Achievements	**Professional Qualifications**
Career Highlights	**Professional Summary**
Career Synopsis	**Profile**
Executive Profile	**Summary**
Expertise	**Summary of Achievement**
Highlights of Experience	**Summary of Qualifications**

Or, as you will see in the first example format that follows (Headline Format), your summary does not have to have any title at all.

Here are five sample Career Summaries. Consider using one of these as the template for developing your Career Summary, or use them as a foundation to create your own presentation. You will also find some type of Career Summary in just about every resume included in this book.

Headline Format

HIGHER-EDUCATION EXECUTIVE / VICE PRESIDENT / DIRECTOR

Strategic Planning / Finance / Marketing / Facilities

MBA—Executive Leadership   MS—Educational Administration
MS—Instructional Systems & Technology

Paragraph Format

CAREER PROFILE

ASSISTANT PRINCIPAL/DEAN OF STUDENTS/COORDINATOR/EDUCATOR/TRAINER offering expertise in the development and teaching of educational programs designed to meet a broad cross-section of learner needs. Experience in teaching, project development, and behavioral management. Counseling and training abilities. Excellent administrative, interpersonal, and communication skills, as well as expertise in identifying instructional requirements and developing effective course curriculum. Positive motivator skilled in educating both student and adult learners. Conversational Spanish.

Core Competencies Summary Format

QUALIFICATIONS SUMMARY

CORPORATE TRAINING & DEVELOPMENT PROFESSIONAL

Advanced Engineering & Technology Industries

- Organizational Needs Assessment
- Program Budgeting & Resource Management
- Trainer Training & Team Leadership
- Change Management & Revitalization
- Business & Process Optimization

- Curriculum Design & Development
- Multimedia Instructional Systems
- E-Learning & Distance Learning
- Training Materials Design
- Public Speaking & Executive Presentations

Guest Speaker, 2004 "Technology Innovation in Education" Conference
Winner, 2003 Pioneer Electronics Award for Excellence

Bulleted-List Format

PROFESSIONAL QUALIFICATIONS

- **Elementary School Educator** with 10 years of professional experience.
- Strengths in **literacy development** and **early language acquisition** for "English as a Second Language" learners.
- Extensive background working with **multicultural, special needs, and at-risk** students and their families.
- **Award-winning** classroom management skills.
- Two years of experience as a **mentor teacher.**
- Outstanding communication, organizational, and project-management skills.

Category Format

PROFESSIONAL CAREER HIGHLIGHTS

Experience: 12 years as a Classroom Educator, Department Chairperson, and School Services Administrator

Education: MS—Educational Administration—University of Wisconsin
BS—Elementary Education—Wisconsin State College

Publications: "Integrated Technology into the Classroom," *Data Processing Management Association Annual Journal*, 2003
"Innovative Curricula to Accelerate Student Learning & Retention," *National Education Association*, 2001

Awards: Teacher of the Year, Milwaukee Public Schools, 2003
Teacher of the Year, Detroit Public Schools, 1995

PROFESSIONAL EXPERIENCE

Your Professional Experience is the meat of your resume—the "courses and curricula," as we discussed before. It's what gives your resume substance, meaning, and depth. It is also the section that will take you the longest to write. If you've had the same position for 10 years, how can you consolidate all that you have done into one short section? If, on the opposite end of the spectrum, you have had your current position for only 11 months, how can you make it seem substantial and noteworthy? And, for people whose experience is in between, what do you include, how do you include it, and where do you include it?

These are not easy questions to answer. In fact, the most truthful response to each question is, "It depends." It depends on you, your experience, your achievements and successes, and your current career objectives.

Here are five samples of Professional Experience sections. Review how each individual's unique background is organized and emphasized, and consider your own background when using one of these as the template or foundation for developing your Professional Experience section.

Achievement Format

Emphasizes each position, your overall scope of responsibility, and the resulting achievements.

PROFESSIONAL EXPERIENCE

LEWISTON HIGH SCHOOL, Lewiston, Maine
MATHEMATICS TEACHER (1998 to Present)

Teach full spectrum of secondary-school mathematics curriculum (7th–12th grades) to a multicultural student body at this 1,200-student public high school. Design/develop new curriculum, create instructional resources, lead two student associations, and serve as back-up for girls' basketball coach.

Achievements

❑ Initiated use of graphic calculators to facilitate introduction of technology-based learning tools, and transitioned students from manual to computerized calculations.

❑ Achieved an 8.2% increase in student test scores across all core mathematics disciplines, and a 6.8% increase in core science disciplines.

❑ Utilized math manipulatives (e.g., geoboards, tangrams) as well as varied assessment tools to supplement structured curriculum.

❑ Won a $25,000 grant from the Ford Motor Company to purchase scientific equipment and technology for chemistry and physics classes.

❑ Selected to train newly hired math and science teachers, precept student teachers, and participate on administrator selection panels.

❑ Coached two students to the finals in statewide trigonometry competition.

Challenge, Action, and Results (CAR) Format

Emphasizes the challenge of each position, the action you took, and the results you delivered.

PROFESSIONAL EXPERIENCE

National Director of Corporate Training (2001 to Present)
National Training Implementation Manager (1997 to 2001)
VISA INTERNATIONAL, Atlanta, Georgia

Challenge:	To lead the design, development, and nationwide launch of a comprehensive employee training and leadership-development program impacting all 15,000 VISA employees worldwide.
Action:	Built a 42-person training and support team, established business infrastructure for training unit, purchased more than $1 million in technology training resources and instructional materials, and launched a nationwide marketing campaign to encourage employee interest.
Results:	☑ Orchestrated design, development, and rollout of 25 new training programs offered in 12 locations throughout the U.S. and Europe. Trained more than 2,000 employees in the first two years.
	☑ Achieved/surpassed all corporate objectives for employee development and performance improvement.
	☑ Conceived, launched, and won executive management support for the development and implementation of a complete Instructor Certification Program.
	☑ Partnered with HP, IBM, and Dell to integrate their technologies into VISA's training curriculum. Received more than $200,000 in technology resources at no charge to the company.
	☑ Featured in the National Education Association's annual publication as one of 2002's *Leaders in Corporate Training*.

Functional Format

Emphasizes the functional areas of responsibility within the job and associated achievements.

EMPLOYMENT EXPERIENCE

Assistant Principal	WILLIAMS HIGH SCHOOL, Beaver Creek, Oregon	1999 to Present

Member of 6-person educational administration and management team of this 800-student public high school in Southeastern rural Oregon. Scope of strategic planning, leadership, and decision-making responsibilities is extensive, with particular emphasis on

Curriculum/Instruction:

- ❖ Supervise instructional planning, goals, and objectives; develop new course offerings in science, mathematics, English, foreign languages, and the creative arts.

- ❖ Direct staff, manage operational budgets, and coordinate all educational activities for GATE, ESL, SB 1882 Staff Development, Advanced Placement, Summer School, and SASI administrative computer system.

- ❖ Develop Master Schedule and direct the entire student scheduling process.

- ❖ Recruit, interview, hire, and direct work performance of 42-person teaching staff.

- ❖ Member of the Williams District Mentor Teachers Association.

Staff Development:

- ❖ Orchestrate professional development opportunities for teaching staff across all curricula and grade levels.

- ❖ Use site-based management principles to support teachers' participation in school-wide decisions and to strengthen their ownership of school results.

- ❖ Conduct regularly scheduled performance reviews of teaching and support staff.

- ❖ Supervise and coordinate work of chairpersons of staff-development committees at all 43 schools throughout the Williams District.

Outreach and Communications:

- ❖ Revitalized fledgling student newspaper, recruited a talented team of student writers and production personnel, and expanded distribution to include all parents.

- ❖ Write and publish press releases, fliers, and other promotional materials to encourage community participation in school-sponsored events.

- ❖ Lead public speaking engagements at area middle schools to raise the level of enthusiasm of incoming freshmen.

Career-Track Format

Emphasizes fast-track promotion, overall scope of responsibility, and notable achievements.

—PROFESSIONAL EXPERIENCE & SELECTED EXAMPLES OF SUCCESS—

UNITED STATES AIR FORCE   May 1975–August 2003

More than 18 years in increasingly responsible positions as a commissioned Air Force Officer, including these recent assignments:

- *Promoted* to **Chief Learning Officer,** Air Force Doctrine Center (1998 to Present)

  The Center provides the basic corporate vision guiding the professional efforts of 371,000 employees worldwide.

  – Turned around a new organization that was swamped with urgent, unfocused tasks for two years. Guided a corporate-level needs analysis that integrated every level of proficiency in 12 major learning areas in our first master training plan.

  – *Payoffs:* Our **credibility—our stock in trade—rose fast**, as did our **productivity.**

- *Promoted* to **Director of Curriculum,** Air Force Extension Correspondence Institute (1996 to 1998)

  The Institute was recognized as the educational institution with the most students in the world. With its $5.5 million budget, it serves learners in hundreds of disciplines at locations around the world.

  – Reignited an organization that had four CEOs in as many years, saw its staffing cut 36% in eight years, and suffered with stagnant budgets for four years.

  – *Payoffs:* Skilled but **"burned out" employees revoked their retirement** papers. **Productivity rose** dramatically. **Conflicts** that had festered for years were **resolved.**

- *Promoted* to **Chief of Distance-Learning Policy,** Doctrine University (1993 to 1996)

  Our office served as the single point of contact for researching, employing, and delivering distance-learning technologies.

  – Went beyond the obvious fix to help our customers who had high-tech distance-learning technologies but not the training to use them. Found and removed potential roadblocks from every level.

  – *Payoffs:* Our combination users' handbook, **strategy** document, and "priority-setter" was in the field in just six months. **Customers very pleased.**

- *Promoted* to **Director of Training & Development,** North American Command Headquarters (1989 to 1993)

  Designed, developed, produced, delivered, evaluated, and validated "soft-skills" training curricula servicing 1,700 people.

  – Overhauled a system that left new team members feeling left out of our organization for their first six months. Based new program on a detailed, organization-wide needs analysis.

  – *Payoffs:* **Spin-up time cut by a third.** Everybody won—from workers to managers.

Experience Summary Format

Briefly emphasizes specific highlights of each position. Best used in conjunction with a detailed Career Summary.

EXPERIENCE SUMMARY

Preschool Teacher, George Mason Child Development Center, Macon, GA—2003 to Present

- Instructed 17 three- and four-year-old children in twice-weekly class.
- Assisted with school's reaccredidation process.
- Coordinated children's classroom literature, including thematic and individual reading.

Preschool Teacher, Green Day School, Valley Glen, GA—2000 to 2003

- Instituted literature-based, early-childhood curriculum at NAEYC-accredited school. Supervised two assistant teachers.
- Presented "Learning Through Literature" workshop at Northern Georgia Regional Teacher's Conference.
- Transformed classrooms with creative decorations that tied in with weekly themes and classroom reading.

Secretary, Village Day Camp, Valley Glen, GA—1997 to 2000

- Managed billing, registration, student scheduling, and site tours.
- Managed accounts payable for five affiliated summer camps.
- Administered employee timesheets, reporting, and payroll.

EDUCATION, CREDENTIALS, AND CERTIFICATIONS

Your Education section should include college, certifications, credentials, licenses, registrations, and continuing education. If any are particularly notable, be sure to highlight them prominently in your Education section or bring them to the top in your Career Summary (as demonstrated by the Headline format in the section on writing career summaries, earlier in this chapter).

Continuing professional education is vital in any industry or profession, and this is particularly true in education, where new teaching methodologies and educational concepts are introduced regularly. Professionals in other fields can briefly summarize their continuing-education courses at the end of their resumes. You, on the other hand, must be much more detailed and include most, if not all, of your courses, particularly those that are recent or demonstrate key qualifications and up-to-date knowledge of current educational trends. Try to consolidate as much as possible, but be thorough.

Here are five sample Education sections that illustrate a variety of ways to organize and format this information.

Academic Credentials Format

EDUCATION

Ph.D., Education Administration, University of Oklahoma, 2001
M.Ed., Secondary School Education, University of Wisconsin, 1991
B.S., Secondary Education, University of Wisconsin, 1987

Highlights of Continuing Professional Education:

- World-Management of the Classroom, Purdue University, 2004
- Technology in Education, Purdue University, 2003
- Executive Leadership Skills, Dale Carnegie, 2001
- Conflict Resolution & Violence Management, Institute for Safety in Education, 1998

Certification:

Certified Secondary School Principal, State of Wisconsin, 1991
Certified Secondary School Teacher, State of Wisconsin, 1987

Executive Education Format

EDUCATION

Executive Development Program	STANFORD UNIVERSITY
Executive Development Program	UNIVERSITY OF CALIFORNIA AT IRVINE
Master of Education Degree	UNIVERSITY OF CALIFORNIA AT LOS ANGELES
Bachelor of Education Degree	UNIVERSITY OF CALIFORNIA AT SAN DIEGO

Certifications Format

TEACHING CERTIFICATIONS & EDUCATION

- Certified Educational Diagnostician (K–12), State of Delaware, 2001

- Certified Generic Special Education Teacher (K–12), State of Delaware, 1997

- Certified Elementary Self-Contained Classroom Teacher (1–8), State of Delaware, 1995

- M.Ed. Candidate, University of Newark, expected 2005

- B.S., Elementary Education, Delaware University, 1995

Professional Training Format

PROFESSIONAL TRAINING & DEVELOPMENT

- *Developing Creative Learners,* National Education Association Annual Conference, 2004
- *Appropriate Use of Behavior Management in the Classroom,* Bedford County Public Schools In-Service Symposium, 2003
- *Issues Impacting Children, Families & School Communities,* Maryland State Teachers' Association, 2002
- *Observation & Assessment Methodologies,* Maryland State Teachers' Association, 2000
- **Education Major,** Catonsville Community College, Catonsville, Maryland, 1991–1993

Non-Degree Format

> **TRAINING & EDUCATION**
>
> **UNIVERSITY OF ILLINOIS,** Urbana, Illinois
>
> **BS Candidate**—Nursing Education (senior class status)
>
> **UNIVERSITY OF MICHIGAN,** Ann Arbor, Michigan
>
> **Dual Majors in Education & Nursing** (2 years)
>
> **Graduate,** 200+ hours of continuing professional education through the University of Illinois, University of Michigan, and University of Wisconsin.

THE "EXTRAS"

The primary focus of your resume is on information (most likely, your professional experience and academic credentials) that is directly related to your career goals. However, you also should include things that will distinguish you from other candidates and clearly demonstrate your value to a prospective employer. And, not too surprisingly, it is often the "extras" that get the interviews.

Following is a list of the other categories you might or might not include on your resume, depending on your particular experience and your current career objectives. Review the information. If it's pertinent to you, use the samples for formatting your own data. Remember, however, that if something is truly impressive, you might want to include it in your Career Summary at the beginning of your resume in order to draw even more attention to it. If you include it there, it's not necessary to repeat the information at the end of your resume.

Honors and Awards

If you have won honors and awards, you can either include them in a separate section on your resume or integrate them into the Education or Professional Experience section, whichever is most appropriate. If you choose to include them in a separate section, consider this format:

> ## HONORS & AWARDS
>
> - Winner, 2003 "Recognition" award from the National Library Association
> - Winner, 2001 "Innovation" award for outstanding contributions to technology innovation from the National Library Association
> - Named **"Librarian of the Year,"** Hofstra University, 2000
> - **Summa Cum Laude Graduate,** Washington & Lee University, 1995

Publications

As an education professional, being published is a true mark of distinction. In fact, for educators at a university, foundation, or research institution, getting published is almost mandatory to further your professional career. Publications validate your knowledge, qualifications, and credibility. Only people in the medical fields have more pressure to publish than those in academia.

As such, if you are published, be sure to highlight your publications prominently on your resume. If you have a short list of publications, you might highlight them in your Career Summary. However, if your list is extensive, we recommend that you mention that you are a published author in your Career Summary and then list all of your publications after your Professional Experience and Education sections.

Remember, publications can include books, articles, online Web site content, manuals, and other written documents. Here's an example:

> **Publications:**
> - "Teachers' Attitudes Toward an Inclusive Classroom," *Journal of Teacher and Special Education,* Vol. 42, pp. 317–328, 2004.
> - "Innovation in Educational Programming & Instruction, *School Psychology,* Vol. 22, pp. 123–135, 2003.
> - "Graduate Curriculum in Learning Disabilities," approved by the Illinois State School District, 2001.
> - Co-Author, "Teacher Technology Training Manual," Skokie Public School District, 2000.

Public Speaking

Experts are the ones who are invited to give public presentations at conferences, seminars, workshops, training programs, symposia, and other events. So if you have public-speaking experience, others must consider you an expert. Be sure to include this very complimentary information in your resume. Here's one way to present it:

> **PUBLIC SPEAKING**
>
> — **Keynote Speaker,** "Introducing Technology Innovation into the Classroom," 2004; National Education Association National Conference, Milwaukee.
> — **Presenter,** "Instructional Technology Finds Its Place in the Classroom," 2003.
> — **National Presenter,** "Management of Children with Behavioral or Emotional Problems," Masterson County Department of Family and Children Services, 2001.

Teaching Experience

If you're a teacher, you'll include your teaching experience in the Professional Experience section of your resume. However, if you're a school administrator, school psychologist, or student services director, teaching is not your primary job function. Depending on your current career objectives, you can handle your teaching experience in one of two ways:

- If your objective is *not* teaching, briefly mention your teaching experience within your job descriptions under Professional Experience.

- If your objective *is* teaching, we recommend that you include a separate Teaching Experience section on your resume. This way, you can visually attract your reader to an entire section devoted to teaching. Just as with everything else you do with your resume, you are constantly trying to push your reader in the direction in which you want to be perceived. If you want to be a teacher, show that you *are* a teacher!

Consider using the following format to present your teaching experience:

TEACHING EXPERIENCE

❖ **Adjunct Faculty,** Department of Education, Maryland State University, 1999 to Present. Teach Learning Disabilities, Cultural Foundations in Education, Classroom Management, and Diagnostic and Prescriptive Education.

❖ **Adjunct Faculty,** Department of Education, Catonsville Community College, 1998 to Present. Teach Psychological Foundations of Education, Methods of Educational Evaluation, and School Administration.

❖ **In-Service Instructor,** Baltimore City Public School System, 1995 to 2004. Taught high school core curriculum for behaviorally disordered students, the learning disabled, and those with severe behavioral and emotional problems.

Committees and Task Forces

Many education professionals serve on committees, task forces, and other special project teams either as part of, or in addition to, their full-time responsibilities. Again, this type of information further strengthens your credibility, qualifications, and perceived value to a prospective employer. Consider a format such as this:

- Member, 2005–06 Corporate Planning & Reorganization Task Force

- Member, 2003–04 Study Team on "Redesigning Corporate Training Systems to Maximize Employee Development"

- Chairperson, 2002–03 Committee on "Curriculum Planning for the Next Decade"

Professional Affiliations

If you are a member of any educational, professional, or leadership associations, be sure to include that information on your resume. It communicates a message of professionalism, a desire to stay current with the industry, and a strong professional network. What's more, if you have held leadership positions within these organizations, be sure to include them. Here's an example:

Professional Affiliations

CALIFORNIA STATE TEACHERS ASSOCIATION
Professional Member (1994 to Present)
Resource Center Development Committee Member (1998 to 2000)
Recruitment Committee Member (1995 to 1996)

NATIONAL EDUCATION ASSOCIATION
Associate Member (2000 to Present)
Professional Member (1994 to 2000)
Curriculum Design Review Committee Member (2001 to 2003)
Instructional Software Development Committee Member (1999 to 2000)

Civic Affiliations

Civic affiliations are fine to include if they

- are with a notable organization,
- demonstrate leadership experience, or
- may be of interest to a prospective employer.

However, things such as treasurer of your local condo association and singer with your church choir are not generally of value in marketing your qualifications. Here's an example of what to include:

> ***Civic Affiliations:***   Volunteer Chairperson, United Way of America—Detroit Chapter, 2000 to Present
> President, Lambert Valley Conservation District, 2001 to Present
> Treasurer, Habitat for Humanity—Detroit Chapter, 1999 to 2000

Technology Skills & Qualifications

Most education professionals will not need to add a separate section on their resumes for technology skills. Rather, you'll most likely incorporate relevant technology skills into your Career Summary with just a brief mention.

However, for candidates in technology-based education careers, this is a critical section. You need to list your experience with hardware, software, applications, operating systems, networks, multimedia, graphics, and more.

You'll also have to consider placement of this section. Depending on your specific objectives, we recommend you insert it immediately after your Career Summary (or as a part thereof) or immediately after your Professional Experience. This is extremely important information to a prospective employer, so be sure to display it prominently. Here's just one of many different formats you can use:

> **Technical Expertise**
>
> | **Operating Systems** | Windows NT — XP — 98 — 95 |
> |---|---|
> | **Networks** | LAN — WAN |
> | **Software** | Microsoft Works — Word — Excel — PowerPoint — Publisher |
> | | Lotus 1-2-3 — Notes |
> | | Netscape Navigator — Internet Explorer |

Personal Information

We do not recommend that you include such personal information as birth date, marital status, number of children, and related data. However, there may be instances when personal information is appropriate. If this information will give you a competitive advantage or answer unspoken questions about your background, then by all means include it. Here's an example:

> ■ **Personal Profile**
>
> - Born in Argentina. U.S. Permanent Residency Status since 1991.
> - Fluent in English, Spanish, and Portuguese.
> - Competitive Triathlete. Top-5 finish, 1992 Midwest Triathlon and 1995 Des Moines Triathlon.

Note in the preceding example that the job seeker is multilingual. This is a particularly critical selling point and, although it might be listed under Personal Information in this example, we think it is appropriate to highlight it in your Career Summary as well.

Consolidating the Extras

Sometimes you have so many extra categories at the end of your resume, each with only a handful of lines, that spacing becomes a problem. You certainly don't want to have to make your resume a page longer to accommodate five lines, nor do you want the "extras" to overwhelm the primary sections of your resume. Yet you believe the information is important and should be included. Or perhaps you have a few small bits of information that you think are important but don't merit an entire section. In these situations, consider consolidating the information using the following format. You'll save space, avoid overemphasizing individual items, and present a professional, distinguished appearance.

PROFESSIONAL PROFILE	
Affiliations	National Education Association Nevada State Teachers Association Las Vegas County Teachers Association
Public Speaking	Speaker, NEA Leadership Conference, Dallas, 2000 Presenter, NEA National Conference, San Diego, 1998 Panelist, NEA National Conference, Chicago, 1996
Languages	Fluent in English, Spanish, and German
Additional Information	• Founder and Program Chair, Detroit Education & Training Professionals Association • Bilingual—Spanish/English • **Available for relocation**

Writing Tips, Techniques, and Important Lessons

At this point, you've done a lot of reading, probably taken some notes, highlighted samples that appeal to you, and are ready to plunge into writing your resume. To make this task as easy as possible, we've compiled some "insider" techniques that we've used in our professional resume-writing practices. We learned these techniques the hard way through years of experience! We know they work; they will make the writing process easier, faster, and more enjoyable for you.

GET IT DOWN—THEN POLISH AND PERFECT IT

Don't be too concerned with making your resume "perfect" the first time around. It's far better to move fairly swiftly through the process, getting the basic information organized and on paper (or onscreen), rather than agonizing about the perfect phrase or ideal formatting. Once you've completed a draft, we think you'll be surprised at how close to "final" it is, and you'll be able to edit, tighten, and improve formatting fairly quickly.

WRITE YOUR RESUME FROM THE BOTTOM UP

Here's the system:

- **Start with the easy things**—Education, Professional Affiliations, Public Speaking, Publications, and any other extras you want to include. These items require little thought and can be completed in just a few minutes.

- **Write short job descriptions for your older positions, the ones you held years ago.** Be very brief and focus on highlights such as rapid promotion; achievements; innovations; professional honors; or employment with a well-respected, well-known school system, university, or corporation.

Once you've completed this, look at how much you've written in a short period of time! Then move on to the next step.

- **Write the job descriptions for your most recent positions.** This will take a bit longer than the other sections you have written. Remember to focus on the overall scope of your responsibility, major projects and initiatives, and significant achievements. Tell your reader what you did and how well you did it. You can use any of the formats recommended earlier in this chapter, or you can create something that is unique to you and your career.

Now, see how far along you are? Your resume is 90 percent complete with only one small section left to do.

- **Write your career summary.** Before you start writing, remember your objective for this section. The summary should not simply rehash your previous experience. Rather, it is designed to highlight the skills and qualifications you have that are most closely related to your current career objective(s). The Summary is intended to capture the reader's attention and "sell" your expertise.

That's it. You're done. We guarantee that the process of writing your resume will be much, much easier if you follow the "bottom-up" strategy. Now, on to the next tip.

INCLUDE NOTABLE OR PROMINENT "EXTRA" STUFF IN YOUR CAREER SUMMARY

Remember the "extra-credit sections" that are normally at the bottom of your resume? If this information is particularly significant or prominent—you won a notable award, spoke at an international conference, developed a new teaching methodology, published a paper, or led a nationwide research study—you may want to include it at the top in your Career Summary. Remember, the Summary section is written to distinguish you from the crowd of other qualified candidates. As such, if you've accomplished anything that clearly demonstrates your knowledge, expertise, and credibility, consider moving it to your Career Summary for added attention. Refer to the sample career summaries earlier in this chapter for examples.

USE RESUME SAMPLES TO GET IDEAS FOR CONTENT, FORMAT, AND ORGANIZATION

This book is just one of many resources where you can review the resumes of other education professionals to help you in formulating your strategy, writing the text, and formatting your resume. These books are published precisely for that reason. You don't have to struggle alone. Rather, you should use all the resources at your disposal.

Be forewarned, however, that it's unlikely you will find a resume that fits your life and career to a "T." It's more likely that you will use "some of this sample" and "some of that sample" to create a resume that is uniquely "you."

INCLUDE DATES FOR YOUR WORK EXPERIENCE?

Unless you are over age 50, we recommend that you date your work experience. Without dates, your resume becomes vague and difficult for the typical hiring manager or recruiter to interpret. A lack of dates often communicates the message that you are trying to hide something. Maybe you haven't worked in two years, maybe you were fired from each of your last three positions, or maybe you never graduated from college. Being vague and creating a resume that is difficult to read will, inevitably, lead to uncertainty and a quick toss into the "not interested" pile of candidates. By including the dates of your education and your experience, you create a clean and concise picture that the reader can easily follow to track your career progression.

An Individual Decision

If you are over age 50, dating your early positions must be an individual decision. On the one hand, you do not want to "date" yourself out of consideration by including dates from the 1960s and early 1970s. On the other hand, it may be that those positions are worth including for any one of a number of reasons. Further, if you omit those early dates, you may feel as though you are misrepresenting yourself (or lying) to a prospective employer.

Here is a strategy to overcome these concerns while still including your early experience: Create a separate category titled "Previous Professional Experience" in which you summarize your earliest employment, without dates. You can tailor this statement to emphasize just what is most important about that experience.

If you want to focus on the reputation of your past employers, include a statement such as this:

> • Previous experience includes tenured professorial positions with the Graduate Business Schools of **Harvard** and **Yale** Universities.

If you want to focus on the rapid progression of your career, consider this example:

> • Promoted rapidly through a series of increasingly responsible teaching and teacher-training positions with the Massachusetts Public School System.

If you want to focus on your early career achievements, include a statement such as this:

> • Member of the 6-person Curriculum Development Team that created the State of Virginia's "Standards of Learning" program, now a statewide institution and the guiding force of all public education initiatives.

By including any one of the above paragraphs, under the heading "Previous Professional Experience," you are clearly communicating to your reader that your employment history dates further back than the dates you have indicated on your resume. In turn, you are being 100 percent aboveboard and not misrepresenting yourself or your career. You're also focusing on the success, achievement, and prominence of your earliest assignments.

Include Dates in the Education Section?

If you are over age 50, we generally do not recommend that you date your education or college degrees. Simply include the degree and the university with no date. Why exclude yourself from consideration by immediately presenting the fact that you earned your college degree in 1958, 1962, or 1966—about the time the hiring manager was probably born? Remember, the goal of your resume is to share the highlights of your career and open doors for interviews. It is *not* to give your entire life story. As such, it is not mandatory to date your college degree.

However, if you use this strategy, be aware that the reader is likely to assume that there is *some* gap between when your education ended and your work experience started. Therefore, if you choose to begin your chronological work history with your first job out of college, omitting your graduation date could actually backfire, because the reader may assume you have experience that predates your first job. In this case, it's best either to *include your graduation date* or *omit dates of earliest experience*, using the summary strategy discussed above.

ALWAYS SEND A COVER LETTER WHEN YOU FORWARD YOUR RESUME

Sending a cover letter each time you send a resume is expected and is appropriate job search etiquette. When you prepare a resume, you are writing a document that you can use for each and every position you apply for, assuming that the requirements for all of those positions will be similar. The cover letter, then, is the tool that allows you to customize your presentation to each school, company, or recruiter, addressing their specific hiring requirements. It is also the appropriate place to include any specific information that has been requested, such as salary history or salary requirements (see the following section for more on this).

NEVER INCLUDE SALARY HISTORY OR SALARY REQUIREMENTS ON YOUR RESUME

Your resume is *not* the correct forum for a salary discussion. First of all, you should never provide salary information unless a **school** or **company** has requested that information and you choose to comply. (Studies show that employers will look at your resume anyway, so you may choose not to respond to this request, thereby avoiding pricing yourself out of the job or locking yourself into a lower salary than the job is worth.)

When contacting **recruiters,** however, we recommend that you do provide salary information, but again, only in your cover letter. With recruiters you want to "put all of your cards on the table" and help them make an appropriate placement by providing information about your current salary and salary objectives. For example, you could write, "Be advised that my current compensation is $55,000 annually and that I am interested in a position starting at a minimum of $65,000 per year." Or, if you would prefer to be a little less specific, you might write, "My annual compensation over the past three years has averaged $50,000+."

ALWAYS REMEMBER THAT YOU ARE SELLING

As we have discussed over and over throughout these first two chapters, resume writing is sales. Understand and appreciate the value you bring to a prospective employer, and then communicate that value by focusing on your achievements. Companies don't want to hire just anyone; they want to hire "the" someone who will make a difference. Show them that you are *that* candidate.

CHAPTER 3

Printed, Scannable, Electronic, and Web Resumes

After you've worked so tirelessly to write a winning resume, your next challenge is the resume's design, layout, and presentation. It's not enough for it to read well; your resume must also have just the right look for the right audience.

The Four Types of Resumes

In today's employment market, job seekers use four types of resume presentations:

- Printed
- Scannable
- Electronic (e-mail attachments and ASCII text files)
- Web

The following sections give details on when you would need each type, as well as how to prepare these types of resumes.

THE PRINTED RESUME

We know the printed resume as the "traditional resume," the one that you mail to a recruiter, take to an interview, and forward by mail or fax in response to an advertisement. When preparing a printed resume, you want to create a sharp, professional, and visually attractive presentation. Remember, that piece of paper conveys the very first impression of you to a potential employer, and that first impression goes a long, long way. Never be fooled into thinking that just because you have the best qualifications in your industry, the visual presentation of your resume does not matter. It does, a great deal.

THE SCANNABLE RESUME

The scannable resume can be referred to as the "plain-Jane" or "plain-vanilla" resume. All of the things that you would normally do to make your printed resume look attractive—bold print, italics, multiple columns, sharp-looking typestyle, and more—are stripped away in a scannable resume. You want to present a document that can be easily read and interpreted by scanning technology.

Although the technology continues to improve, and many scanning systems in fact can read a wide variety of type enhancements, it's sensible to appeal to the "lowest common denominator" when creating your scannable resume. Follow these formatting guidelines:

- Choose a commonly used, easily read font such as Arial or Times New Roman.

- Don't use bold, italic, or underlined type.

- Use a minimum of 11-point type size.

- Position your name, and nothing else, on the top line of the resume.

- Keep text left-justified, with a "ragged" right margin.

- It's okay to use common abbreviations (for instance, scanning software will recognize "B.S." as a Bachelor of Science degree). But, when in doubt, spell it out.

- Eliminate graphics, borders, and horizontal lines.

- Use plain, round bullets or asterisks.

- Avoid columns and tables, although a simple two-column listing can be read without difficulty.

- Spell out symbols such as % and &.

- If you divide words with slashes, add a space before and after the slash to be certain the scanner doesn't misread the letters.

- Print using a laser printer on smooth white paper.

- If your resume is longer than one page, be sure to print on only one side of the paper; put your name, telephone number, and e-mail address on the top of page two; and don't staple the pages together.

- For best possible results, mail your resume (don't fax it), and send it flat in a 9 × 12 envelope so that you won't have to fold it.

Scannable resumes are becoming less common and less in demand as the majority of career documents are transmitted by e-mail or pasted into online applications. It is only when your resume pages need to physically pass through a scanner that you will need a scannable resume. We recommend that you not worry about this format until and unless you are required to produce one for a specific company. For electronic resume guidelines, see the next section.

THE ELECTRONIC RESUME

Your electronic resume can take two forms: e-mail attachments and ASCII text files.

E-mail Attachments

When including your resume with an e-mail, simply attach the word-processing file of your printed resume. Because a vast majority of businesses use Microsoft Word, it is the most acceptable format and will present the fewest difficulties.

However, given the tremendous variety in versions of software and operating systems, not to mention printer drivers, it's quite possible that your beautifully formatted resume will look quite different when viewed and printed at the other end. To minimize these glitches, use generous margins (at least 0.75 inch all around). Don't use unusual typefaces, and minimize fancy formatting effects.

Test your resume by e-mailing it to several friends or colleagues, and then having them view and print it on their systems. If you use WordPerfect, Microsoft Works, or another word-processing program, consider saving your resume in a more universally accepted format such as RTF or PDF. Again, try it out on friends before sending it to a potential employer.

Although employers can easily open, view, and print a PDF (Portable Document Format) file, we do not recommend this as your primary electronic format. A PDF file is viewed as a graphic rather than an editable file, and therefore the data from your resume cannot be read into a company's resume-storage system unless it is printed and physically scanned. PDF is an excellent option if your resume has an unusual design, and especially if design skills are an important part of your qualifications. But for the most part, the PDF format will be less useful than a word-processing file format (such as .doc) for the companies receiving your resume.

ASCII Text Files

You'll find many uses for an ASCII text version of your resume:

- To avoid formatting problems, you can paste the text into the body of an e-mail message rather than send an attachment. Many employers actually prefer this method. Pasting text into an e-mail message lets you send your resume without the possibility of also sending a virus.

- You can readily copy and paste the text version into online job application and resume bank forms, with no worries that formatting glitches will cause confusion.

- Although it's unattractive, the text version is 100 percent scannable.

To create a text version of your resume, follow these simple steps:

1. Create a new version of your resume using the Save As feature of your word-processing program. Select "text only" or "ASCII" in the Save As option box.

2. Close the new file.

3. Reopen the file, and you'll find that your word processor has automatically reformatted your resume into Courier font, removed all formatting, and left-justified the text.

4. To promote maximum readability when sending your resume electronically, reset the margins to 2 inches left and right, so that you have a narrow column of text rather than a full-page width. (This margin setting will not be retained when you close the file, but in the meantime you can adjust the text formatting for best screen appearance. For instance, if you choose to include a horizontal line to separate sections of the resume, by working with the narrow margins you won't make the mistake of creating a line that extends past the

normal screen width. Plus, you won't add hard line breaks that create odd-length lines when seen at normal screen width.)

5. Review the resume and fix any "glitches" such as odd characters that may have been inserted to take the place of "curly" quotes, dashes, accents, or other nonstandard symbols.

6. Remove any tabs and adjust spacing as necessary. You might add a few extra blank lines or move text down to the next line.

7. If necessary, add extra blank lines to improve readability.

8. Consider adding horizontal dividers to break the resume into sections for improved skimmability. You can use any standard typewriter symbols such as *, -, (,), =, +, ^, or #.

To illustrate what you can expect when creating these versions of your resume, on the following pages are some examples of the same resume in traditional printed format, scannable version, and electronic (text) format.

THE WEB RESUME

This newest evolution in resumes combines the visually pleasing quality of the printed resume with the technological ease of the electronic resume. You host your Web resume on your own Web site (with your own URL), to which you refer prospective employers and recruiters. Now, instead of seeing just a "plain-Jane" version of your e-mailed resume, with just one click an employer can view, download, and print your Web resume—an attractive, nicely formatted presentation of your qualifications.

What's more, because the Web resume is such an efficient and easy-to-manage tool, you can choose to include more information than you would in a printed, scannable, or electronic resume. Consider separate pages for achievements, technology qualifications, equipment skills, honors and awards, management skills, and more, if you believe they would improve your market position.

For those of you in technologically related professions, you can take it one step further and create a virtual multimedia presentation that not only tells someone how talented you are, but also visually and technologically demonstrates it. Web resumes are an outstanding tool for people seeking jobs in technologically or visually related professions.

Your Web resume can also include all of the items (and more) that you would normally include in your professional portfolio. If you are an elementary teacher, you might include lesson plans, thematic units, customized curriculum, photographs, and other artwork. If corporate training is your expertise, your portfolio could showcase some of your handout materials, group exercises, and summary reports of your post-training evaluations. Testimonials and letters of reference can be another powerful part of your professional portfolio.

Depending on your technology skills, you might decide to create and manage your own Web resume/portfolio. Another option is to outsource this project to a firm that specializes in career portfolios. A few we like are Blue Sky Portfolios (www.blueskyportfolios.com), Brandego (www.brandego.com), and Portfolio Vault (www.portfoliovault.com).

A simplified version of the Web resume is an online version of your Microsoft Word resume. Instead of attaching a file to an e-mail to an employer, you can include a link to the online version. This format is not as graphically dynamic as a full-fledged Web resume, but it can be a very useful tool for your job search. For instance, you can offer the simplicity of text in your e-mail, plus the instant availability of a printable, formatted word-processing document for the interested recruiter or hiring manager. For a demonstration of this format, go to www.e-resume-central.com and click on "SEE A SAMPLE."

Laura Greystone

672 Oaklawn Drive
Cincinnati, Ohio 45242
(513) 555-0202

Lgreystone23@netscape.net

Expertise SENIOR-LEVEL UNIVERSITY ADMINISTRATION & LEADERSHIP

Experience DEAN OF ADMISSIONS & FINANCIAL AID, 1998–2004
ASSISTANT DEAN OF ADMISSIONS, 1996–1998

MORRISON COLLEGE, Cincinnati, OH

Planned and directed the reorganization and refinement of the Admissions and Financial Aid departments. Redesigned core process, streamlined operations, and accelerated program growth. Directed a staff of 14 and managed a $300,000 annual operating budget.

> **Recruitment:** Created and launched a multifaceted recruitment program, including high school visitations, open house visitations, targeted direct mail and e-mail, guidance counselor cultivation, and alumni admissions networking. Results included 185% increase in admissions inquiries, 53% increase in applications, and 10% increase in matriculants.

> **Strategic Planning:** Appointed to senior management team that developed and implemented the college's strategic planning processes for enrollment, facilities, curriculum, personnel, finances, and public relations.

> **Committee Memberships:** Served on the Middle States Accreditation Committee, Centennial Athletic Committee, College Retention Committee, Marketing Task Force, and Budget Advisory Committee.

The print version of the resume section.

Laura Greystone

672 Oaklawn Drive
Cincinnati, Ohio 45242
Lgreystone23@netscape.net
(513) 555-0202

Expertise   Senior-Level University Administration and Leadership

Experience   Dean of Admissions and Financial Aid, 1998–2004
Assistant Dean of Admissions, 1996–1998
Morrison College, Cincinnati, OH

Planned and directed the reorganization and refinement of the Admissions and Financial Aid departments. Redesigned core process, streamlined operations, and accelerated program growth. Directed a staff of 14 and managed a $300,000 annual operating budget.

RECRUITMENT: Created and launched a multifaceted recruitment program, including high school visitations, open house visitations, targeted direct mail and e-mail, guidance counselor cultivation, and alumni admissions networking. Results included 185 percent increase in admissions inquiries, 53 percent increase in applications, and 10 percent increase in matriculants.

STRATEGIC PLANNING: Appointed to senior management team that developed and implemented the college's strategic planning processes for enrollment, facilities, curriculum, personnel, finances, and public relations.

COMMITTEE MEMBERSHIPS: Served on the Middle States Accreditation Committee, Centennial Athletic Committee, College Retention Committee, Marketing Task Force, and Budget Advisory Committee.

The scannable version of the resume section.

LAURA GREYSTONE

----

672 Oaklawn Drive
Cincinnati, Ohio 45242
Lgreystone23@netscape.net
(513) 555-0202

EXPERTISE

Senior-Level University Administration and Leadership

EXPERIENCE

Dean of Admissions and Financial Aid, 1998-2004
Assistant Dean of Admissions, 1996-1998

MORRISON COLLEGE, Cincinnati, OH

Planned and directed the reorganization and refinement of
the Admissions and Financial Aid departments. Redesigned
core process, streamlined operations, and accelerated
program growth. Directed a staff of 14 and managed a
$300,000 annual operating budget.

--- Recruitment: Created and launched a multifaceted
recruitment program, including high school visitations, open
house visitations, targeted direct mail and e-mail, guidance
counselor cultivation, and alumni admissions networking.
Results included 185 percent increase in admissions
inquiries, 53 percent increase in applications, and 10
percent increase in matriculants.

--- Strategic Planning: Appointed to senior management team
that developed and implemented the college's strategic
planning processes for enrollment, facilities, curriculum,
personnel, finances, and public relations.

--- Committee Memberships: Served on the Middle States
Accreditation Committee, Centennial Athletic Committee,
College Retention Committee, Marketing Task Force, and
Budget Advisory Committee.

The electronic/text version of the resume section.

The Four Resume Types Compared

This chart quickly compares the similarities and differences between the four types of resumes we've discussed in this chapter.

	PRINTED RESUMES	**SCANNABLE RESUMES**
TYPESTYLE/ FONT	Sharp, conservative, and distinctive (see our recommendations in chapter 1).	Clean, concise, and machine-readable: Times New Roman, Arial, Helvetica.
TYPESTYLE ENHANCEMENTS	**Bold,** *italics,* and <u>underlining</u> for emphasis.	CAPITALIZATION is the only type enhancement you can be certain will transmit.
TYPE SIZE	10-, 11-, or 12-point preferred… larger type sizes (14, 18, 20, 22, and even larger, depending on typestyle) will effectively enhance your name and section headers.	11- or 12-point, or larger.
TEXT FORMAT	Use centering and indentations to optimize the visual presentation.	Type all information flush left.
PREFERRED LENGTH	1 to 2 pages; 3 if essential.	1 to 2 pages preferred, although length is not as much of a concern as with printed resumes.
PREFERRED PAPER COLOR	White, Ivory, Light Gray, Light Blue, or other conservative background.	White or very light with no prints, flecks, or other shading that might affect scannability.
WHITE SPACE	Use appropriately for best readability.	Use generously to maximize scannability.

ELECTRONIC RESUMES	WEB RESUMES
Courier.	Sharp, conservative, and distinctive... attractive onscreen and when printed from an online document.
CAPITALIZATION is the only enhancement available to you.	**Bold,** *italics,* and underlining, and color for emphasis.
12-point.	10-, 11-, or 12-point preferred... larger type sizes (14, 18, 20, 22, and even larger, depending on typestyle) will effectively enhance your name and section headers.
Type all information flush left.	Use centering and indentations to optimize the visual presentation.
Length is immaterial; almost definitely, converting your resume to text will make it longer.	Length is immaterial; just be sure your site is well organized so viewers can quickly find the material of greatest interest to them.
N/A.	Paper is not used, but do select your background carefully to maximize readability.
Use white space to break up dense text sections.	Use appropriately for best readability both onscreen and when printed.

Are You Ready to Write Your Resume?

To be sure that you're ready to write your resume, go through the following checklist. Each item is a critical step that you must take in the process of writing and designing your own winning resume.

- ❑ Clearly define "who you are" and how you want to be perceived.

- ❑ Document your key skills, qualifications, and knowledge.

- ❑ Document your notable career achievements and successes.

- ❑ Identify one or more specific job targets or positions.

- ❑ Identify one or more industries that you are targeting.

- ❑ Research and compile key words for your profession, industry, and specific job targets.

- ❑ Determine which resume format suits you and your career best.

- ❑ Select an attractive font.

- ❑ Determine whether you need a print resume, a scannable resume, an electronic resume, a Web resume, or all four.

- ❑ Secure a private e-mail address.

- ❑ Review resume samples for up-to-date ideas on resume styles, formats, organization, and language.

PART II

Sample Resumes for Teachers and Educators

CHAPTER 4

Resumes for Early-Childhood Educators

- Child Care Directors
- Preschool Teachers
- Kindergarten Teachers
- After-School Program Coordinators
- Preschool Enrichment Consultants
- Children's Librarians
- Head Start Teachers
- Nursery School Directors

RESUME 1: BY ANITA RADOSEVICH, CPRW, JCTC

PENNY CONWAY
973 Corbin Way • Modesto, California 95350 • (425) 881-3201

Director / Teacher / Early Childhood Education
~ Natural gift to relate to children ~

PROFILE

An enthusiastic, warm, and caring educator/administrator who wants all children to be successful learners and works to create an atmosphere that is stimulating, encouraging, and adaptive to their emotional needs. Follower of traditional teachings and values. Energetic and decisive leader able to successfully merge and develop effective communications between provider, parent, and child through unique triangular, team-centered concept.

PROFESSIONAL EXPERIENCE AND ACHIEVEMENTS

Director, APPLEBEE HOUSE CHILD CARE CENTER, Omaha, Nebraska   1993–2005

Management/Administration
Established start-up operating procedures for an eight-child in-home child care center that grew into a 45-child facility. Retained 92% of the children and continued to grow facility with an annual revenue of more than $100,000. Ensured smooth-running operations concerning administrative, menu planning, scheduling, policies and procedures, and educational program elements. Recruited staff of 10 to 12 assistant directors and child care assistants for each shift. Consistently provided more staff than the "state-required ratio of children" in order to provide a quality child care center.

Communications/Training
Encouraged parent participation in creative craft-based activities (Jell-O, finger painting, blowing bubbles, baking, cooking, shaving cream, flour and water to create volcano foam, math, creative writing). Ensured all materials were biodegradable and non-toxic. Initiated and developed "triangular concept of communication," which strengthened communications and interaction among parent, child, and provider.

Trained and directed parents, assistant directors, and child care assistants to emphasize an active, positive learning environment. Worked with children to gain confidence and trust. Encouraged open communication and freedom of expression. Achieved measurable successes with all children, including at-risk and "problem" children. Increased parent involvement through regular communications and invitations to participate in classroom activities and field trips such as fishing, camping, and visiting the elderly.

Creativity/Imagination
Designed music programs using a variety of musical instruments including the harp, piano, and organ. Encouraged creative music style using pots, pans, and skillets to build hand dexterity skills. Developed build-up and tear-down exercises to stimulate their imaginations.

Dividing professional experience into functional paragraphs is a good way to keep the information manageable and easy to understand.

PENNY CONWAY

Page 2

LICENSES

In-home Child Care: 45 children, State of Nebraska
Foster Care: Ages 0–18, 1988–2001

PRESENTATIONS

Lectured on the "Triangular Concept of Communication" among parent, child, and provider for an audience of 3,000 at "Excellence in Early Childhood" conference.

SPECIALIZED TRAINING

UNIVERSITY OF OMAHA COOPERATIVE EXTENSION, Omaha, Nebraska

Certificates:

CPR/First Aid

Developing Creative Learners

Issues Affecting Children and Families

ADHD/ADD Workshop Early Intervention Team

Appropriate Use of Behavior Management

Good Stuff for Kids

Observation and Assessment in Early Childhood Programs

Encouraging Responsibility in Young Children Through Choices/Consequences of Raising Children in a Socially Toxic Environment

COMPUTER SKILLS

PC computer literate: Windows 98, MS Office, and scanner

BEATRICE WRIGHT

648 Yale Drive
Alexandria, VA
22314
Home 703.579.6492

Cell 703.528.3164
BWright@aol.com

CAREER FOCUS

Creative and resourceful early childhood/elementary educator **dedicated to child and adult literacy.** Possess extensive **knowledge of children's literature** and **balanced literacy programs.** Experienced in multicultural classroom settings. Strong desire to work at grassroots level to educate inner-city children and adults on the importance of reading and literacy. Seeking admission to a graduate program specializing in **children's literature, language,** and **reading programs.** Expertise includes

Balanced Literacy Programs • Curriculum Development • Course Design
Classroom Management • Educational Administration • Lifelong Learning
Accreditation • Grant Administration • Training & Development
Curriculum Mapping • Parent/Teacher Conferences • Student Retention

EDUCATION

B.A. George Mason University, Fairfax, VA, anticipated May 2005 with honors & distinction
Major: Honors English • Minor: History

EXPERIENCE

Preschool Teacher, George Mason Child Development Center, Fairfax, VA, 2004
- Instructed 17 three- and four-year-old children in twice-weekly class.
- Assisted with school's reaccreditation process.
- Coordinated children's classroom literature, including thematic and individual reading.

Preschool Teacher, Village Green Day School, Great Falls, VA, 2000–02
- Instituted literature-based, early childhood curriculum at NAEYC-accredited school. Supervised two assistant teachers.
- Presented *Learning Through Literature* workshop at Northern Virginia Regional Teacher's Conference.
- Transformed classrooms with creative decorations that tied in with weekly themes and classroom reading.

Camp Director, American Camping Association, Great Falls, VA, Summers 2002–04
- Supervised activities for 200 children at nationally accredited children's camp. Chaired curriculum-development efforts.
- Recruited, trained, and managed staff of 40 counselors and 8 administrative assistants.
- Implemented First Aid, CPR, and Blood-Borne Pathogen certification for staff members.
- Camp earned first-ever 100% rating from evaluator with 17 years of experience.

Manager, Children's Hour, New Orleans, LA, Summers 2001–02
- Directed non-profit literacy-awareness program for hospitals, schools, and pediatricians.
- Coordinated community book events and author visits.
- Promoted literacy awareness through seminars for teachers and administrators.

Summer Camp Director, U.S. Embassy, Community Service Association, Cairo, Egypt, 1997
- Orchestrated camp events and activities for 183 children from around the world.
- Created ethnically harmonious curriculum for diverse student group.
- Organized field trips to educational sites such as the Giza Pyramids.

AFFILIATIONS & COMMUNITY SERVICE

NAEYC Member • Undergraduate English Society, George Mason University
Golden Key National Honor Society and English Honors Society
Virginia Association for Early Childhood Educators • Read to Your Bunny Campaign
Northern Virginia Women's Shelter—Organized new children's library
Crescent House, New Orleans, LA—Raised $800 in book donations for women's shelter

"Once in a while a natural teacher is born and Beatrice is truly that person."
Linda A. Rodgers
Village Green Day School Director
Great Falls, VA

"(Beatrice created) an innovative, totally integrated literature-based curriculum ... the children waited with anticipation to see where they would be visiting next... (Beatrice) presented an environment where children entered the world of a story ..."
Patricia L. Dezelick
Parent & Teacher
Herndon, VA

"...an incredible role model for the staff."
Lynne Simmons
President & Founder
Village Green Day School
Great Falls, VA

This resume uses a creative format, reserving the left column for contact information and testimonials. There is a strong keyword summary in the Career Focus section.

FREDERICK R. RICHARDS
134 Ridgefield Street
Framingham, Massachusetts 01701
508-877-8216
frichards@mediaone.net

EDUCATOR / INSTRUCTOR — EARLY CHILDHOOD

11 years of hands-on experience in early childhood education... Nominated by parents of children in my care for Scholastic National Teacher of the Year... Outstanding communication skills... Readily establish rapport with wide range of people of various ages... Adapt presentation of material/coursework to ensure complete comprehension by students... Software proficiency includes Microsoft Word, PowerPoint, and QuickBooks.

Sought out by organizations to **present workshops** at statewide and regional conferences to early childhood educators on various topics, e.g., science for young children, professionalism for child care providers, development of handbooks and contracts.

PROFESSIONAL EXPERIENCE

Apple Tree Child Center—Sudbury, Massachusetts   1994–Present
OWNER / DIRECTOR

- Oversee three staff members in care of 10 children aged infant–11 in nationally accredited (NAFCC) child care program. Prepare and serve nutritional meals; teach good eating habits and personal hygiene.

- Help children explore interests, develop talents and independence, build self-esteem, and learn how to behave with others in child-centered, child-directed environment.

- Develop curriculum based on NAEYC standards for developmental appropriateness to stimulate children's physical, emotional, intellectual, and social growth. Nurture, motivate, and teach children.

- Assess children to evaluate their progress and discuss parents' involvement in their child's learning and developmental process.

Marlborough Hospital—Marlborough, Massachusetts   1998–Present
CPR INSTRUCTOR / TRAINER, per diem
Teach pediatric safety and CPR to expectant parents, early childhood professionals, grandparents, and others.

PROFESSIONAL ORGANIZATIONS

National Association for the Education of
Young Children (NAEYC)

National Association for Family Child Care (NAFCC)

Mass. Alliance of Family Child Care Providers,
Treasurer, 1 term; President, 2 terms

Office of Child Care Services, Mentor

CERTIFICATION
Commonwealth of Massachusetts Teacher Certification, K–8

EDUCATION / CONTINUING EDUCATION
M.Ed., Early Childhood Curriculum and Instruction, 1998, Suffolk University—Boston, Massachusetts
B.S., Special Education and Elementary Education, 1977, Lowell State College—Lowell, Massachusetts

With a colorful graphic and creative headline font, this resume for an early-childhood educator stands out from the ordinary.

RESUME 4: BY MARTIN BUCKLAND, MRW, CPRW, CJST, JCTC, CEIP

Mary Ann Lancaster

2104 Evergreen Avenue, Toronto, Ontario M4E 1S8
Phone: 416.555.9874
E-mail: mlancaster@sympatico.ca

Early Childhood Educator

Resourceful, innovative, and dedicated educator with the ability to design and deliver stimulating age-appropriate lesson plans. Energetic and enthusiastic; actively promote values and traditional teaching practices coupled with the introduction of technology into the classroom. Articulate; communicate effectively with students, parents, peers, and other stakeholders. Well-traveled and culturally sensitive. Assess students with respect to their personalities; committed to building self-esteem and motivation and creating a relaxed and harmonious environment. Recently appraised by parent with the following testimonial:

> *"Miss Lancaster has provided inspiration, guidance, and support to my son; we have been highly impressed with her ability to enrich his life with her wisdom, caring, and sharing...*
> *She is a true teaching professional and we wish her well in her new teaching appointment."*

Professional Experience

Pine Point Elementary School, Burloak, Ontario   2001–2004
KINDERGARTEN TEACHER

- Designed and facilitated an interactive and theme-based curriculum focussing on monthly calendars to senior and junior kindergarten students.
- Utilized diverse instructional methods and resource materials to emphasize individual learning capabilities.
- Oversaw, with assistant and parent volunteers, two physically challenged students with cerebral palsy and spina bifida requiring extra support and attention.
- Acknowledged by Principal for actively contributing to staff meetings and other school activities and encouraging parents to take on a more responsible role in supervision during critical financial restrictions.

Education

McMaster University, Hamilton, Ontario   2001
MASTER OF EDUCATION—Early Childhood Education

D'Youville College, Buffalo, New York   1999
STUDENT TEACHER
TEACHER'S CERTIFICATE

Completed the following modules: August–December 1999:

ᛣ Methods of Elementary Reading and Writing (A)	ᛣ Meeting the Needs of Exceptional Learners (A)
ᛣ Elementary School Strategies (A)	ᛣ Curriculum Planning (A)
ᛣ Major Themes in Early Childhood Education (B+)	ᛣ Theories of Learning (B+)

Assigned student teaching positions include the following:
Wilfred Laurier School, Burlington, Ontario   March–May 1999
- Developed curricula, assembled teaching materials, prepared goals and agendas, created lesson plans, and taught Grades 1 & 2.

Chelsea School, Hamilton, Ontario   January–March 1999
- Prepared and delivered programs encompassing stories and crafts including a Valentine's Day theme.

University of Western Ontario   1998
BACHELOR OF ARTS—History

Not only eye-catching, the format of this resume helps guide the reader through the document. Up-to-date education is highlighted in a table format.

Joanne Cavanagh

60 Orchard Terrace, Bronxville, NY 10708
(914) 961-9823 Home ✶ (610) 896-8969 College
joanne.cavanagh@haverford.edu

Objective

Kindergarten Teacher. Qualified by academic training as an educator, extensive experience working with young children, and leadership roles.

Education

Bachelor of Science, English Education (expected May 2005)
Haverford College, Haverford, PA
✶ Major: Education—Minor: English—GPA in Major: 3.4
✶ Admitted to the National Honor Society in high school

Ongoing training/certification:
✶ CPR for the Professional Rescuer (2004)
✶ Lifeguard Training and Community First Aid & Safety (2002)

Relevant Experience

Co-Facilitator (2004–2005)
Haverford College, Haverford, PA
✶ Selected to lead weekly group meetings with 20 freshmen to discuss issues related to adjusting to college life.

Swim Instructor (Summers 2003–2004)
Lake Isle Country Club, Eastchester, NY
✶ Taught young children to swim one-on-one and in small-group lessons.
✶ Utilized self-taught techniques acquired through 12 years of competitive swimming experience and book research.
✶ Entrusted with simultaneously managing head lifeguard duties.

Head Lifeguard/Lifeguard (Summers 1999–2003)
Lake Isle Country Club, Eastchester, NY
✶ Promoted to Head Lifeguard in 2000 based on demonstrated work ethic.
✶ Ensured a safe environment by scheduling coverage, supervising lifeguards, and testing pool water regularly.
✶ Organized special holiday games for children.

Junior Achievement Kindergarten Teacher (Spring 2004)
St. Mary's Elementary School, Broomall, PA
✶ Conducted educational activities that followed the curriculum.
✶ Selected books to read based on coursework in children's literature.

Community Service

Special Olympics Volunteer, Haverford, PA (2001–2003)
✶ Supported an assigned group throughout all games and meals.
✶ Participated as "Team Hugger" for two years, hugging participants at the conclusion of their events.

Catholic Worker, West Philadelphia, PA (2001–2002)
✶ Mentored group in an after-school program, providing structured play and individual homework help.

This resume shows quite a bit of experience for a newly graduated kindergarten teacher and clearly relates this youthful experience to her new role.

RESUME 6: BY FRAN KELLEY

Chloe Kelley

7 Oak Lane, Waldwick, NJ 07463   201-555-1212

**Child Care
Professional**

Excellent ability to establish and maintain rapport with both children and parents based on superb interpersonal and communication skills. Provide facilitated learning environment with well-planned and organized curriculum. Able to assess each child to determine their personalities and relate to them as individuals. Intuitive ability to control children while providing a relaxed and fun atmosphere for them. Solve problems quickly and well with total focus on the welfare of the child.

**Professional
Employment**

AFTER-SCHOOL PROGRAM COORDINATOR
YWCA of Old Hills, Old Hills, NJ   1999–present
Design and deliver after-school programs for 35–40 children from K–7th grade.
- Develop age-appropriate curriculum linked to monthly themes.
- Cultivate respect of children through consistent deployment of policies while creating an atmosphere where children can relax and have fun.
- Establish and maintain good working relationships with parents through constant communication regarding vacations, policies, and upcoming events.
- Develop and maintain solid relationships with principals, school nurses, and secretaries.
- Recruit, develop, train, and supervise four to five staff members.
- Ensure compliance with state regulations for child care, administration of medications, staff-to-children ratio, attendance books, and fire drills.
- Implement parental requests regarding supervision of homework and participation in sports and recreational activities.

SECRETARY—NURSERY SCHOOL and CAMP
- Coordinate billing, registration, site tours, and word processing.
- Order all supplies and snacks.
- Manage accounts payable for five separate nursery school sites.
- Administer employee time sheets.
- Schedule day classes and trips for camp.
- Manage all details for special parties, including booking, billing, scheduling, and staffing.

TEACHER
Happy Times School, Inc., Oakland, NJ   1997–1999
Supervised the activities of 12–13 children ranging from two to three years old at this privately owned pre-school.
- Developed and delivered thematic monthly curriculum appropriately geared to age ranges with reinforcement through all bulletin boards and banners throughout the school.
- Taught colors, shapes, numbers, weather, and science.
- Conducted walking trips and organized fund-raisers.

ASSISTANT DIRECTOR
- Conducted tuition billing for 60 families.
- Created and administered staff schedules.
- Performed diverse administrative duties: word processing, filing, and answering telephones.
- Conducted site tours.

A strong introduction focusing on educational philosophy is a notable feature of this well-organized resume.

Chloe Kelley

201-555-1212

page two

Professional Employment, cont.

ASSISTANT TO DIRECTOR
The Exceptional Child Pre-School, Rye, NJ   Summer 1997
- Designed bulletin boards and classrooms around monthly themes.
- Served as half-day floating teacher in afternoons for classes with infants through kindergarten.
- Conducted daily projects and various lesson plans.

ART TEACHER
Ridge Hills Recreation Commission, Ridge Hills, NJ   Summer 1996
- Instructed art for 20 three-year-olds at this morning summer recreation program.

ASSISTANT TO PROGRAM COORDINATOR
YMCA of Middletown, Middletown, NY   1992–1996
- Assisted in the after-school latchkey program for 20–25 children in 1st through 5th grades.
- Supervised homework, indoor/outdoor games, special classes, and craft projects.
- Served as summer camp counselor.
- Supervised vacation programs.
- Acted as birthday party hostess for weekend programs.

Education

Associate Degree—Early Childhood Education
Ramapo Community College, Oak Ridge, NJ   1997
Student Teaching:
— Supervised all room centers and activities and conducted various lesson plans for a class composed of 20 three- and four-year-olds.
Relevant coursework:
— *Early Childhood Education I and II, Child and Educational Psychology, Sociology of Family, Human Service, Parenting Young Children, Curriculum Materials & Methods, Developing and Implementing Curriculum, Supervised Field Work Experience I and II, Field Work Seminar I and II; Infants and Toddlers.*

Languages

Spanish: some knowledge

Computer Skills

Microsoft Windows, Word: high level of proficiency
Excel, PowerPoint: some knowledge

Certifications

First Aid Level 1; CPR Adult, Child, and Infant; National Safety Council

Professional Affiliations

NJ Association for the Education of Young Children (NJAEYC)

RESUME 7: BY BEATE HAIT, CPRW, NCRW

Joyce A. Morrison

133 Bertram Island Road
Hopatcong, New Jersey 07843
973-398-1832

PRESCHOOL ENRICHMENT CONSULTANT / CHILDREN'S LIBRARIAN

Dynamic professional career promoting literacy and language development through programs encouraging parent/child interaction… Knowledge of wide variety of information sources to assist patrons in locating information for use in their personal and professional lives… Communicate effectively with people of all ages… Recognize opportunities for outreach; develop and implement programs… Excellent research and organizational skills.

Toddler Presentations — Hopatcong, New Jersey   2000–Present
PROGRAM LEADER / CONSULTANT

- Design specific single-day or multi-session programs for children ages 2 and up. Present home workshops for children ages 6 and up during school vacations. Promote interaction between parent(s) and child(ren). Programs include a story and craft focusing on a specific theme:

Storytime with Simple Science	Holiday Sampler for Young Children
Red Is Best (Valentine's Day)	You're So Silly (April Fool's)
Mother's Day Coffee/Story Hour	Tea Party

- Develop and present customized party activity related to party theme, child's age and interests. Offer complete party planning services. Make quality-time happen.

Sussex County Public Library — Hopatcong, New Jersey   1994–Present
CHILDREN'S LIBRARIAN

- Manage children's department; supervise circulation; train children's department staff. Contributed to development of training manual and library policy.
- Manage budget of $10K–$15K; preview and purchase print and non-print materials. Follow trends and consider patrons' requests to effectively oversee selection and organization of library materials.
- Design and present all programs for ages 2 through 10 and family, focusing on stimulating children's emotional, intellectual, and social growth. Write all press releases for children's programs.
- Interface with school and community to develop informational programs and systems to meet needs of patrons. Complete reference inquiry interview through information retrieval. Assist users with searching techniques, including use of Internet.
- Assisted in grant writing to obtain Community Partnerships Grant through the New Jersey Department of Education. Developed and implemented outreach program to promote literacy for children in a day-care setting while concurrently providing support for caregivers.

Randolph Public Library — Randolph, New Jersey   1990–1994
ASSISTANT DIRECTOR / CHILDREN'S SERVICES

- Supervised children's department and encouraged teamwork to ensure quality service to the public. Assisted Director in administrative duties.

MEMBERSHIPS / VOLUNTEER ACTIVITIES

Lenape Valley Early Childhood Advisory Council	Netcong Arts Council, Chairperson
Hopatcong Parks Department, Volunteer Coordinator	Executive Board of HCC, Past Treasurer

EDUCATION

M.S., 1989, Early Childhood and Child Development, Montclair University — Montclair, New Jersey
B.A., 1978, English Major, Drew University — Madison, New Jersey

An owl reading a book is the perfect graphic to enhance this resume for a children's librarian.

Tanisha Jones

14000 Sixth Avenue   Sun City, PA 16000
Home: 724.555.8735   Work: 724.555.8004   E-mail: Teacup@searchforth.net

Objective: To continue my track record for dedication, responsibility, and leadership in education as an Early Childhood Education Teacher with County Head Start.

Education & Certification

Pennsylvania State University
University Park, PA
- Bachelor of Science Degree in Elementary / Kindergarten Education
- Pennsylvania Instructional 1 Teaching Certificate
- Pennsylvania Private Academic School Certificate (Early Childhood Elementary)

Scholastic Highlights
- Dean's List: 5 semesters.
- Chaired / sat on relevant committees.
- Attended education seminars: Penn State Cooperative Extension—Middle County.
- Maintained continuous employment to fund education.

Relevant Employment

Community Child Care Center (Present)
Hudson, PA
- Center Supervisor
- Preschool Teacher

Pierre Indian Learning Center
Pierre, SD
- Teacher

Ferguson Township Elementary School
Pine Valley, PA
- Teaching Internship

Townsend Primary School
Townsend, PA
- Teaching Internship

Teaching Qualifications

Class Instruction
- Capable of providing expert instruction for students ranging from learning-disabled to gifted.
- Responsibly lead daily learning activities based on development of monthly themes.
- Ably contribute to building new curriculum framework / units.
- Successfully initiate classroom management plans promoting individual responsibility / positive reinforcement.
- Provide tactful, stern classroom mediation whenever necessary.
- Innovate and test stimulating educational games.
- Build excellent, productive relationships via daily contact with parents and guardians.
- Create clear monthly calendars to aid students and parents in coordinating school activities.

Administrative Strengths
- Possess superior time-management skills.
- Perform above and beyond daily requirements to achieve project success.
- Professionally versatile working in a team effort or independently.
- Active participant in staff meetings, in-services; serve on and chair committees.
- Easily adapt to new assignments / willing to take extra time to learn skills.
- Expertly assemble staff schedules and calendars to increase efficiency.
- Lead others and take initiative.
- Coordinate peer-tutor programs.

Committee Involvement

- College Women's Association: President 2003-04
- Young Authors Conference: Chair, 2001
- Year-Round Schooling: Research Committee Member
- School Scheduling: Committee Member
- Peer Tutoring Program: Coordinator

Computer Proficiency

Windows, Works, Word,
WordPerfect,
Internet navigation,
Graphics versatility

Personal Highlights

Mature and Stable / Thorough / Innovative / Pleasant / Professional / Conscientious

A multicolumn format makes the most of the available space. Note the interesting addition of a Personal Highlights section at the very bottom.

Jennifer R. Haglund

1861 Pascal Avenue
Roseville, MN 55113
651-555-3892
jrhaglund@uminn.edu

Profile

✳ Enthusiastic, committed educator with innate ability to understand and motivate children.
✳ Keen interest in and hands-on experience working with students who have special needs.
✳ Strive to build student self-esteem and encourage understanding of cultural diversity, gender differences, and physical limitations.
✳ Create a cooperative community in the classroom; model for students the importance of mutual respect and cooperation among all community members.
✳ Skilled in adapting to students' diverse learning styles.

Education

Macalaster College • St. Paul, MN
Pursuing **Master's Degree—Special Education**
  • Anticipated completion: Fall 2006
  • Working toward Emotionally Impaired specialty

University of Minnesota • Minneapolis, MN
Bachelor of Science in Education (2000)
  • Language Arts major; Math and Early Childhood Education minors
  • Earned *Class Honors* and named *Gopher Scholar*

Certification

Minnesota Provisional Elementary with Early Childhood Specialty (K–8)

Relevant Experience

Preschool Teacher—Ready, Set, Succeed! Program/Perry Community Schools • Perry, MN (1999–Present)
  • Oversee all aspects of state-funded program for at-risk four-year-olds modeled after Head Start.
  • Plan and implement age-appropriate curriculum to academically prepare students for kindergarten and provide opportunity for development of socialization skills.
  • Utilize wide range of instructional techniques (centers, cooperative groups, individual work) with emphasis on providing a language-rich environment.
  • Interview parents; determine eligibility for program based on income and other guidelines.
  • Make home visits; build rapport with families as well as students.
  • Administer four-year-old Brigance screening to assess students' developmental levels.
  • Developed duties for and direct program assistant.
  • Trained in and taught Minnesota Literacy Progress Profile to five-year-olds (Summer 1999).

Substitute Preschool Teacher—College Child Development Center • Minneapolis, MN (1997–1999)
  • Interacted with infants and children up to kindergarten age.

Student Teacher—King Elementary/Roseville Community Schools • Roseville, MN (1997)
  • Taught all subjects to 17-member first-grade classroom.
  • Organized and facilitated reading group.

Student Intern—United Way First Call for Help & Volunteer Center • St. Paul, MN (1997)
  • Referred callers in need to community service agencies and directed volunteers to assignments.

Tutor Aide—Columbia Middle School/Columbia Community Schools • Columbia, MN (1998)
  • Assisted 6th-grade Language Arts teacher with lesson plan preparation and instruction.
  • Tutored students individually and in small groups.

Tutor—Self-employed (1996–1998)
  • Privately tutored high school student in all subjects.

Volunteer Tutor—Brooklyn Middle School/Brooklyn Community Schools • Brooklyn, MN (1994–1998)
  • Completed Lit Start program and tutored middle school students.

References available on request

Note how professional, student, and volunteer experiences are blended to present a substantial Relevant Experience section.

Helen F. Shalk

2 Rigel Road, Kingston, ON K1C 0B2 (613) 777-9999
Chillin@hotmail.com

PROFILE

A self-directed, action-oriented professional with more than 10 years of experience in education and community service. Proven abilities in problem solving, people management, and motivation. A self-starter with high energy enabling maximum and efficient work under pressure.

"This individual gives her all to everything she does. Her participation in a project is like having your own King Midas!" — quote from her performance appraisal as Nursery School Director (2001).

SUMMARY OF QUALIFICATIONS

Organizational Skills
As a leader, organized, coached, and lead people of all ages in a variety of activities and events.
- Coordinated the National Capital Marathon route control by planning for the protection of the participants, **recruiting resources from the community,** and assigning roles and responsibilities at various geographic locations throughout the National Capital Region (secured route of 21 kilometres).
- Recruited, trained, and supervised a volunteer staff of 20 responsible for registering more than 1,500 children in Gloucester Recreational soccer league.
- Managed family needs in the context of an absent spouse, which involved **facilitating the development and education of special-needs children,** managing the family finances, coordinating special-needs child care, and orchestrating all related logistics.
- Established the T-Ball league at Rockcliffe that involved scheduling games and acquiring equipment and uniforms. For 2 years, guided the coaches and ensured all participants, including coaches, received acknowledgement and trophies. **Set budgetary goals** to maintain previous years' expenses. The program resulted in happy kids and satisfied parents in the community.

Administrative Functions
- Performed Nursery School Director duties at Rockcliffe Army Base for more than 2 years and Trenton Army Base for more than 4 years, planning activities, teaching children, and **maintaining a daily log on each child.**
- Volunteered with St. John Ambulance as a brigade member, attending weekly meetings to review skills, drills, and equipment usage following strict protocols with the purpose of **providing quality patient care.**
- Managed medical records, answered inquires, directed people to appropriate locations, managed file system, handled mail, performed word processing (self-taught), and coordinated other **administrative tasks** associated with the gymnasium.
- Pooled resources to transport people and children to events and activities in the community and **coordinated child care for families** within the community.

A functional style worked well for this individual, whose primary professional experience had taken place on military bases. A quote from the job seeker herself is a nice touch at the end of the resume.

Helen F. Shalk
page 2

Community Service

More than 10 years of active service within the community in a variety of capacities.

- Participated in the needs assessment and **facility planning** for the community centre at Rockcliffe Army Base.
- Recruited and coordinated volunteers for the community centre.
- Performed councillor duties, enforcing community bylaws and supporting the mayor in **policy development** and implementation.

"The professional attitude that Helen portrays is evident in the way she approaches everyone she comes in contact with." —Mayor of Rockcliffe Army Base

WORK AND VOLUNTEER EXPERIENCE

Nursery School Director   2001–current
Rockcliffe Base, Ottawa, Ontario

Registrar   2002
Gloucester Recreational Soccer, Gloucester, Ontario

Volunteer Coordinator   2001
National Capital Marathon, Ottawa, Ontario

Mayfair Coordinator   2000
Manor Park Elementary School, Ottawa, Ontario

Community Councillor   1999–2002
Rockcliffe Base, Ottawa, Ontario

Gymnasium Clerk and Secretary   1995–1999
National Defence, Trenton, Ontario

PROFESSIONAL DEVELOPMENT AND EDUCATION

Early Childcare Certificate   2002–2003
Algonquin College, Ottawa, Ontario

Business Management   2003
Ottawa Carleton Night School, Ottawa, Ontario

French Language Training   2000
Berlitz School of Language

Bachelor of Arts, Psychology   1991
University of Manitoba

REFERENCES AVAILABLE UPON REQUEST

"Children help supply the energy that warms our hearts; without them, the world would be a mighty cold place." —Quote from Helen Shalk

CHAPTER 5

Resumes for Elementary Educators

- Elementary Teachers
- Bilingual Educators

COMMITTED TO THE CARE AND EDUCATION OF YOUNG CHILDREN

LINDSAY M. SHULL

lindsayteaches@primenet.com

5963 Oakview Circle
Oklahoma City, Oklahoma 59109

405.134.8163

This four-page resume with a distinctive cover can be printed on single sheets of paper or in a "book-let" style. Inside, good organization makes the pages highly readable.

PROFILE

Professional Educator with diverse experience and strong track record fostering child-centered curriculum and student creativity. A warm and caring teacher who wants all children to be successful learners and works to create a classroom atmosphere that is stimulating, encouraging, and adaptive to the varied needs of students. Committed to professional ethics, standards of practice, and the care and education of young children.

Certifications	*Oklahoma Department of Education, 1998*	*Elementary K through 12*
	Endorsement: TESL—in progress	*(Teaching English as Second Language)*
	Texas Department of Education, 1996	*Elementary K through 8*
	Spalding Method—a reading program	

ACHIEVEMENTS

- **CERTIFICATE**—Developmentally Appropriate Music Experiences for Young Children.
- Originated and developed **CHILDREN'S ACTIVITY GROUP CENTER:**
  — Provided children from the ages of 4 to 12 with educational activities.
  — Designed and implemented programs for crafts and science experiments.
  — Planned and directed field trips encompassing *"How The World Works"* venues.

SUMMARY OF QUALIFICATIONS

- Successfully develop and instruct child-centered, integrated, thematic unit curriculum, utilizing multiple intelligences, to create an atmosphere of learning and fun.
- Demonstrate ability to consistently individualize instruction, based on students' interests and needs, at the most appropriate level.
- Positive coaching and motivational proficiencies.
- Key member in designing and developing operating procedures for the opening of a new school.
- Implement strategies to create innovative units enabling students to master academic skills.
- Utilize solid organizational, work, and time management skills.
- Strong interpersonal relations and effective oral and written communication skills with students, colleagues, principal, parents, and individuals on all levels.
- Perform effectively both as an autonomous, self-motivated individual and as an active, contributing team member.
- Demonstrate decision-making skills with problem-solving abilities.

Computer Skills: Mac and Windows OS, word processing, Internet search, e-mail procedures.

EDUCATION

UNIVERSITY OF OKLAHOMA **MASTER'S PROGRAM**—in progress	Norman, Oklahoma
UNIVERSITY OF TEXAS **BACHELOR OF SCIENCE DEGREE**—2000 *Major:* Elementary Education	Dallas, Texas
UNIVERSITY OF TEXAS—1996 to 2000 *Major:* Elementary Education; *Minor:* History	Austin, Texas

LINDSAY M. SHULL
COMMITTED TO THE CARE AND EDUCATION OF YOUNG CHILDREN   PAGE 1

TEACHING EXPERIENCE

JACKSON ELEMENTARY SCHOOL, July 2003 to current Oklahoma City, Oklahoma
TEACHER—FIRST GRADE
- Year-round school with *Back to Basics* academic curriculum.
- Effectively instruct at-risk students.
- Implemented Accelerated Reading Program (ARP). Assess students for tier placement, perform ongoing testing, and evaluate comprehension improvement.
- Integrate multiple subjects and provide students with hands-on projects, creating an atmosphere of learning and fun.
- Maintain a structured, monitored environment, including adhering to mandated mps (minutes per subject) requirements, and setting and achieving daily student goals.
- Provide weekly progress reports assessing student comprehension on subjects taught.
- Work effectively in team-teaching situations.

DUNCAN LIBERTY SCHOOL, August 2001 to June 2003 Stillwater, Oklahoma
TEACHER—K THROUGH EIGHTH GRADE
- Head teacher, reported directly to school board, supervised three employees.
- In addition to teaching duties, created lesson plans for eight grade levels adhering to Oklahoma Academic Standards; performed office manager functions; allocated time to teach P.E., Music, Art, Social Skills; responsible for application and evaluation in all subject areas.
- Coordinated services for special-needs children (i.e., OT, PT, Speech Therapist, Special Education teacher) with community agencies.
- Performed administrative responsibilities, including reporting to Oklahoma Department of Education on various compliance issues for the school district.

CAHLAN CHARTER SCHOOL, August 2000 to June 2001 Irving, Texas
TEACHER—PRIMARY (K–3), MIDDLE (4–8), SECONDARY (9–12)
- Prepared and administered lesson plans in all levels. Developed and implemented multiple intelligence and learning modalities in lesson planning.
- As *Career Development Advisor* for upper grades, provided guidance/counseling to address students' academic and emotional needs.
- Accountable for Learning Center activities and programs.

VALLEY SCHOOL DISTRICT, August 1998 to June 2000 Ft. Worth, Texas
STUDENT TEACHER—KINDERGARTEN
- Resourceful at working with special-needs children: behavioral problems, ADD, and at-risk.
- Collaborated with community resource and child support personnel.

HARRIS COUNTY SCHOOL DISTRICT, 1997 to 1998 Austin, Texas
TEACHER AIDE—ADD, BEHAVIORAL DISORDERS, AND AT-RISK CHILDREN
- Performed evaluations and assessments for referral and mainstreaming.
- Designed and implemented programs to involve children in creative expressions of art and music.

TEXAS COUNCIL OF GOVERNMENTS, 1996 Austin, Texas
INSTRUCTOR
- Assisted preschool students from three years through five years old.
- Developed, designed, and implemented indoor and outdoor children's activities and teaching lessons.
- Extensive knowledge of community resources, support systems, and social services.

PROFESSIONAL AFFILIATIONS
National Science Teachers Association
Big Brothers–Big Sisters Organization

LINDSAY M. SHULL
COMMITTED TO THE CARE AND EDUCATION OF YOUNG CHILDREN PAGE 2

CONTINUING EDUCATION AND PERSONAL DEVELOPMENT

March 2004	Classroom Management Seminar	Norman, Oklahoma

- Methods and new strategies to motivate children toward positive learning behavior
- Teaching students consistency and structure

February 2004	Super Teaching Workshop	Norman, Oklahoma

- Teaching students how to learn
- Teaching test-taking strategies

January 2004	Reader's Theater	Norman, Oklahoma

- Strategies and techniques for educators
- Methods and strategies for enabling students to become independent readers
- Educational styles that enforce "Round Robin" instruction

July 2003	Language Acquisition Workshop	Tulsa, Oklahoma

- Methods for teaching English to second-language learners

June 2003	G.E.M.S. Society—Math and Science Workshop	Oklahoma City, Oklahoma

OKLAHOMA STATE UNIVERSITY
- Using Math and Science to solve "real world" problems
- Environmental Issues and Our Children

August 2002	Project Wild—Creating Environmental Activities	Stillwater, Oklahoma

- People, Culture, and Wildlife
- Responsible Human Actions

April 2001	Texas Mathematics & Science Consortium	Dallas, Texas

- Problem Solving in Math and Science

February 2000	Early Childhood Education Conference	Irving, Texas

- Early Learning Difficulties
- Assessment in Early Childhood Education
- Creative Thinking for Early Learners

August 1999	Accepting Individual Differences and Change	Dallas, Texas

- Insights into Listening and Communication
- Developing Appropriate Activities for Special-Needs Children
- Family Changes in Changing Times

April 1998	Linguistic Bias	Austin, Texas

- Language Reflecting Culture Values
- Gender Bias Relating to Interaction with Children
- Traditional and Historical Usage of Language

GRACE TAYLOR

76 Columbia Street
Frankfort, NY 13340

Home 315.249.2309
Mobile 315.890.1276

EXPERIENCED ELEMENTARY TEACHER

Energetic and dedicated teacher with a solid foundation in subject matter instruction (particularly science) and active involvement in creating change. Offering an optimistic attitude and a strong commitment to shaping reflective, self-directed learners who think critically and creatively. Experienced with the most up-to-date instructional methodologies and exposed to a variety of collaborative teaching approaches. Excellent knowledge of the needs of students requiring remedial reading instruction. Continuously strive to enhance the educational environment and promote school unity.

- Character Education
- Two-Year Looping Program
- Differentiated Classroom
- Technology Integration
- Enrichment Programs
- Authentic Assessments
- Diversity Curriculum
- Curriculum Mapping
- Departmentalization

HIGHLIGHTS OF QUALIFICATIONS

→ Experienced with a full range of exceptional children from high-needs remedial students to highly advanced enrichment students. Proven ability to ease the transition of bilingual students into the mainstream school system.

→ Actively engaged in sharing new models of learning and collaborating with other educators to promote innovation and exemplary practices. Continuously seek professional development to expand and reaffirm classroom techniques.

→ Involved in educational improvement initiatives (i.e., Micro Society) that focus on building classroom and school-wide cultures of "thinking" by fostering the attitudes, values, and skills that support good critical and creative thinking.

→ Able to recognize and develop students' multiple intellectual strengths, adapting instruction to individual differences, cultural backgrounds, and developmental levels. Also able to assess their work in ways that promote further learning.

→ Possess useful current insights to make sound educational judgments, focus standards, and respond to state frameworks to strengthen teaching and learning of both general education and special education.

TEACHING EXPERIENCE

Mohawk Central School District, *Mohawk, NY*   **1997 to Present**
(Middle-class suburban community and the largest school district in Herkimer County, with a student population of 9,350)

<u>Fisher Elementary</u>   **6th Grade**—*2000 to Present (Tenured 2000)*   **5th Grade**—*1997 to 2000*

Implement district programs in 4th through 6th grade school. Strive to shape classroom and instruction materials to help students develop valuable thinking skills and encourage a deeper understanding of concepts within and across disciplines. Curriculum marked by diversity of education practices and innovative approaches to learning.

- Rewrote the district's science curriculum and piloted the use of science kits for the district.
- Serve as 6th Grade Yearbook Advisor and as Head Coordinator for the annual science fair.
- Rewrote the English/Language Arts curriculum to align district program and assessments to state frameworks.
- Coordinator for 6th grade activities, school-wide fairs, and field trips.
- Member of various leadership teams involved with curriculum restructuring.

EDUCATION & CREDENTIALS

<u>**M.S. Elementary Education; Emphasis: Reading**</u>
Marist College, Poughkeepsie, NY

<u>**B.A. Social Science and Elementary Education**</u>
Marist College, Poughkeepsie, NY

To avoid repetition of job duties, two teaching positions covering eight years are grouped together. This strategy also leaves room for a strong "Highlights of Qualifications" section while keeping the resume to one page.

MADDIE PRIOR

"A dedicated educator who makes learning fun"

55 Rock Falls Road
Naperville, Illinois 60540

773-455-5555 Cellular
mprior@mxn.net

PROFESSIONAL GOAL

Elementary (K–6) Special Education Teacher
Endorsements in Special Education—Multi-Categorical Resource and Reading

QUALIFICATIONS

- Teaching experience in multicultural public and parochial environments in Colorado and Illinois.
- Ability to relate well with students, teachers, and parents; committed to educational excellence.
- Hands-on teaching style that offers learning opportunities through a myriad of teaching strategies.
- Approach that challenges, stimulates, and motivates students to do their best.
- Natural ability to spark students' interest, engage them in learning, and build lifelong learners.
- Genuine concern for the educational development of students of all ages and abilities.
- Valued by staff, administration, and parents as a teacher who has a wonderful sense of humor.
- Characterized as passionate about teaching, vibrant, energetic, supportive, and fair.

EDUCATION

Bachelor of Arts—Honors Graduate, University of Denver, Denver, Colorado, 2004
- Major: Education (K–6) with Special Needs Concentration
- Minor: Spanish
- Cumulative GPA: 3.92/4.0

Endorsements:
- Special Education Endorsement—Multi-Categorical Resource Level 1, 2004
- Reading Endorsement, 2004

STUDENT TEACHING

Dinlan Elementary School, Springfield, Illinois   **January 2004–May 2004**

Special Education—Multi-Categorical Resource—Student Teacher, Grades 2–5
- Wrote and implemented Individual Educational Plans (IEP) for students. Evaluated and recorded IEP goals. Gained experience with DIBBLES evaluation testing. Developed and implemented creative lesson plans, i.e., Jeopardy, Time-O, Sight Word Concentration, and Pecci. Taught students subject areas of Reading, Math, Spelling, Writing, and Cooking.

Hope Education Center, Denver, Colorado   **January 2003–May 2003**

Special Education—Directed Observation, Grades K–6
- Created and taught functional life skills and geography classes. Developed and incorporated rubrics in lesson plans.

> *"Maddie is an outstanding young educator who has excellent rapport with individuals regardless of their age or ability. She is able to create an atmosphere where others feel capable and cared about while maintaining appropriate social interactions with them."*
> — Julia Rosenblank, Ph.D., Principal, Dinlan Elementary School, Springfield, Illinois

A slogan and a testimonial "bracket" this resume for strong impact from beginning to end.

JUDY CASSIDY

724 West South Street
Philadelphia, PA 19110
215-745-3372 ▪ judyc@aol.com

PROFILE

ELEMENTARY EDUCATOR with more than 20 years of experience fostering academic learning and enhancing critical-thinking abilities. Incorporate effective cooperative learning techniques and unique classroom management style to establish creative and stimulating classroom environment. Dedicated, resourceful teacher skilled in building rapport and respect with students and student teachers.

Honored with **New Teacher Mentor Award** for Outstanding Service (2004).

"Miss Cassidy is an exceptional teacher. She is respectful to and of her students, and that respect is reciprocated. Using a variety of materials and techniques, Miss Cassidy challenges her students to excel. Her classroom is a warm, nurturing atmosphere where children are called to be their best selves."   A.F., School Administrator

EDUCATION AND CERTIFICATIONS

Instructional II—Permanent Certification, **State of Pennsylvania** (2002)

Master of Arts—**LaSalle University** (1994)

Bachelor of Science, Elementary Education—**Chestnut Hill College** (1988)

CAREER HIGHLIGHTS

- Developed and executed **Everyday Math Program** at John Smith Elementary School (1999). Program resulted in 180-point improvement in overall math grades in 2002 (versus previous year's scores). Participated in ongoing staff development and district training sessions to ensure utilization of hands-on, cooperative learning approach along with reinforcement and assessment techniques.

- Served as **Middle States Team Evaluator** for Brooklyn Diocese School System (1998). Collaborated with four colleagues in accreditation process that included interviewing teachers/committee, writing evaluation report, and creating recommended action plan. Conducted comprehensive academic assessment in similar capacity as Catholic Elementary School Evaluator for Diocese of Camden (1995).

- Achieved 90% passing rate in students graduating to fifth grade by directing and facilitating promotional requirements for **Multidisciplinary Learning Project** at John Smith Elementary School (1999–2002). Through intensive interaction, students developed research, writing, and computer skills to accomplish long-term school project with City Year members. Initiative strengthened student knowledge, pride, and enthusiasm for learning.

TEACHING EXPERIENCE

Philadelphia Public School District   1999–Present
John Smith Elementary School
ELEMENTARY TEACHER, Fourth Grade

Plan, implement, and evaluate various curriculum areas. Encourage cooperative learning, peer interaction, and increased achievement levels among disadvantaged and challenged students.

Appointed by principal as **Grade Chairman and Mentor** (2000–2003).

A notable award, a testimonial, and a Career Highlights section create a strong introduction to this teacher's chronological work history.

Judy Cassidy
Page Two

TEACHING EXPERIENCE (continued)

St. Agnes–Sacred Heart School   1995–1998
<u>ELEMENTARY TEACHER</u>, Third Grade

Instructed students in Reading, Integrated Language Arts, Religion, and Social Studies. Coordinated and implemented Language Arts Program for first- to fourth-grade students.

New Jersey Area Parochial School System   1989–1995
<u>ELEMENTARY TEACHER</u>, Third and Fourth Grade

- Saint Joseph Regional School
- Blessed Sacrament School
- Our Lady of Perpetual Help

Philadelphia Parochial School System   1978–1988
<u>ELEMENTARY TEACHER</u>, First and Second Grade

- Immaculate Heart of Mary School
- Our Lady of the Holy Souls School
- Saint Timothy School

TEACHING TESTIMONIALS

"Judith has, from the outset, displayed a level of professional competence and a striving for professional development that has benefited her students, our staff, and the entire school community in concrete ways. She introduced and implemented a variety of innovative classroom management strategies, such as Workshop Way and Integrated Language Arts, having been the first to pilot such a program in our school. She has challenged and motivated students to achievement and activities that have not only developed each child's personal gifts and talents, but also developed cooperative learning strategies to foster collaboration and interaction among her students." G.S., Principal

"Judy's professionalism, enthusiasm, and talent as a teacher are evident on a daily basis. Judy employs a thematic approach, and the varied learning experiences the children have to showcase their talents are not just one-time activities but are related to all curriculum areas. Judy is comfortable with and flexible in following many different styles of administration and has been recommended to assume leadership roles many times during her career." F.B., School Administrator

PROFESSIONAL DEVELOPMENT COURSES

<u>Attended and participated in various courses from 1998–2004, including</u>

- The Middle Years Literacy Framework
- Middle Years Balanced Literacy
- Academy of Reading Program
- Bringing Curriculum to Life
- Accelerated Reading Program

- Professional Education for Central-East AAO
- Rigby Guided Reading and Literature Circles
- Improving Decision-Making/Values Clarification
- Improving Ability to Communicate Mathematically
- Everyday Math Program and PowerPoint for Educators

RESUME 15: BY ROLANDE L. LAPOINTE, CPC, CIPC, CPRW, IJCTC, CCM, CSS, CRW

RHONDA L. LeCOMPTE
202 Arborway
Jamaica Plain, MA 02130

Telephone: (617) 555-3571   E-mail: RLecompte@aol.com

CREDENTIALS:

- Certified to Teach Bilingual Education (K–8)
- Certified to Teach Special Education
- Certified to Teach Elementary Education (K–8)

EDUCATION:

M.A. Applied Linguistics (Bilingual, ESL Education)   **Summa Cum Laude, 2003**
    — University of Massachusetts, Boston, Massachusetts

B.S. Special Education   **Magna Cum Laude, 1994**
Dual Major: *Special Education, Mental Retardation & Elementary Education*
Concentration: *Psychology*
    — University of Maine at Farmington   1990–1994
    — Université du Maine, LeMans, France   Spring Semester 1992
    — University of Maine, Orono, Maine   1989–1990

Academic Awards / Achievements:
    — Certificates of Award for Highest GPA in MR Major (1993, Spring)   UMF
        & Outstanding Academic Achievement (1992, Spring)
    — Alpha Lambda Delta / National Scholastic Honor Society for Freshmen   UMO
    — Selected (1 of 3 Students at the University) to participate in a
        Special Education Delegation to the People's Republic of China   UMF

QUALIFICATIONS:

- Bilingual (English & Spanish).
- Experience in one-on-one tutoring and group instruction of ESL.
- Experienced in client assistance working with the mentally retarded—teaching living skills to adolescents and adults.
- Designed and implemented a new program for teaching life skills that is currently successfully being used in a high school setting.
- Experienced in conceptualization, consultation, and presentation of varied-level educational workshops/conferences.
- Serve as a teaching consultant to other teachers involved in the process of integrating students into other programs and classes.
- Published in *Racenicity: The Whitewashing of Ethnicity* by Pepi Leistyna (Chapter 6) / Publisher: Roman & Littlefield (forthcoming)

(Continued on Page Two)

This resume for a bilingual/special/elementary teacher was very effective in generating interviews for positions in highly competitive school districts.

Rhonda L. LeCompte   Curriculum Vitae (Page Two)

TEACHING EXPERIENCE:

Bilingual (Spanish) Special Education Teacher   **Fall 2003–Present**
Cambridge High School (Cambridge, Massachusetts)
— Designed, implemented, and administer new Life Skills Program.
— Mentor to several high school students.

Spanish Instructor   **Summer 2002**
UMASS, Boston, Massachusetts / Veteran's Upward Bound Program

Substitute Teacher   **2001–2003**
Boston School System (Boston, Massachusetts)

ESL Instructor   **2000–2002**
Cambridge Center for Adult Education (Cambridge, Massachusetts)

Bilingual Special Education Teacher   **1999–2000**
Thomas Jefferson Elementary School (Boston, Massachusetts)
— K–3 Self-contained language room

Peace Corps Volunteer (Cuenca, Ecuador)   **1997–1999**
Special Education Teacher Consultant
Instituto Psicopedagogico Agustin Cueva Tamariz (Cuenca, Ecuador)
— Total program conducted in the Spanish language, grades K–6.
— Consulted with multiple teachers, classrooms, and students.
— Implemented/presented individual and classroom consultation programs
   for teachers.
— Demonstrated planning/presentation of lessons through model teaching.

Special Education Teacher (Behaviorally Impaired)   **1994–1997**
Montello Jr. High School (Lewiston, Maine)
— Self-contained classroom for 7th and 8th grade students.
— Supervised 1–2 Education Techs.
— Outstanding Teacher Award (1996–1997), Lewiston Teacher's Association.

RESUME 16: BY LERACHEL BUFFKINS, CPRW, GCDF, FJST, CFRWC

DENNIS WATSON, SR.

5877 Anchor Way ◆ Rockville, MD 20902 ◆ (301) 495-1111 ◆ dwatsonsr@yahoo.com

SPECIAL EDUCATION PROFESSIONAL

**More than 15 years of classroom and field experience
with the K–12 special-needs student population**

- Educational knowledge and teaching skills include student-centered instruction, educational technology, parental involvement in student learning strategies, reflective teaching, critical-thinking instructional activities, individual learning plans, student motivation strategies, and active and meaningful learning activities.
- Proficiently implement principles, methods, and procedures for diagnosis, treatment, and rehabilitation of physical and mental dysfunctions, and for counseling and guidance.
- Experienced in curriculum and training design, teaching, and instruction for individuals and groups, and the measurement of training effects.
- Highly motivated and dedicated with a commitment to quality education; enforce rules for behavior to maintain order among the students.
- Characterized as a strong communicator with effective presentation skills.

HIGHLIGHTS OF QUALIFICATIONS

**Individualized Education Programs (IEP) • Counseling • Curriculum Building
Testing & Assessment • Case Management • Training and Supervision
Organizational Development • Crisis Intervention**

EDUCATION & CERTIFICATION

**Master of Science, Special Education, with Emphasis on
Collaborative Vocational Evaluation Training**
George Washington University, Washington, D.C., 2004

Bachelor of Science, Special Education K–12
University of the District of Columbia, Washington, D.C., 1988

Teaching Certificate, K–12 Special Education, State of Maryland (Valid: 1998–2005)

TEACHING EXPERIENCE

Itinerant Special Education Resource Teacher
P.G. County Public Schools, Ace Road Special Education Office, 1999–Present

- Provide special education procedural and technical support to 11 school teams in reference to the assessment, identification, placement, and program review of students receiving special education services and support.
- Design and implement IEPs for developmentally disabled students; administer Woodcock-Johnson assessments for initial and re-evaluation referrals.

Written for a highly experienced special-education teacher, this resume follows a classic chronological format but places impressive education up front and starts off with a strong summary.

Dennis Watson, Sr. **Page 2**

- Communicate frequently with parents, social workers, school psychologists, occupational and physical therapists, school administrators, and other teachers.
- Initiate, plan, and coordinate programs such as the support group for parents of students with learning disabilities and attention-deficit disorder.
- Act as the designated Assistant Instructional Supervisor for Special Education designee at Multidisciplinary Team meetings per request.

Special Education Resource Teacher and Special Education Department Chair
P.G. County Public Schools, Spring Hill Middle School, 1995–1999

- Provided special education intensive resource instruction for 7th and 8th grade levels in the areas of Reading, Language Arts, and Social Studies.
- Supported the school staff by providing special education procedural and technical assistance in reference to the assessment, identification, placement, and program review of students receiving special education services.
- Developed IEPs and assisted with specific needs regarding implementation.
- Revised assessments for initial and reevaluation referrals.
- Coordinated placement of students with special needs into mainstream classes.

Special Education Learning Center Teacher
P.G. County Public Schools, Langley Park Elementary School, 1993–1995

- Instructed students in 4th, 5th, and 6th grade levels in the areas of Reading, Language Arts, Math, Science, and Social Studies.
- Designed curricula, assigned work geared toward each student's ability, and graded papers and homework assignments.
- Provided a highly structured academic environment using a variety of behavior management techniques.
- Facilitated the multidisciplinary team and weekly school instructional team meetings.

Special Education Learning Center Teacher
D.C. Public Schools, Garrison Elementary School, 1988–1993

- Instructed special-needs students on K–3rd grade levels in the areas of Reading, Language Arts, Math, Science, and Social Studies.
- Designed student IEPs and administered Brigance, Berry VMI, and Key Math assessments for initial and reevaluation referrals.
- Partnered with colleagues regarding curriculum modifications and behavior management strategies and techniques, as well as pre–referral intervention strategies.

ADDITIONAL PROFESSIONAL TRAINING

- P.G. County Public Schools:
    - Drug Awareness, 2000
    - MS Excel, 1999
    - Intro to Hispanic Culture, 1999
    - Teaching Students with Special Needs, 1996
- Trinity College Off-Campus, Teaching the Responsive Classroom, 1992
- D.C. Public Schools Teacher Training, Computer Literacy, 1989
- George Washington University, Technology in Special Education, 1988

ANNE C. ELLIS

210 Candlewood Court, Lacey, Washington 98509
ellisedu@earthlink.com   378-245-1256

OBJECTIVE

A position as an Elementary School Teacher that will utilize strong teaching abilities to create a nurturing, motivational, and stimulating learning environment to help children achieve their potential.

PROFILE

- Highly motivated, enthusiastic, and dedicated educator who wants all children to be successful learners.
- "Believe in the impossible"; continually research educational programs and procedures to benefit students.
- Committed to creating a classroom atmosphere that is stimulating and encouraging to students.
- Demonstrated ability to consistently individualize instruction, based on each student's needs and interests.
- Exceptional ability to establish cooperative, professional relationships with parents, staff, and administration.

EDUCATION

B.S. in Elementary Education, Troy State University, Troy, Alabama   2004
- Summa Cum Laude—President's Honor List—Kappa Delta Phi
- National Collegiate Education Award Winner
- Who's Who Among Students in American Universities and Colleges
- Participated in the Test for Teaching Knowledge field project, 2004

A.A. in Arts and Sciences, Pierce College, Tacoma, Washington   1999

CREDENTIALS

Elementary Education: 1–6:   Alabama License (Pending)—Washington License (Pending)

STUDENT TEACHING

Student Teacher, Harrand Creek Elementary School, Dothan, Alabama   Fall 2004
- Completed 200 hours hands-on teaching; resulting in a total of 488 hours experience in a first grade classroom. Utilized children's literature to teach and reinforce reading, writing, grammar, and phonics. Coordinated and taught math lessons and activities. Collaborated with teacher in planning, preparing, and organizing thematic units. Observed the use of teaching techniques to meet the needs of visual, kinesthetic, and auditory learners for all subject areas. Assisted in the quarterly grading.

Classroom Intern, Harrand Creek Elementary School, Dothan, Alabama (60 hours)
2nd Grade, Reading, Clover Park Elementary School, Dothan, Alabama
4th Grade, Reading, Science, Social Studies, Headland Elementary School, Dothan, Alabama
4th Grade, Math, EastGate Elementary School, Dothan, Alabama
5th Grade, Art & Social Studies, EastGate Middle School, Ozark, Alabama
1st Grade, Reading Tutor for student at-risk program, Troy State University, Alabama

RELATED EXPERIENCE

Director, Kinder-Care Learning Center, Lacey, Washington   1997 to 1999
Oversaw day-to-day operations of child care center for 65 children. Ensured all local, state, and federal rules and regulations were adhered to.

AFFILIATIONS

Member, National Council for Exceptional Children
Leader, Girl Scouts of America

This resume for a newly qualified teacher makes a strong visual impression through use of unusual fonts and a striking graphic.

The *ABCs* for Hiring TYLER TORRES

2349 Gold Street
Scottsdale, AZ 86254

602-349-7654
tyler@net.com

Qualified for a position as a **Substitute Elementary School Teacher.** Certified to teach children from kindergarten to eighth grade. Hold a Bachelor of Science in Elementary Education and a Master of Arts in Education.

Highlights of Qualifications A–L

Attitude is geared towards empowering children to learn to their fullest potential.

Believe every child has the ability to learn if placed in a nurturing environment.

Create and implement lesson plans for students with special needs; adapt teaching style to accommodate different levels of learning.

Demonstrate ability to engage students in the educational process and facilitate learning.

Employment history—**Teacher, Pine Park Elementary (2 years), Twin Pines Elementary (18 years).**

Foster an encouraging educational setting to meet the objectives of each student.

Girl Scout Leader for 5 years.

Hands-on teaching style; take an active interest in the progression of each student.

Interact with parents, teachers, and administrators, establishing open oral and written communication.

Judged Spelling Bees.

Keen ability to pique students' interest by providing a creative and supportive environment.

Led successful parental workshops that focused on how to improve homework habits and nurture a love for reading.

continued...

With a unique format that makes the connection between teaching and the "ABCs," this resume is a real attention-getter. Note how essential information is in boldface to ensure that the reader absorbs it in a quick skim of the resume.

TYLER TORRES page 2

Highlights of Qualifications M–Z

Maintain a stimulating and nurturing classroom setting. Promote free thinking and expression of ideas.

Natural talent for engaging students.

Open-minded and culturally sensitive.

Prepare lesson plans to meet the needs of the individual student and the curriculum set forth by the state.

Qualified educator with an impressive teaching ability.

Respected teacher with more than **20 years of experience.**

Served on the PTA to help bridge the gap between parents and teachers.

Team-taught various subjects, including **Math, English, Science, and History.**

Undeniably powerful, compassionate, and dedicated.

View teaching as an opportunity to enrich the lives of children.

Wear many hats; one of teacher, motivator, and role model.

Xtremely conscientious when developing classroom material.

Yawns are nonexistent in the classroom.

Zest for educating!!

RESUME 19: BY GAIL FRANK, NCRW, CPRW, JCTC, CEIP, MA

Kalista Jabert

555 Adams Street, Lowell, MA 01852 • 978-453-9988 • kjabert@verizon.net

"...Kalista has been a godsend for my son... her attentiveness and commitment have resulted in him making progress we never dreamed of..."

—Parent of Student, 2003

Sensitive, creative, and patient Special Education teacher with more than 12 years of experience in championing educational and developmental student needs. Master's-prepared professional who works collaboratively to develop innovative, age-appropriate solutions for behaviorally and emotionally challenged K–4 students.

Determined and tireless worker who forges strong relationships with other educators, administrators, and parents. Additional experience in delivering presentations, writing grants, and providing full-time care for special needs children.

EDUCATION

Fitchburg State College, Fitchburg, MA
M.Ed. in Early Childhood Education, 1997

Lesley College, Cambridge, MA
B.S. in Education
Dual Certification in Moderate Special Needs and Elementary Education with a Minor in Psychology

TEACHING EXPERIENCE

Special Education Teacher, Grades 1–4
Todd Alternative School—Lowell, MA
Fall 1998–Present
- Design and implement curricula to meet the individual needs of behaviorally/emotionally challenged special needs students.
- Brainstorm and strategize comprehensive behavioral management plans with teachers, aides, and parents.
- Chosen as Team Chairperson to lead development and implementation of individualized educational plans.

Fourth Grade Teacher
Summer School Program—Lowell, MA
Summer 2003
- Implemented and supplemented age-appropriate curricula to meet the needs of fourth-grade students working below grade level.
- Received *"Excellence in Teaching"* award from school principal.

Inclusion Specialist
Concord Public Schools—Concord, MA
Summer 2001
- Designed interactive workshop to facilitate understanding of daily disability challenges faced by students.
- Trained staff of 25 to work with children of varying disabilities in a regular camp setting.
- Collaborated with staff and designed activities to include a 7-year-old girl with tuberculosis in the regular Concord Recreation Program.

A strong endorsement from a parent, used as a quote in the left margin, lets this candidate "toot her horn" without seeming to brag about herself.

Kalista Jabert • PAGE 2

Third Grade Teacher
Donahue Elementary School—Lowell, MA
1995–1998

- Implemented and supplemented curricula in a regular third-grade classroom.
- Teamed with Chapter I, ESL, and Special Education teachers and devised curricula to meet the individual needs of the student population.
- Developed and taught thematic units to enhance student involvement and participation.

Behavior Management Program Teacher
Reilly Elementary School—Lowell, MA
1992–1995

- Developed a behavior management program that provided a positive and nurturing environment for students in grades 1–4.
- Implemented strong, comprehensive behavior modification programs to coincide with individualized academic programs.
- Conducted home visits that linked home and school as partners in development.

RELATED EXPERIENCE

Grant Recipient
Innovative Teacher Mini-Grant, The Reynolds Foundation
- Wrote extensive grant request that won funding for a teacher-developed unit to match the Massachusetts Curriculum Frameworks. Titled *Creating the Sky*, it was a program that allowed children to create a sky consistent with the Earth and Space Science Strand.

Camp Fatima Counselor, Exceptional Citizens' Week
Meredith, NH
Summers 1996–Present
- Selected as counselor at Camp Fatima, a charitable overnight summer camp for disabled children. Requested to return for 9 consecutive summers.
- Paired with one severely disabled camper and performed all living, health, and personal care needs for an entire week.
- Led local fund-raising events, such as bake sales and donor drives, throughout the year to benefit camp.

Behavioral Consultant
Lowell Public Schools—Lowell, MA
Spring 2002
- Developed and presented 5 interactive workshops for teachers and administrators on behavioral management at the Sullivan Elementary School.

Shayla Miller

3211 Pine Grove Lane • Richmond, Virginia 23219
804-555-9278 • smiller02@richmond.com

OBJECTIVE

To obtain a teaching position in Elementary Education, K–6

SUMMARY OF QUALIFICATIONS

- Initiate programs to foster inclusivity and respect among students.
- Collaborate with other educators to create new learning experiences for students.
- Use creativity and the arts to promote enjoyment of learning.
- Gear teaching style to include students with various abilities and functional levels.

PROFESSIONAL EXPERIENCE

9/2004–present
Pine Grove Elementary School, Richmond School District, Richmond, Virginia
Teacher, Grade 3, Leave Replacement Position

- Plan and implement Virginia Standards in all subject areas.
- Encourage extra reading by developing extensive classroom library.
- Utilize manipulatives in mathematics and science for hands-on understanding.
- Participate in district's math curriculum writing team.
- Direct third grade Drama Club.
- Team-teach with fourth grade teacher for combined-group reading lessons.
- Participate in PTA.
- Initiated and continue weekly inclusion of students from Boces special education class.

12/2003–6/2004
Madison Central School District, Madison, Virginia
Substitute Teacher, Grades K–6

- Managed classroom as appropriate to each grade level.
- Implemented lesson plans and added personal expertise to classroom activities.

STUDENT TEACHING EXPERIENCE

9/2003–12/2003
Centerton Elementary School, Madison, Virginia
Student Teacher, Grade 3 and Kindergarten

- Enacted strategic planning procedures to facilitate students' meaningful engagement with curriculum.
- Developed personal teaching approach centered on active engagement and cooperative learning.
- Created instructional materials and strategies consistent with students' learning and behavioral needs.
- Evaluated and analyzed students with special needs; attended instructional support meetings.

This highly readable resume concentrates on teaching experience on page 1 and then includes other work experience and qualifications on page 2. The pencil border strikes just the right note.

Shayla Miller   **Resume – page 2**

ADDITIONAL WORK EXPERIENCE

6/1998–2/2002
Lazarus, Columbus, Ohio
Sales Manager

- Responsible for all aspects of daily operation: recruitment, training of personnel, store presentation, inventory control, scheduling, and customer relations.
- Assumed New Store Coordinator position with additional responsibilities of organizing and opening of all new stores in Tri-State area, including recruitment, staffing, employee development, receiving, and store setup.

ARTISTIC BACKGROUND

- Classically trained in voice and piano.
- Various recitals in Chicago area; performed with Chicago Opera Company and various regional and national opera companies.
- Fifteen years of theatrical training: directing, acting, cabaret, and improvisation.

COMPUTER SKILLS

- Microsoft Word
- Microsoft Excel
- Internet browser and e-mail applications

EDUCATION AND CERTIFICATION

Richmond University, Richmond, Virginia
- *Master of Science in Elementary Education*, 12/2003
  GPA: 3.8/4.0
- *Certification Program of Reading*, in process

Ashland University, Ashland, Ohio
- *Bachelor of Fine Arts*, 5/2002
  Major in Opera Performance

Virginia State Provisional Certification, Grades K–6, 5/2004

Virginia State Provisional Certification, Grades K–12, Music, 5/2004

Family Math Training Workshop, 10/2003

Identification and Reporting of Child Abuse and Maltreatment, 3/2003

MIDORI TAKASAKI

31 Masters Road
Augusta, Ontario A2B 3C4

Phone: (905) 333-4455
Email: mtakasaki@sprint.ca

QUALIFICATIONS AND PERSONAL STRENGTHS

"Midori has very high expectations for her students and she teaches them study skills and organizational skills that will make them independent learners."

Extremely organized, resourceful, and dedicated teacher with more than 21 years of classroom experience. Consistently recognized for ability to create exciting and enriching classroom environments in which students are motivated to achieve and develop into independent learners.

- Extremely resourceful and self-sufficient—independently created exhaustive in-class student resources to complement curriculum and facilitate research and learning.
- Consistently able to engage students, meet their collective and individual learning needs, and assist them in reaching or exceeding their learning goals.
- Exceptional sensitivity working with special needs children, including Gifted, Remedial, ADD, and other unique or identified students.
- Participated as a Marker in the scoring of Grade 3 Assessment (Mathematics).

PROFESSIONAL DEVELOPMENT

"Midori sets clear rules and expectations for her class and communicates frequently with parents to share the good news as well as the problems."

In-Service Training
Technology & Learning with Computers (TLC)	Augusta Board of Education	2003
First Steps Training	Cedar Bay Public School	2001

Certification
Certified Kumon Instructor—Reading and Mathematics	2003

Qualifications
Primary (Summer 2000), Junior, Intermediate, and Senior

Graduate / Post-Graduate Education
Bachelor of Education (French Language, Literature)	University of Augusta	1983
Master of Arts Program (French Language, Literature)	University of Pinehurst	1982
Bachelor of Arts (Honours French)	University of Augusta	1981

ACCOMPLISHMENTS

"Midori is extremely well organized and her long-range plans and weekly plans are meticulously prepared. She is always on the lookout to find new ideas, new strategies, new rewards to make her class more interesting and to motivate her students."

- Compiled, prepared, and submitted comprehensive proposal for Hilroy Fellowship Program entitled *Please Teach Me How to Read and Write*. Designed to increase oral/written communication and reading comprehension for Grade 4 French Immersion students, the proposal recommended a unique teaching methodology based upon the compilation and integration of most successful personal teaching strategies and resources.

- Independently opened Augusta Kumon Centre in 1999 and received full instructor certification. Current enrollment exceeds 50 part-time students instructed by a staff of 7 student instructors. Responsible for teaching and overseeing all aspects of business, including hiring, supervision, training, and administration.

- Successfully self-taught on recorder and developed extremely effective teaching approach based upon three accepted methodologies: *Je m'amusique*, *Musicabec*, and the *Ed Sueta Baroque Recorder Method*. Grade 4 and 5 students able to write their own pieces and perform in school functions, including Augusta Citizenship Celebration.

This classic-style resume is enhanced through the addition of testimonials in the left column.

Midori Takasaki   *(905) 333-4455*   2

PROFESSIONAL EXPERIENCE

Professional teaching career dedicated to designing and implementing highly structured and effective programs in accordance with Provincial curricula guidelines. Lessons are highly structured yet specifically designed to permit the flexibility required to meet the particular needs of students. Methodologies employed include cooperative learning strategies, modeling, and outcome-based approaches designed to encourage self-learning and independence.

"Midori aims at perfection, and the materials that she prepares for her class, her classroom decorations, [and] her art projects…are always perfectly polished."

CEDAR BAY PUBLIC SCHOOL, Augusta, Ontario   1999–Present
Positions/Responsibilities:
Teacher—Grade 4 French Immersion, Grade 4 English
French Remedial Teacher—Grades 1–6
Junior Arts & Crafts Club

- Created comprehensive in-class Sciences research library on index cards—students encouraged to use, administer, and maintain all materials.
- Successfully implemented in-class use of *Math Concepts & Skills* computer-based learning program. Currently instructing school staff on use and benefits.
- Presented a variety of French Immersion information sessions to parents and incoming students, discussing all aspects of the program and fielding all inquiries.

"Mme Takasaki's greatest strength lies in her planning and organization skills. She is always in complete control of the class and is the epitome of a poised and confident teacher."

SOUTHWOOD PUBLIC SCHOOL, Pinehurst, Ontario   1992–1999
Positions/Responsibilities:
Teacher—Grades 4/5, 5, 5/6 French Immersion, Grade 4 English
French Immersion Teacher/Librarian
French Immersion Art Teacher—Grades 1–5
French Immersion Academic Resource Assistant—Grades 2–6
School Display Coordinator
Junior Arts & Crafts Club
Concours Oratoire
Fetons la Parole

- Independently developed "Mille Mots Merveilleux," a comprehensive 70-page vocabulary development handbook designed to enhance student writing proficiency.
- Contributed to development of Durham Board's French Language Curriculum.

"Her classroom management skills are refined…no difficulty, at any time, getting the students' attention."

FRENCHMAN'S BAY ACADEMY, Warwick, Bermuda   1983–1991
Positions/Responsibilities:
Teacher—Grades 9–12 French, Grade 9 English

- Created and implemented dynamic lessons to prepare students for the University of London General Certificate of Education Ordinary level examination.

LANGUAGE SKILLS

- Fluent in French
- Knowledge of German, Italian, and Spanish

References and supplemental information available upon request.

Jennifer K. Masters

1235 Amberton Drive
Cincinnati, OH 45211

Home: (513) 243-1720
Cellular: (513) 505-2073

Objective

To have a positive influence on the lives of students as a teacher in a Christ-centered school.

Qualifications

🔔 Veteran educator with diverse experience and innate ability to understand and motivate children.

👌 Strong classroom management skills; model for students the importance of following the teachings of Jesus in all that we do.

☎ Excellent communication and organizational skills.

📖 Unwavering commitment to helping young children develop the skills needed to become lifelong learners.

✂ Skilled in adapting lessons to students' diverse learning styles.

Experience Profile

➤ Provided expert instruction for students with abilities ranging from special needs to gifted (K–4).

➤ Presented and led daily learning activities, created themed units, and encouraged parental involvement to reinforce and enrich classroom learning.

➤ Successfully initiated classroom management plans that promoted a Christ-centered approach, individual responsibility, working cooperatively, and positive reinforcement.

➤ Introduced stimulating educational games, manipulatives, and activities to supplement traditional textbooks.

➤ Provided fair and consistent discipline, in accordance with school policy.

➤ Developed and taught a full-day kindergarten curriculum that met or exceeded Ohio state standards.

➤ Initiated improvements to a church-based latchkey program that enabled it to benefit more families.

➤ Identified the need for, created, and taught a pre-K program for children who were kindergarten age–eligible but not developmentally ready. Helped children develop social, emotional, and readiness skills for kindergarten. Expanded the program to include younger preschoolers who were ready for more challenging work.

Certifications

STATE OF OHIO, DEPARTMENT OF EDUCATION
➤ *Permanent Teaching Certificate*
➤ Long-term Substitute Teacher, Multi-age (Pre-K through 12).

Continued —

To position herself for a role in the growing field of Christian education, this teacher includes several religious references to add even more value to her stellar teaching qualifications.

RESUME 22, CONTINUED

Jennifer K. Masters   Page 2

Teaching History

"Jennifer Masters is truly an outstanding primary-grades teacher...is a warm and caring educator who commands the utmost respect and diligence from her students..."

**Tom Smithson
Principal
St. Mary School**

"She is a hardworking teacher. She is dedicated to doing her task well..."

**Jim Thompson
Director of Education
St. Lucy Learning Center**

"I have observed Jennifer to be a patient, caring, and focused teacher... Mrs. Masters has also done an extremely good job of identifying students who are in need of psychological/medical/ educational evaluation to determine the need for specific interventions..."

**Marilyn Jones
Speech/Language
Pathologist
Tri-State Public Schools**

Education

Licensure

ST. MARY SCHOOL, Cincinnati, OH   1982–1985, 1994–Present
Teacher, Kindergarten (1994–Present)
Teach half-day and full-day kindergarten.

Latchkey Program Director (1996–2001)
Concurrent with daily teaching duties, managed latchkey program. Responsibilities included budget planning and control, hiring, training, and staff development.

Teacher, Grades 2, 3, and 4 (1982–1985)
Taught all subject areas in two multi-age classrooms: grades 2–3 and grades 3–4.

ST. LUCY LEARNING CENTER, Cincinnati, OH   1989–1994
Teacher, Preschool and Kindergarten
Started as an interim teacher to fill in for a teacher on maternity leave. Demonstrated flexibility by moving into the 3-year-old classroom when several sudden teacher departures necessitated the need for a stable influence to reaffirm the children's confidence. Created, then taught the pre-K program for four years.

SMART KIDS, Cincinnati, OH   Summers 1989–1993
Tutor
Established and operated a tutoring program for students in grades K–5. Prepared students for the upcoming academic year, with focus on developing reading and mathematics skills. Worked with individuals and small groups.

SAVIOR LUTHERAN SCHOOL, Cincinnati, OH   1976–1982
Teacher, Preschool and Kindergarten
In addition to daily teaching of the preschool and kindergarten programs, witnessed to public school children through a voluntary release-time religion program.

ST. PAUL SCHOOL, Washington, IL   1974–1976
Teacher, Grades 1, 2, and 3
Taught all subject areas to students in grades 1–3 in a multi-age classroom.

PROFESSIONAL DEVELOPMENT   Ongoing
Continuing education has included courses, seminars, and workshops on topics ranging from Reading and Writing for Kindergartners to incorporating new Ohio state standards into the curriculum. Comprehensive course listing furnished on request.

UNIVERSITY OF CINCINNATI, Cincinnati, OH   1976
Completed Kindergarten Practicum and Mathematics course to obtain Ohio teaching certificate.

REGIONAL TEACHERS COLLEGE, Washington, IL
Bachelor of Arts in Education. Magna Cum Laude   1974

State of Ohio, Provisional, Grades K–8

CHAPTER 6

Resumes for Secondary-School Educators

- Middle School Teachers
- High School Teachers
- Coaches

RESUME 23: BY DAYNA FEIST, CPRW, CEIP, JCTC

BILL ANDERSON
265 Charlotte Street
Asheville, NC 28801

(828) 254-7893 *home*
(828) 314-7893 *cell*
banders@hometown.net

HISTORY TEACHER
North Carolina License, Social Studies 9–12

PROFILE

Proactive, uncompromising focus on improving reading, writing, and critical thinking skills. Use flexibility, resourcefulness, and organizational and interpersonal skills to assist that learning through a positive, encouraging environment.

Strengths

"A page of history is worth a volume of logic."—Oliver Wendell Holmes

- Capable teacher thoroughly grounded in U.S., Middle East, World, and European History.
- Rapport-builder with parents (they think they're all alone out there), able to gain their involvement, trust, and respect in creating a participative environment.
- Adept, available, and adaptable classroom manager—combine discipline plan with effective procedures and varied lessons to attract the inattentive and enforce student accountability.
- Student motivator—can use cooperative learning and other student-directed/process learning techniques to cultivate inclusivity and build teamwork and goal-setting skills.
- Develop useful daily lesson plans and instructional resources.
- Friendly, interactive, and dependable.
- Some fluency in Spanish (can read Spanish newspaper).

EDUCATION

B.A., History, *Magna Cum Laude,* December 2003
North Carolina University, Polk, NC

Coursework

- US. History, Medieval Europe, Politics of the Middle East, Political Science, Chinese History (Revolutionary China), Afro-American History, Human Rights & International Politics, Humanities. Dean's List every eligible semester.

Student Teaching

"I teach skill in asking questions through my skill in asking the right question...."

- Hall High School, spring and fall 2003—11th grade college prep classes in U.S. History. Despite novice ranking, selected to teach AP U.S. History class due to knowledge of material.

  - Contributions included judging senior projects, proctoring end-of-course tests, and sponsoring the fledgling Debate Club.

  - Because my co-op was on the school improvement team, was able to observe planning and goal-setting functions in the effort to meet constantly changing requirements.

  - Participated positively in parent-teacher conferences.

Honors & Affiliations

Cited by department faculty for original, critical thinking....

- Selected for Phi Alpha Theta History National Honor Society (high GPA and faculty recommendation).

- Selected by History Department faculty for the Mike Bolson History Scholarship as a promising student in the field of history, despite being on an education track.

- Participant, NCU History Association.

- Alpha Phi Omega National Service Fraternity—Chapter President; as Vice President of Service, initiated projects involving boys' and girls' clubs; fundraising.

This job seeker returned to school to earn teaching credentials after a 30-year career in manufacturing. Page 1 of the resume could stand on its own; page 2 provides details of earlier experience and community activities.

RESUME 23, CONTINUED

banders@hometown.net • (828) 314–7893 *cell* • (828) 254–7893 *home*   **BILL ANDERSON**

Prior Education	**Diploma, Welding** (one-year program), 1980 WNC Technical Community College Coursework in Anthropology, Biology, Spanish, 1973 University of Massachusetts–Boston
PRIOR EXPERIENCE	BOILER OPERATOR: Culverton Textiles, Foster, NC—1981–1998 Operated steam- and electric-generating utility for largest textile mill of its kind in the world (on 10 acres), with its own waste treatment and water filtration system. A self-contained mini-city, it generated much of its own power. Member of 2-man team: managed electrical control room, maintenance, welding, machinery repair, pipefitting. ENGINEER: 100-foot Bluestocking fishing boat, Gloucester, MA—1971–1980 MACHINIST MATE: United States Navy—1967–1971 Served on the U.S.S. *Georgetown* (traveled to Mozambique Civil War; the Indian Ocean; and Havana, Cuba) and U.S.S. *Severn* (oil tanker refueling ships at sea in the Mediterranean). Trained Navy personnel (including firemen and 3rd class petty officers) to work with tools and operate equipment.
COMMUNITY REINVESTMENT	■ Coached Roller Hockey for boys' and girls' clubs, ages 13–18, in league competition. ■ Tutor, Afterschool Club, Salvation Army. ■ Big Brothers/Big Sisters, 1981–1983. Mentored 7–year–old boy (gardening, movies, sports, homework).

RICHARD OLSON
3605 North 86th Street
Superior, Wisconsin 54880
(715) 555-1692 or olson@cc.com

OBJECTIVE:

Elementary or Middle School Social Studies Teacher

HIGHLIGHTS OF QUALIFICATIONS:

- ❑ Numerous practica experiences in local schools.
- ❑ Total commitment to students, district, school, and community.
- ❑ Highly effective communicator.
- ❑ Compassionate and sensitive to needs and emotions of children.
- ❑ 11 years of experience coaching boys' baseball. Expertise in both on-field coaching and off-field administration of game.
- ❑ Committed to personal lifelong learning as well as offering quality education to children.

LICENSE:

Wisconsin teaching license. Certified to teach elementary education and Social Studies Grades 7–9.

EDUCATION:

University of Wisconsin—Superior (UWS)
BS, Elementary Education with **Social Studies** minor, May 2004.
GPA: 3.79. Involved in Future Teachers Association.

AWARDS:

UWS, Dean's List of Academic Achievement, 2002–2003; Fairbrother Academic Scholarship, 2003–2004; Lakehead Pipeline Company, Incorporated, Academic Scholarship, Spring 2003; Maurice Brown Academic Scholarship, 2002–2003; and UWS Foundation Academic Scholarship, 2001–2002.

PRACTICA:

Social Studies Methods, Lester Park Middle School, Duluth, MN, Spring 2003
Language Arts Methods, St. James Elementary School, Superior, WI, Fall 2002
Reading Methods, St. James Elementary School, Superior, WI, Fall 2002
Physical Education Methods, Cooer Elementary School, Superior, WI, Spring 2002

COACHING:

Baseball, Boys Legion (ages 16–18), Great Falls, MI, Youth Baseball Association, 1991–1997
Baseball, Boys Senior Little League (ages 13–15), Great Falls, MI, Youth Baseball Association, 1987–1990

- ❑ American Legion Baseball Program experienced phenomenal growth during tenure. Player enrollment increased to such an extent as to necessitate need for Junior Varsity Club. Promoted Legion baseball in community, raising awareness of it to higher level.
- ❑ Assisted several players to continue playing in college through on-site coaching and personal contacts with college coaches.
- ❑ Effectively assisted American Legion Club members in securing funds for program allowing for expenditures to be used in more beneficial manner.
- ❑ Work, tireless commitment, and knowledge of game earned me position with Atlanta Braves as Associate Scout.

There is a lot of information packed into this resume for a newly qualified teacher. It was important to include coaching and employment activities that gave him lots of experience working with children.

Richard Olson   **Page 2**

EMPLOYMENT:

School District of Superior, WI
Intern, January–June 2004
Interning in 6th grade classroom at Great Falls Elementary School. Assume responsibilities of regular classroom teacher: recording attendance, teaching all subjects, administering and correcting tests, and exercising needed discipline. Already employed as substitute teacher where I have interacted with other teachers and school employees in various capacities.

❑ Coordinated 6th grade fundraiser that raised more than $2,000.
❑ Co-director of district-wide spelling bee that involved communications with district principals and teachers.
❑ Participated in after-school "Math Olympiad" program, a supplemental math activity for students seeking additional challenges.
❑ Assisted in school's participation in nationwide oration and writing contests.

University of Wisconsin–Superior
Game Management, 2001–Present
Administer smooth, effective execution of all sports programs. Welcome visiting teams and provide necessary assistance. Secure and supervise workers for events.

❑ Key player in significantly improving UWS's hospitality image through hard work, effective planning, and personable communication.
❑ Successfully assisted in staffing 2004 NCAA Division III Men's Hockey National Finals Tournament.

VISTA (Volunteers in Service to America), Superior, WI
Summer Associate, May–August 2003
Strived to improve literacy of at-risk students. Created and learned about several literacy assessment tools used to select appropriate literacy experiences and assessed impact of total summer school experience on students. Served as resource person for paraprofessionals and helped prepare resource materials for other tutors.

❑ Effectively tutored 4 primary grade students in reading and writing daily.
❑ Developed evaluation tools, including rubrics, surveys, and other assessments, that were used as before-and-after measures for program.
❑ In conjunction with other summer associates, developed recruitment and training plan.

City of Great Falls Parks Department, Great Falls, MI
Park Maintenance Worker, Summers 1997–2001
Resurrected and maintained beauty of 22-acre city baseball complex.

Sheridan Lanes, Great Falls, MI
Assistant Manager, 1990–2001
Successfully ensured customer satisfaction for business by establishing rapport and communication. Managed leagues and maintained facility.

❑ Reestablished youth bowling leagues.
❑ Successfully managed/hosted annual tournaments.
❑ Remained loyal during several ownership changes.

RESUME 25: BY JANET BECKSTROM, CPRW

Ronald P. Carlson

345 Chelsea Circle   dramaguy@network.com   *Residence:* 734-555-8514
Ann Arbor, MI 48108   *Cellular:* 734-555-2104

SECONDARY EDUCATOR *&* THEATER INSTRUCTOR

Ten years of instructional experience with students from diverse socio-economic backgrounds; broad-ranging skill levels in classroom and nontraditional settings. Experience in developing, implementing, and evaluating curriculum, especially the integration of performing arts into reading and language arts. Demonstrated ability to creatively interpret abstract concepts; foster student creativity, curiosity, and self-confidence; and identify and promote others' talents. Ability to "make a connection" with others. Complete list of directorial and acting credits on attached Addendum.

Classroom Experience

FATHER GABRIEL RICHARD HIGH SCHOOL • Ann Arbor, Michigan   1999–Present
     Teacher—English, Public Speaking & Theater (9th–12th grades)
     Director—Theater Program
- Provide instruction for five classes.
- Produce three shows each year: a production targeting elementary and middle school audiences as well as the public; a major musical involving 50–75 students as actors, vocalists, and crew; and a more challenging ensemble piece encompassing a smaller cast within a tighter time frame.
- Introduced concept of casting elementary and middle school students in productions, resulting in casts of more diverse ages while cultivating future interest in the theater program.
- Recruited and developed an active network of parents and community members providing support to all aspects of the theater program, both on- and off-stage.
- Serve on Peer Evaluation Committee; former member of Articulation Committee (mandated as part of accreditation by the North Central Association).

WASHTENAW COMMUNITY COLLEGE • Ypsilanti, Michigan   2002–Present
     Instructor—Theater Department (Courses 160/164)
- Provide instruction in theater performance to theater and non-theater majors.
- Prepare students for and direct student production at end of course.

ANN ARBOR COMMUNITY SCHOOLS • Ann Arbor, Michigan   1992–1999
     Teacher (Angell Creative Arts School)—Creative Drama (5th) and Advanced Drama (6th)
     Substitute Teacher (District-wide)—Including month-long assignment in Creative Drama (8th–9th)
     Student Teacher and **Director** (Huron High School under supervising teacher Miranda Powell)—Theatre History, Improvisation, Acting and Stagecraft (9th–12th)

ANN ARBOR YOUTH THEATRE • Ann Arbor, Michigan   1997–1999
     Resident Artist—Creative Drama (1st–12th), Acting Workshop (7th–12th)
     Drama Specialist—Mini-Theater program for grant-funded Day Camp

CHELSEA COMMUNITY SCHOOLS • Chelsea, Michigan   1995–1997
     Volunteer Teacher—Chelsea Middle School (6th–8th and Extracurricular)

GREENHILLS SCHOOL • Ann Arbor, Michigan   1993–1995
     Teacher—Creative Movement (K–2nd), Creative Drama II (5th–7th), Acting 1 (7th–8th), Language Arts (8th), Public Speaking (12th)

Certification

State of Michigan Professional Secondary Teacher Certification

- continued -

Well-organized categories showcase this job seeker's wealth of experience, both in the classroom and in theatrical performance and directing.

Ronald P. Carlson   734-555-8514

Education

EASTERN MICHIGAN UNIVERSITY • Ypsilanti, Michigan
Bachelor of Arts—Secondary Education   1993
Major: Theater/Speech   *Minor:* English

Related Experience

❖ **Founder/Director** (2002–Present)—*Two Times Two,* a children's performance troupe. Create story dramas based on children's literature and bring them to life. Performance venues have included Camp Ti-Pi-Donodo for grieving youth and Washtenaw County's 2004 *Children First* Conference. Student participants range from elementary to college age.

❖ **Creative Drama Specialist** (1999)—*Partners Program,* involving the University of Michigan School of Music and the John F. Kennedy Center, and funded by the Ann Arbor Arts Foundation. Provided drama activities and instruction for students of all ages (including some determined to be at-risk) in Ann Arbor and Washtenaw County schools.

❖ **Drama Instructor** (1999)—*Arts & More* program. Worked with developmentally and physically impaired classes at Roberto Clemente Student Development Center. Collaborated with teachers to integrate drama into their respective curricula.

❖ **Drama Club Sponsor** and **Director** (1987–1995)—*Chelsea High School.* Re-energized faltering theater program as extracurricular activity. Directed or co-directed 13 productions. Managed all aspects of productions, including set construction, costuming, sound, lighting, and publicity. Organized club and facilitated activities that raised $1,200 for the club. Taught theater workshops for high school students. Developed Chelsea chapter of the International Thespian Association. Presented *Inside/Out* at the Michigan State Thespian Conference (1990); production was recommended for presentation at the prestigious International Thespian Conference.

❖ **Director** (1989)—*Dexter High School.* Directed 2 productions that were ultimately selected for the Michigan Interscholastic Thespian Competition. Raised awareness of performing arts within the school and the community, thereby increasing audience attendance.

Special Projects

❖ **Actor** (2003)—Homeless Empowerment Relationship Organization's *Living on the Streets* project. Starred in video that demonstrated the impact of homelessness on children. Posed for still photos for inclusion in soft-cover book on which the video was based.

❖ **Actor/Dancer** (2002–2003)—Role of "Grandmother" in the University Musical Society's *Nutcracker* at Powers Center.

❖ **Freelance Director** (1999–2003)—Directed 3 productions for Chelsea Community Players.

❖ **Director** (1997)—Directed *Just Don't Do It!,* a video featuring students from New Directions Alternative Education School, produced by the King Agency and sponsored by the State of Michigan Office of Highway Safety Planning. Served as coach for subsequent live touring production.

- References available on request -

RESUME 26: *BY RHODA KOPY, BS, CPRW, JCTC, CEIP*

THOMAS B. KLEIN

89 Kensington Road • Manahawkin, NJ 08050 • 609-612-8985 • tbklein@verion.net

— **High-School English Teacher for Your Most Challenging Students** —
— **Football Coach** —

SUMMARY

Spirited, optimistic education professional with an excellent reputation for spurring dramatic improvements in the classroom performance, behavior, and attitude of lower-track high-school students deemed "unteachable." Able to gain the trust and respect of youngsters and convey confidence in their abilities. Successful in using innovative, unconventional approaches to engage students' interest, strengthen reading and writing skills, develop an appreciation for literature, and achieve high passing rates on standardized proficiency tests. Initiator and manager of a unique, highly effective in-school suspension program. Extensive coaching background.

SKILLS AND ACCOMPLISHMENTS

Classroom Teaching

- Consistently sought the challenge of teaching and inspiring lower-track high-school students.
- Achieved outstanding success in strengthening their reading and writing abilities, building life skills, and motivating them to consider job / career goals; 25% of students pursued higher education.
- Encouraged students to become active classroom participants and join in the decision-making process.
- Attained an HSPT passing percentage in the upper 80% range among students who had previously failed.
- Effectively used comic books and other unconventional resources to build grammar and punctuation skills.
- Organized spirited debates on controversial topics.
- Sparked students' interest in literature through role playing and lively discussions.
- Arranged for monthly guest speakers to address career topics.

Behavior Management / Counseling

- Achieved one of the lowest rates of discipline problems in the school.
- Created a fun, free-spirited environment in which students adhered to stated rules of conduct.
- Worked closely with parents to reinforce behavior management.
- Developed trusting relationships with students and frequently served as a sounding board for problems.
- Helped students develop a better outlook and a solution-oriented approach to dealing with challenges.

Program Development and Management

- Initiated the introduction of a learning-based in-school suspension program to deal with a high rate of daily suspensions; later instituted the program at a middle school based on outstanding results.
- Coordinated each student's assignments with classroom teacher and provided one-on-one instruction in all subject areas. For the first time in the school's history, required suspended students to perform schoolwork.

Coaching

- Coached several undefeated football teams, including one that went on to win the state championship.
- Helped sharpen the skills of many players who later played college football.
- Oversaw the entire football program for 6 Pop Warner teams; interacted with local school coaches to integrate their philosophies into the program, so players are well-prepared for high school football.

PROFESSIONAL EXPERIENCE

Pomeranz High School, Newark, NJ:
Director of In-School Suspension Program / Teacher (2000–Present)
English Teacher, Grades 9–12 (1980–2000)
Assistant Football Coach (1986–1990) / Head Football Coach (1990–1992) / Head Baseball Coach (1992)
Assistant Coach, Football / Baseball / Wrestling (1990–1991)

COMMUNITY SERVICE / AWARDS

Football Commissioner, Angels Athletic Association / Pop Warner Football, Manahawkin, NJ (1998–Present)
Football Coach, Pop Warner Football, Manahawkin / Newark, NJ (1985–1998)
Community Service Award, Kaitland County Chamber of Commerce (2003)

CERTIFICATION / EDUCATION

Certification as Teacher of High School English, State of New Jersey
B.A., English / Communications, 1980 • Rutgers University, New Brunswick, NJ
Graduate Credits in Curriculum and Administration • Monmouth University, W. Long Branch, NJ

This high school teacher wants to take on a school's "most challenging students," and the functional Skills and Accomplishments listing effectively highlights his ability to do so.

David Dumas
555 Overland Drive
Union City, NJ 07087
(201) 583-5555
dd322@hotmail.com

GOAL
High School Teacher
and / or Coach

PROFILE
➤ More than three years of experience in teaching, coaching, and motivating.

➤ Demonstrated gift for inspiring individuals and teams toward higher achievements.

➤ Poised and competent; able to maintain a sense of humor under pressure.

➤ Reputation for excellence; enthusiastic, high-energy, and creative professional.

EDUCATION
2001 BA, History
Southern University
South Grove, SC

COMPUTER SKILLS
Windows XP, 98, and 95
Microsoft Office:
– Word
– Excel
– Access
– Outlook
– Explorer

EXPERIENCE
2002–Present **Teacher / Coach / Moderator**
Union City High School, Union City, NJ

Teacher–World History, Government, and Contemporary Issues
- Teach 3 classes of 9th–12th graders, engaging their curiosity and analytical problem-solving abilities in structured classroom activities.
- Plan and create innovative lesson plans and learning environment emphasizing relevancy and group task cooperation.
- Participate in staff meetings, addressing problems including family relations, staff cooperation, community support, and problem issues with individual children.
- Selected to serve on the Discipline Board (3 years); actively involved as judge and as student advocate.
- Conduct interviews for incoming freshmen in person and by telephone, screening applicants for high school admittance.

Coach–Football, Winter & Spring Track
- Successfully built cooperative athletic teams and promoted winning attitudes in teams, including co-ed teams and varsity sports, by
  – treating athletes with respect and maintaining a sense of humor;
  – welcoming constructive criticism and input on improvements;
  – encouraging athletic, social, and team skill development.
- Produced impressive record of winning teams in the last 3 years:
  – girls' track team achieved state championship every year;
  – boys' track team was champion in 2 of the last 3 years;
  – varsity football team made state playoffs twice.
- Provided coaching and oversight for the annual summer football camp of 6th and 7th graders.

Moderator–African-American Student Union
- Oversee all facets of this extracurricular program, including
  – arranging for college prep and career days with speakers;
  – planning, organizing, and conducting two field trips per semester;
  – designing and implementing successful fundraising activities.
- Revitalized and increased student and parent involvement in the African-American Student Union, building it into a high-profile program on the campus and within the community.
- Acted as liaison between the African-American Student Union, parents, community groups, and school administrative hierarchy.
- Initiated the establishment of a Parents' Association for support, communication, and networking.

This resume highlights the three important roles (teacher, coach, and student union moderator) this educator fills in his current position. The narrow left column makes good use of space on the page to present his credentials.

Paul Mannington
1234 Hodges Road, Apt. 222
Marlboro, NJ 07746
732.555.7892   pmann@aol.com

SECONDARY SCHOOL TEACHER/COACH

A championship coach taking his winning approach into the classroom. Demonstrated ability to deliver individualized instruction appropriate to each student's abilities. Committed to creating a classroom atmosphere that is stimulating and encouraging to students. Exceptional ability to work harmoniously with parents, school, and community.

PRACTICUM AND RELATED COURSEWORK

Literature Class, Base Middle School, Marlboro, NJ   **Winter 2001**
Assisted literature teacher with discussion sessions, homework assignments, correcting papers, and recording grades. Assisted in preparing students for upcoming CSAP standardized proficiency tests.

- ✓ Developed rapport with students, earning their respect and trust.
- ✓ Sparked students' interest in literature through interactive, lively discussions.
- ✓ Encouraged students to become active participants, joining the decision-making processes.

Reading Methods, The Learning Hub, Manalapan, NJ   **Fall 2000**
Extracurricular reading program for ESL elementary students.

- ✓ Strived to improve literacy of ESL students.
- ✓ Applied reading techniques and methods; verified comprehension and retention.
- ✓ Achieved success in strengthening reading abilities, helping students achieve parity in the classroom.

Coursework at the School of Education, Rutgers University, New Brunswick, NJ

- ✓ Teaching in American Schools
- ✓ School and Society
- ✓ Literature for Middle and Secondary School Teachers

COACHING HIGHLIGHTS

More than 20 years of coaching experience, creating an energizing, educational environment that motivated students to athletic achievement and personal accomplishment. Designed programs for learners of varying needs; assessed individual performance levels and adopted different approaches to maximize results. Supervised staff and administered budget resources for program implementation.

- ✓ Guided the Rutgers Men's and Women's Alpine Ski team to the Division III Championships.
- ✓ Directed racing program at Black Mountain. Managed 4 coaches, 50 J-1 through J-5 racers, operating budget, and equipment.
- ✓ Selected by Sno Engineering to train employees in Service-Based Leadership Program.
- ✓ Led Killington Ski Club to the Junior Olympics.
- ✓ Selected as Eastern Team Coach for J1–J2 Olympics, Black Mountain.
- ✓ Designed, developed, and implemented "Team Sugarbush," children's weekend ski program.
- ✓ Created Junior Enrichment through Sports (JETS), a low-cost program introducing local children to skiing, offering instruction and building self-confidence and personal achievement.

This resume begins with a strong "personal branding statement" that conveys this job seeker's dual teaching/coaching expertise.

Paul Mannington
Page 2

EDUCATION

Rutgers University, New Brunswick, NJ
Bachelor of Arts and Sciences, English Literature, May 2004

University of Vermont, Burlington, VT
Liberal Arts, English Concentration, 1995–1998

CERTIFICATIONS

PSIA Level III (Certified in 1980)
USSCA Level II Race Coach (Slalom, Giant Slalom, Super G, Downhill)
USSA Certified Race Official

MEMBERSHIPS

Professional Ski Instructors of America
United States Ski Coaches Association
United States Ski and Snowboard Association

WORK HISTORY

Assistant Coach, Rutgers University, New Brunswick, NJ	2000–Present
Landscape Foreman, Middlesex Landscape Nursery, Middlesex, NJ	1996–2000
Ski Instructor, Killington Ski Area, Killington, VT	1996–1999
Technical Director, Waterville Valley Ski School, Waterville Valley, NH	1995–1996
Program Director, Head Coach, Black Mountain Race Team, Jackson, NH	1992–1995
Marketing Director, Sugarbush, Warren, VT	1988–1989
Head Race Coach, Mount Snow, West Dover, VT	1983–1988
Race Coach/Coordinator, Okemo Mountain, Ludlow, VT	1982–1983

RESUME 29: BY DEBORAH WILE DIB, CCM, NCRW, CPRW, JCTC

Mirriam Weissman

30 Darwin Drive, Patchogue, NY 11763   (631) 521-7245

Secondary-level English and Social Studies Teacher

Eager to bring students into the twenty-first century using a unique combination of 20 years of real-world experience in business and drama coupled with 5 years' background as secondary-level substitute teacher.

Bring a passion for teaching to the classroom and engage students in an energized learning process. Utilize a variety of instructional methods, including the use of drama and the arts, to create a contemporary and relevant forum for learning that is grounded in the curriculum.

Education and Certification

New York State Certification in Secondary Education: Social Studies and English

Certification studies: twelve credits in Education and student teaching, 1996
State University of New York at Stony Brook

Bachelor of Arts in English, 1990
Dowling College, Oakdale, NY

Master-level drama and theater production classes, 1983 to 1986
The Actor's Studio, New York, NY

Areas of Knowledge and Experience

- Use of the arts for instruction
- Drama and performance
- Communication arts
- Public speaking and debate
- Current events lessons
- Classroom management
- Thematic instruction
- Motivational program design
- Strategic curriculum planning
- Use of computers for instruction

Summary of Qualifications

Provide students with an imaginative education thoroughly grounded in the curriculum, yet looking forward to the realities of higher education and the challenges of the workplace.

Prepare students to become productive citizens with global vision by using innovative and traditional methodologies to teach the communication, creative thinking, and writing skills necessary for success in today's marketplace.

Enhance teaching methods by use of experiences from diverse employment background that includes communication-oriented work as news feature writer, executive secretary, and real estate salesperson.

Frequently utilize dramatic arts in the classroom by applying experience gained as actor doing regional theater, Off and Off-Off-Broadway, radio voice-overs, and daytime television.

"O, this learning, what a thing it is!"

William Shakespeare

The Taming of the Shrew

This is an unusual and highly effective resume for someone whose only teaching experience is as a substitute teacher—but you'd never know that by reading her first-page presentation of qualifications. Original formatting adds to the appeal.

Mirriam Weissman page 2

Representative Methodologies and Lessons

As a substitute teacher, immediately try to develop a rapport with students and engage in discussion of current events. Facilitate the discussion to steer towards daily lesson plan. Discussion and debate keeps topic relevant, and keeps students centered, entertained, and open to learning.

Construct creative lessons to maintain interest, yet thoroughly cover curriculum. As a student teacher, planned vocabulary lessons that removed the "boredom" factor and utilized creative writing to enhance learning of vocabulary. Students used vocabulary words in contextual sentences to create exciting weekly class stories. Lessons were a great success.

Observed a student lunch-time incident and used it to develop a discussion on respect and compassion. Discussion became a two-day theme culminating in a better understanding of the phrase "walking in another person's shoes." Lesson was so effective that compassion theme was carried throughout quarter.

Always maintain students' curiosity about "what will happen next." Keep a keen focus on the tempo of the class to maintain control and flow of work. Deal with disruptive students immediately and firmly; will not tolerate inconsiderate behavior. Built excellent relationships and still have contact with some students from earliest teaching days.

Experience in Education

Substitute Teacher, grades 7 through 12   2000 to present
Patchogue-Medford School District
Sachem School District

Additional Experience

Licensed Real Estate Salesperson   1998 to present
Caldwell-Banker, Inc., Patchogue, NY

Feature Writer   1992 to 1993
The Advance Newspapers, Coram, NY
(Clippings available upon request)

Storyteller   1986 to 1991
Patchogue-Medford Library, Patchogue, NY

Dream Pursuer (Actor and Drama Student)   1983 to 1986
New York, NY

Executive Secretary to the Vice President of Operations   1980 to 1984
Saks Fifth Avenue, New York, NY

Assistant to the Vice President of Advertising   1979 to 1980
Banker's Trust Company, New York, NY

RESUME 30: BY ROSS PRIMACK, CPRW, CEIP, GCDF

Sarah Elizabeth Keane

123 Winter Tree Drive • Litchfield, CT 06759-3324
860-555-5555 • sekeane@aol.com

STUDENT-FOCUSED FAMILY AND CONSUMER SCIENCE TEACHER
OFFERING HANDS-ON EXPERIENCE

• *Child Development*	• *Foods/Nutrition*	• *Interior Design*	• *Menu Planning*
• *Parenting*	• *Life Skills*	• *Budgeting*	• *Sewing*

PROFILE

Classroom Instruction—Enthusiastic, committed educator with innate ability to understand and motivate students. Continuously strive to build self-esteem and encourage understanding of cultural diversity, gender differences, physical limitations, and learning ability. Committed to creating a classroom atmosphere that is stimulating and encouraging. Safety conscious and observant of student behavior and actions. Demonstrated ability to individualize instruction.

Education Relationships—Team player adept at establishing and fostering cooperative professional relationships with parents and administration. Diplomatic approach to parent-teacher relationships. Actively solicit and encourage parents' participation to ensure student progress.

Personal Attributes—Outstanding interpersonal skills, having dealt with a broad diversity of education professionals, students, and parents. Easily establish rapport and trust. Highly motivated to expand knowledge and skills. Enjoy keeping current with new developments and trends in education. Well-organized and adept at multitasking and prioritizing. Powerful communication skills, verbal and written. Computer skills include Word, Excel, PowerPoint, Publisher, and Internet.

"Sarah is a quality teacher in every sense of the word and would add a high degree of improvement to any facility. She has worked with difficult students and has not only managed to control and educate them, but also gain their respect."

Stanley Ward, *Director*
Prospect Continuing Education

"Her forte is her ability to connect with children and parents alike. She is able to establish a working relationship with children of all identities. She is reliable, trustworthy…and is valued and respected by her students, co-workers, administration and our community."

April Carr, *Special Education Teacher*
Sanswood Elementary School

"She has the ability to encourage academic growth in students while enhancing their self esteem. Her knowledge, ability to teach, compassion, and eagerness to motivate students is inspiring."

Fred Turner, *Teacher*
Conard High School

"(Sarah) is astute in her recognition of and awareness of individual student needs. She uses consulting time effectively and is creative in her approach to problem solving. Sarah is a great team player. She is a good listener and effectively offers input in group collaboration."

Patrick Shatner, MSW, *School Social Worker*
Conard High School

EDUCATION

WESTERN CONNECTICUT STATE UNIVERSITY, Danbury, CT
Currently pursuing coursework towards a Master of Science in School Counseling (2000 to Present)

UNIVERSITY OF BRIDGEPORT, Bridgeport, CT
Master of Science—Education (1992)
Certification—Provisional Educator Certificate Pre K–8
Consumer and Family Science K–12 (3.8 GPA)

UNIVERSITY OF CONNECTICUT, Storrs, CT
Bachelor of Science—Human Development and Family Relations

A very strong profile, supplemented by exceptional testimonials, creates a blockbuster opening for this resume. Extensive teaching experience is detailed on page 2.

Sarah Elizabeth Keane   Page Two

CAREER HISTORY

RAFFIN MIDDLE SCHOOL   Hartford, CT   2003 to Present
Grade 7 Reading Teacher

- ❑ Coordinate efforts with colleagues to develop and implement reading strategies.
- ❑ Provide students with comprehensive preparation for Connecticut Mastery Tests.
- ❑ Develop and modify lesson plans. Administer tests and grade student papers.
- ❑ Create visually appealing and informative bulletin boards.
- ❑ Review student records and prepare PPTs.
- ❑ Process paperwork from the Department of Children and Family Services.

HARPER ELEMENTARY SCHOOL   Woodbury, CT   1998 to 2003
Grade 5 Teacher

- ❑ Developed, taught, modified, and assessed lessons for class of 22 students.
- ❑ Implemented structured behavior modification plans.
- ❑ Conducted semiannual conferences with parents.
- ❑ Coordinated all facets of field trip planning, including reservations, fundraising, and chaperoning.
- ❑ Served as 5th grade SAT team representative to address and develop strategies for special needs students.
- ❑ Represented 5th grade on faculty council. Met monthly with colleagues to address issues and concerns. Disseminated issues for discussion with principal.

CONARD HIGH SCHOOL   West Hartford, CT   1997 to 1998
Child Development Teacher

- ❑ Taught child development unit to high school students.
- ❑ Coordinated efforts with Naugatuck Valley Community College to enable participants of high school class to receive college credit for completed coursework.

PROSPECT ADULT EDUCATION   Prospect, CT   1994 to 1995
Part-Time Facilitator/Instructor

- ❑ Facilitated adult education programs on topics including cooking and custom decorating.

SANSWOOD ELEMENTARY SCHOOL   Woodbury, CT   1992 to 1998
Title 1 Teacher

- ❑ Teamed with classroom teachers to develop and implement remedial and enrichment curriculum for grades K–5.
- ❑ Assisted with all facets of student evaluations.
- ❑ Chaperoned field trips.

PROFESSIONAL DEVELOPMENT

- *Meeting Individual Student Needs*
- *Health Curriculum K–12*
- *Student Portfolio Assessment*
- *Health Curriculum Committee*
- *Writing Project (Grade 5)*
- *Classroom Management*

RESUME 31: BY SUSAN GUARNERI, NCC, NCCC, CPRW, CCMC, CEIP, MCC

Cecilia M. Diaz
55 Magnolia Lane, Oakland, NJ 07436
201-405-5555 ▪ cmdiaz@net.com

Career Target

Middle School Science Teacher in a child-centered school district.

Summary

☑ Highly motivated, energetic educator with 15 years of middle school teaching experience.
☑ Strong track record of fostering student curiosity, creativity, and enhanced learning.
☑ Enthusiastic, warm, and caring professional, sensitive to students' specialized and changing needs.
☑ Demonstrated ability to deliver individualized instruction, appropriate to each student's abilities.
☑ Ability to act as liaison, harmoniously and effectively, between parents, school, and community.

Key Skill Areas

Instructional Strategies
- Designed and developed integrated, thematic physical science curriculum for middle school students, aligned to meet core content and state standards.
- Use cross-curriculum, cooperative learning, motivational environment, team planning, and "real-world" examples to stimulate learning and learner retention.

Learning Styles
- Achieve educational goals by incorporating learning modality principles into all instruction. First special-service teacher incorporated into an inclusion class.
- Emphasize an active learning environment, high student expectations, and individualized instruction in a student-centered, heterogeneous classroom.

Educational Technology
- Championed innovative physical science programs and activities utilizing instructional media to enhance the scope and quality of education.
- Accomplished in the use of hands-on materials, manipulatives, and technology (electron microscopes, research on the Internet, video cameras, software).

Leadership
- Pioneered "Scientists in the Classroom" Program, partnering with local companies to provide scientific demonstrations and Q&A sessions.
- Selected as judge for state-run program, "21st Century Science"—3 years.

Student / Parent Relations
- Fostered parent involvement through regular communication (telephone calls or notes daily) and invitations to participate in classroom activities and events.
- Natural gift for getting young students excited about learning.

Certifications and Education

New Jersey Permanent Certification K–8 Elementary
New Jersey Permanent Certification K–12 English

1995 M.Ed., Stockton State College, Stockton, NJ
1983 B.S., Elementary Education & English, Clemson University, Clemson, SC

Continuing Education:
2001 Meteorology Course, Union College, School of Meteorology
1998 Certificate, Computer Educator, Passaic County College, Passaic, NJ
1996 Materials Science Conference, sponsored by Rutgers University
1992 Cooperative Learning, Conference on Scientific Curriculum

Computer Skills

Macintosh PCs	MS Word	MS Works	Netscape Navigator
ClarisWorks	MacGrade	Internet	E-mail

This two-page resume devotes as much attention to activities leadership as it does to teaching descriptions. It also uses a broad Key Skill Areas section to emphasize relevant achievements.

Cecilia M. Diaz
201-405-5555 ▪ Page 2

Experience
1989–present   **Morris County Middle School,** Morristown, NJ
Science Teacher—8th **Grade**
- Teach Chemistry, Physics, Geology, and Meteorology as well as enrichment classes for 3 classes daily, with up to 30 students per class, utilizing curriculum compacting and tiered instruction with 5 tiered teams in a block-scheduling system.
- Designed self-learning and small-group cooperative learning activities as well as hands-on science activities such as the Cliffton House archeological excavation.

2003   **Central State Middle School,** Harrison, NJ
Substitute Teacher—Physical Science

1988–1989   **Oakland Township School District,** Oakland, NJ
Substitute Teacher—K–12, primarily 6th **Grade**

1984–1988   **Tiny Tots Pre-school,** Rahwah, NJ
Kindergarten Teacher / Director
- Full administrative, staffing, and budgeting responsibility for this mini-school within the district, with 13 teachers, aides, cook, and school bus driver, in addition to duties as kindergarten teacher.

Activities
1989–2001   **Advisor, MCMS Newspaper: <u>The Tiger Ledger</u>**
- Provided proactive leadership for this student-run newspaper. Introduced students to assignments as cartoonists, reporters, photographers, proofreaders, and editors.
- Collaborated with <u>Morristown News</u> to meet quarterly production deadlines. Upgraded original cut-and-paste layout to computer layout. Forged parent partnerships for fundraising activities.

1989–2000   **Advisor, MCMS Video Imaging Program Production**
- Led creative team of student volunteers in the design, editing, and production of an annual 8th grade video production, a reprise of their 8th grade year, which was shown to parents, faculty, administration, and students at the end of the school year.
- Spearheaded successful fundraising campaign that raised $10K within one year for multimedia equipment. Spun-off to become the MCMS TV Studio, a fully functioning studio with a network of TV monitors installed in every classroom.

1989–1995   **Advisor, MCMS Yearbook: <u>The Tiger</u>**
- Oversaw this student-run production by 7th and 8th graders, culminating in a hardcover yearbook. Students learned photography, layout, cropping, editing, and the entire production process. Raised funds to support this annual activity.

Committees & Awards
Discipline Committee—established demerit system
Mission Statement Committee—Morristown Township "Millennium Mission"
Who's Who in American Education
Board of Education Honoree—for contributions to MCMS newspaper

Professional Associations
National Education Association (NEA)
New Jersey Education Association (NJEA)
New Jersey Science Teachers Association (NJSTA)

RESUME 32: BY IGOR SHPUDEJKO, B.S.I.E., MBA, CPRW, JCTC

Ann Thomas

10 Henry Street, Wycoff, New Jersey 07401
H: (201) 886-1125 — E-mail: Athomas@yahoo.com

OBJECTIVE	A position as a Middle School Mathematics Teacher where I can create an energized learning environment that focuses on individual understanding and expression.
PROFILE	Dedicated, talented, resourceful teacher skilled in building rapport and respect with students. Possess the ability to establish a creative and stimulating classroom environment. Experienced in using innovative computer software to enhance learning process. Background includes tutoring in high school, student teaching in high school and middle school, and serving as a mathematics teaching assistant at the college level.

SUMMARY OF QUALIFICATIONS

- More than 8 years of experience as a mathematics teacher and tutor.
- Introduced "Studio Calculus" at Dover Institute of Technology (DIT) as a new teaching tool utilizing Maple Software.
- Received award for "Outstanding Teaching Assistant" from DIT student body.
- Tutored students in high school and college in mathematical principles.
- Able to make subject material "come alive" for students through enthusiasm and creativity.

EDUCATION
2000-Present
1997-2000

DOVER INSTITUTE OF TECHNOLOGY, Jersey City, New Jersey
Ph.D. work in Mathematics. Stanley Fellowship recipient.
Master of Science in Applied Mathematics (GPA 4.0)

1994-1997

WILLIAM PATTERSON UNIVERSITY, Wayne, New Jersey
Bachelor of Arts in Secondary Education (GPA 4.0), magna cum laude

EXPERIENCE
1998-Present

DOVER INSTITUTE OF TECHNOLOGY, Jersey City, New Jersey
<u>Teaching Assistant/Lecturer</u>
Prepared curriculum and materials for Freshmen Precalculus and Calculus courses. Served as recitation instructor for Mathematical Analysis up to senior level. Recitation instructor for Logic and Discrete Mathematics. Explained solutions, administered tests and quizzes, and fielded questions about material.

- Recipient of "Outstanding Teaching Assistant Award" from student body for both 98-99 and 99-00 school years.
- Utilized Maple Computer Software to implement "Studio Calculus."
- Presented statistics paper on "Time Series Analysis" to faculty and guests.

1997-1998

SHARPE CAPITAL, New York, New York
<u>Researcher</u>
Responsible for encapsulating financial news in fact sheets for client use.

1995-1997

WILLIAM PATTERSON UNIVERSITY, Wayne, New Jersey
<u>Mathematics Tutor</u>
Tutored in university's "drop-in" math-help center.

CERTIFICATIONS

New Jersey Teaching Certificate in secondary education.

AFFILIATIONS

American Mathematical Society (AMA)
Mathematics Association of America (MAA)
American Statistical Association (ASA)

COMPUTER SKILLS

Proficient in Microsoft Word, Excel, and PowerPoint;
Maple Software (mathematical software package); C++; and FORTRAN.

This is an efficient one-page format for an experienced teacher. Note the effective Profile and Summary of Qualifications.

John Mettle

Mobile: (860) 213-3333
E-mail: John_Mettle@emails.com
16 Terryville Avenue, Hartford, CT 06401

TECHNOLOGY EDUCATION TEACHER

Extensive previous career in design and manufacturing engineering & operations management.

EDUCATION

Teacher Certification in Technology Education: University of Connecticut, Storrs, CT
Candidate for **Certification** in **Middle School Mathematics;** completed / passed Praxis II
M.S. Management, Rensselaer/Hartford University, Hartford, CT
M.S. Mechanical Engineering, Worcester Polytechnic Institute, Worcester, MA
B.S. Mechanical Engineering, University of India
Additional credits in **Electrical Engineering,** University of Connecticut, Storrs, CT

TEACHING EXPERIENCE

Martin Luther King Middle School, Bristol, CT   2/02–Present
Technology Education Teacher (8/02–Present)
Mathematics Teacher: grades 7 and 8 (2/02–6/02)
- Instruct 225 technology students, 15 classes per week, in technology education. Previously taught 180 students in mathematics. These are inner-city students of all socioeconomic and academic levels.
- Initiated technology curriculum in department previously offering only wood shop.
- Participated in K–8 curriculum development for technology education.
- Hired five 8th-grade students (out-of-pocket) to work in technology department after school. Results: I have benefited from their help; the students are learning new skills and a good work ethic.

Central High School, Southington, CT   10/30/01–12/14/01
D.F. Jones Middle School, Glastonbury, CT   8/28/01–10/25/01
Student Teacher, Technology Education
Taught five classes including **Project Lead the Way** classes:
- Aero Lab—7th grade; World of Motion—8th grade; Computer Geometry I—9th grade; Engineering Design—9th grade; Principles of Engineering—11th grade.

West Hartford School District, West Hartford, CT   9/99–1/00
Long-term substitute position: **Technology Education Teacher,** grades 9, 10, and 11, Loughby High School.

Southington School System, Southington, CT   10/98–6/99
Permanent Substitute Teacher: taught mathematics at all levels in grades 9 through 12.

BUSINESS EXPERIENCE *(Full details upon request)*

D&K INDUSTRIES, INC., Southington, CT   1995–1998
Served in several capacities including **Manager of Engineering and Quality** (4/97–10/98)
METTLE ENTERPRISES (Family sign business), Bristol, CT   1992–1994
Standardized manufacturing methods. Redirected marketing focus, resulting in 50% increase in sales.
WIRE FORMS COMPANY, West Hartland, CT   1981–1992
Steadily promoted through increasingly responsible positions highlighted by **Technical Director** (1989–1992).

AFFILIATIONS and INTERESTS

Member of International and Connecticut Technology Education Associations; past member, Technology Student Association. Interests include ballroom dancing and instructing, yoga, and meditation.

This teacher had made a successful career transition after nearly 10 years in business. Now, his business experience appears on the resume as "added value" rather than a primary qualification.

SHARON WELLS

4344 East Franklin Street, Apt. 5
New Haven, Connecticut 06525
(203) 336-8041   Email: germanteach@home.com

GOAL:

High School German Teacher, In-service Instructor, or Computer Technician.

EDUCATION:

Southern Connecticut State University
B.A. Education—Anticipated 2005
Major: **German**
Minor: **Educational Computing & Technology Certificate**—May 2002
GPA: 3.31

Coursework for the Educational Computing & Technology Certificate: The Computer in Education, Teaching with Technology, Utilizing Technology for the Administrative Tasks of Teaching, Current Issues in Computers and Educational Technology, and Advanced Educational Media Production.

COMPUTER SKILLS:

Hardware
Public access terminals, Macintosh and Windows PCs with Ethernet LAN connections, Sun workstations running UNIX operating system, X-terminals, laser and color printers, scanners, video phones, video conferencing, and digital cameras.

Software
MS Word, MS Excel, MS PowerPoint, WordPerfect, ClarisWorks, Claris Home Page, Hyper Studio, Avid Videoshop, Fetch, PageMill, Top Class, PageMaker, QuarkXPress, Photoshop, Swivel 3D, Director, Illustrator, MiniCad, FileMaker Pro, Telnet, Netscape, and TurboGopher.

LANGUAGES:

German. Intermediate to advanced proficiency. Able to read, write, speak, and understand.

VOLUNTEER:

Taught English as a Second Language at the New Haven Adult Learning Center, Fall 2001. Worked in small groups with adults with various languages and 2 Bosnian students.

EXPERIENCE:

2000–Present: **DELI CLERK**
Gala Jubilee, Hamden, CT

Merchandise products, order food, and work events. Relate well to a wide variety of people.

1998–2000: **WAITRESS/CASHIER**
Bonanza, West Haven, CT
Sold more side orders than anyone previously at restaurant. West Haven Bonanza rated top in nation. Performed other tasks as needed.

1997–2002: **VISUAL SPECIALIST MERCHANDISER**
JCPenney, West Hartford, CT
Promoted from Hamden store because of excellent merchandising skills.

Ordered merchandise via computer. Maintained a monthly budget that varied seasonally.

Worked cooperatively with other merchandisers in store as well as district managers.

Continually planned for future events/seasons.

Utilized self-management skills. Managed 2 employees.

1997–1999: **SALES ASSOCIATE**
JCPenney, Hamden, CT
Sold in various departments. Merchandised store products.

A two-column format makes this well-organized resume stand out. For a soon-to-be-qualified teacher, education and volunteer activities are as important as work experience.

CHAPTER 7

Resumes for Specialty Teaching Positions

- Art Teachers
- Drama Teachers
- Dance Teachers
- Music Teachers
- Japanese-Language Instructors
- Reading Teachers
- English as a Second Language (ESL) Teachers
- Physical Education Teachers
- Outdoor Skills Teachers
- Computer Instructors
- Distance-Learning Professionals
- Community Health Educators
- Educational Assistants

RESUME 35: BY DONNA FARRISE, JCTC

Lisa D. Messina

23 Beverly Drive, Greenlawn, NY 11740
Home (631) 757-3221 • Cell (516) 321-6795

Profile

Enthusiastic, self-motivated **ART EDUCATION TEACHER** who uses creativity and innovation to motivate, impart knowledge, and facilitate learning. Effectively incorporate the love of literature and art history into all lessons, creating an enriched learning environment. Possess outstanding interpersonal, presentation, and classroom management skills. Continually encourage diversity among children to accomplish a common goal—"a Love of Art." These qualities have earned the respect of faculty, peers, and students.

"One hundred years from now it will not matter what my bank account was, the sort of house I lived in, or the kind of car I drove. But the world may be different because I was important in the life of a child."
—Anonymous

Certifications

New York State Art Certification K-12 (pending)
Certification in Interior Design, Parsons School of Design, 1988

Education

Long Island University, C.W. Post, Brookville, NY
☑ **Bachelor of Arts in Art Education**   December 2004
G.P.A. 3.87 • Dean's List

Student Teaching

<u>MURPHY JUNIOR HIGH SCHOOL</u> • Stony Brook, NY   11/04 to 12/04
☑ **Student Teacher, Seventh through Ninth Grade**
— Taught studio art, drawing and painting, sculpture, and multimedia.
— Designed and implemented well-received lessons utilizing various techniques, and developed cooperative learning strategies and interdisciplinary learning.
— Established learning environments that met the intellectual, social, and creative needs of students.
— Developed murals, displays, and presentations of artwork.
— Utilized slide presentations and audio/visual equipment.
— Created multicultural diverse lesson plans.
— Incorporated technology into the classroom.
— Exercised a positive and assertive approach to discipline for modeling behaviors.

<u>NASSAKEAG ELEMENTARY SCHOOL</u> • Setauket, NY   9/04 to 11/04
☑ **Student Teacher, Kindergarten through Sixth Grade**
— Utilized a literature-based approach; facilitated learning consistent with the diverse needs and interests of all students while following the curriculum according to New York State and District Art Standards.
— Taught clay, sculpture, drawing, painting, and graphic design classes.
— Incorporated art history, art appreciation, and art criticism in all lesson plans.
— Created interdisciplinary lessons, i.e., incorporated language arts (poetry) and color theory (palettes), integrating the expressive quality of color.
— Maintained an active, disciplined classroom while activities occurred simultaneously.

Design elements and a relevant educational quote work together to create a unique resume for an art teacher.

RESUME 35, CONTINUED

Lisa D. Messina
_____Page 2

Related Art Experience

Employment History

DEBORAH VASSAR INTERIORS • Nissequogue, NY   1/92 to 6/93
☑ **Residential Department Manager**
— Developed design layouts and blueprints for residential projects.

ZORBA THE GREEK RESTAURANT • Oakdale, NY   2/86 to 6/01
(Two Full-service Greek Restaurants • 70 Seats)

☑ **Owner / General Manager**
— Co-directed the daily operations of this restaurant chain with two
   locations.
— Pioneered and launched innovative advertising campaigns; created logo
   design.
— Directed all aspects of interior design needs, new construction, and
   renovations.
— Diverse responsibilities were expansive and included ordering
   food/beverages, handling all aspects of menu design, booking/catering
   parties, promotions, P&L, inventory control, labor controls, profit margins,
   and forecasting.
— Oversaw payroll procedures and developed/monitored budgets.
— Interviewed, hired, fired, trained, and scheduled 15-20 employees, i.e.,
   managers, cooks, server staff, and hostesses.

Community Service

— Setauket PTA
— Girl Scouts—Brownie Leader
— Unitarian Universalist Fellowship at Stony Brook
— Three Village Character Counts Coalition—Character Development
— Senior Seminar—Community High School Group

Professional Development

— P.R.A.I.S.E.—Parents Raising Adolescents, Increasing Self-Esteem
— Character Development Classes
— Facilitated Parenting Skills Classes

Interests

— Museums
— Literature
— Traveling
— Salsa Dancing
— Physical Fitness
— Tennis

RESUME 36: BY PETER MARX, JCTC

Enter, stage center

ROGER O. TAYLOR, JR.

89 Old Memorial Blvd.
Zephyr Hills, FL 22867
(814) 392-8292
rogerot@msn.com

Seeking a Drama / English / Language Arts teaching position
with Pasco County School System

Prelude ("Gains Credentials")

Certified in Florida to teach Drama (Grades 6–12).
Certified in Florida to teach Middle School English (Grades 5–9).
Will complete full state certification requirements in April 2005.

Act 1 ("Earns Secondary Education")

Master of Science in Educational Administration, Wilkes University, Wilkes Barre, PA, 2002
Bachelor of Arts in Theater, Jacksonville University, Jacksonville, FL, 1984

Act 2 ("Gathers Supporting Training")

Equal Opportunity	1999
Instructor Training	1997
Total Quality Management	1995
Improvisational Performance	1994
Theater Management	1989

- 2 years of experience teaching 25–50 students in a classroom or lecture environment.
- Completed a 4-semester-hour Linguistics course at the University of Florida, July 1999.
- Currently enrolled in Adolescent Literature. Expected completion December 2004.

Intermission ("United States Army, 1984–2004")

Act 3 ("Applies Global Experience")

Assistant Scoutmaster, Boy Scout Troop 11, Zephyr Hills, FL, 1999–2002
Assistant Cubmaster, Cub Scout Pack 610, Zephyr Hills, FL, 1997–1999
Master of Ceremonies for official events at Camp Zama, Japan, 1994–1996
Play-by-play Announcer for the Camp Zama High School Fighting Trojans Football Team, 1996
Youth Recreation Director, Seoul, Korea, 1992–1993
More than 20 years of work as an amateur actor throughout the world

Exit, stage left

This individual retired from a military career that had absolutely nothing to do with his dream job. But he had prepared himself over the years and devised a creative format that perfectly matched his goal of teaching drama in public schools.

CLAIRE JEAN MONET

DANCE TEAM DIRECTOR

Jazz (including Character, Lyrical, Modern) • *Hip-Hop* • *Ballet* • *Tap*

CREATIVE Team Leader and Dancer experienced in all phases of dance from **choreography and instruction** to successfully creating and directing **star-quality performances.**

PROFESSIONAL DANCE PROFILE

- **Professional Dancer and Instructor with more than 20 years of experience** in all facets of dance.
- **Danced 3 years for NBA Salt Lake City Dixie Twisters dance team.**
- **Choreographed NBA Denver Power Dancers jazz routine,** Denver, CO (1996–1998).
- **Studied Modern and Jazz Dance** at Utah State University (1986–1990).
- **Excellent teaching skills** encompassing all styles, levels, and students ages 5 to 40.

...................................CHOREOGRAPHY BACKGROUND..............................

- *The Wizard of Oz,* Children's Jazz Productions, Salt Lake City, UT (2001–2002)
- *A Lyrical Jazz Solo,* Salt Lake City, UT (2001)
- *Evita,* Procter's Theatre, Salt Lake City, UT (2000)
- *USA NBA Jazz Dance Camps,* all styles, one-minute routines, various cities in U.S. (1999–2002)
- *Betty Morris Dance Company,* Lyrical Jazz piece, Salt Lake City, UT (2002)

...................................PROFESSIONAL PERFORMANCES..............................

- Solo artist (Lyrical Jazz), *The Looking Glass Theater,* Salt Lake City, UT (2001)
- *Martin Shore Dance Art* (Modern Jazz, Lyrical Jazz, Character Jazz, Jazz, Tap, Hip-Hop), Sacramento, CA (1998)
- *NBA Salt Lake City Dixie Twister's Dance Team* (Jazz, Lyrical Jazz, Hip-Hop, Character Jazz), Salt Lake City, UT (1994–1997)
- *Martin Shore Dance Art* (Modern Jazz), Salt Lake City, UT (1992–1994)
- *Betty Morris Dance Company* (Jazz, Modern Jazz, Lyrical Jazz, Character Jazz), Utah State University, Salt Lake City, UT (1992–1993)

...................................PROFESSIONAL EXPERIENCE..............................

The Blue Moon Dance Studio, Salt Lake City, UT   1993–2004
DANCE INSTRUCTOR/DIRECTOR-OWNER

United Spirit Association (Road tour of several U.S. cities)   1991–1993
JAZZ DANCE INSTRUCTOR

1613 East Glenn Terrace, Salt Lake City, UT 84109
Phone: (801) 276-6299   E-mail: cmonet@us.net

This concise, well-organized resume for a dance teacher and director is enhanced by an appropriate graphic.

ALAN W. DAVIDSON

4003 Sunset Lane
Richmond, Texas 77469
(281) 549-2190
Email: gmusic@msn.com

PROFILE

An accomplished **Guitar Instructor** and **Musician** with more than 15 years of guitar playing and singing experience and 10 years of guitar instruction experience. Committed to providing students with a solid foundation in music fundamentals while making music education fun and interesting.

EDUCATION & TRAINING

UNIVERSITY OF HOUSTON—Houston, TX
Currently pursuing Bachelor of Fine Arts in Music and a Teaching Certificate

EAST DETROIT CONSERVATORY OF MUSIC—Detroit, MI
Basic guitar and music studies

THE FAUNT SCHOOL OF CREATIVE MUSIC—Los Angeles, CA
Ear training, rhythm training, and theory

Private instruction for *Classical* guitar with Paul Huber, Detroit, MI, and Terry Gashuan, Houston, TX.

Studied *Jazz* theory and guitar with Mike Wheeler, Dave Nichols, and Paul Chester, Houston, TX.

TEACHING EXPERIENCE

L & H MUSIC AND UPBEAT SCHOOL OF MUSIC—Houston, TX
Full-time Guitar Instructor with an average of 60 students per week (1994 to Present).

Instruct in all styles of music from *Classical* to *Rock* for both electric and acoustic guitar with an emphasis on music fundamentals, including rhythm, ear training, sight-reading, and technique.

PERFORMING EXPERIENCE

Performed as a solo artist and played with several cover bands in the Detroit, MI, area.
Currently performing with *Juniper* in Houston, TX.

This resume for a guitar instructor was posted on his Web site, distributed to music schools, and used to apply for employment as a high-school music instructor.

Keiko Taniguchi

5555 Hula Lane, No. 5555 • Honolulu, Hawaii 96826
Tel: (808) 595-3209 • E-Mail: ktaniguchi@hawaii.rr.com

Seeking Position As...

Japanese Language Instructor

Profile: Recent M.A. degree graduate with 5 years of practical teaching experience. Demonstrated ability to design developmentally appropriate curriculum. Expertise in selecting effective methodologies to teach Japanese language and culture based on students' objectives and proficiencies. B.A. in International Business. **Core Skills:**

- Course Design
- Textbook Selection
- Supplemental Materials Design/Selection

- Classroom Management
- Testing Design/Administration
- Student Advising

**Native Japanese Speaker**
**Advanced Oral and Written English Fluency**
**Resident of Hawaii**

Education

M.A., Japanese Linguistics (Pedagogy emphasis), 5/2004
University of Hawaii—Honolulu, Hawaii
GPA 4.0/4.0

B.A., International Business, 8/1992
Women's College of Miami—Miami, Florida
Who's Who Among International Students
Graduated Cum Laude; GPA 3.56/4.0

Teaching Background

Japanese Teacher   Spring 2004
Japanese Practicum. Direct hands-on teaching in JPN 101 class.
University of Hawaii—Honolulu, Hawaii

- Collaborated with three other graduate students to teach listening, speaking, reading, and writing skills to class of up to 14 students.
- Designed, administered, and graded oral and written quizzes and mid-term and final examinations. Provided appropriate feedback to students.

ESL Teacher   5/1996–4/1998
Nagoya City Junior College—Nagoya, Japan

- Taught English in language lab for classes of up to 50 students at a time. Designed listening skills curriculum. Developed mid-term and final examinations.
- Advised interested students on living/studying abroad and related test preparation.
- Substituted for professors and assistant professors in English Department.

In this resume, teaching experience and international business experience are presented separately; both add value to this Japanese-language instructor's skills.

Keiko Taniguchi
Page 2 of 2

ESL Teacher   5/1993–5/1996
NEON English Conversation School—Nagoya City, Japan

- Taught English conversation and grammar to Japanese students of English. Included TOEFL, TOEIC, and national English proficiency test courses.
- Planned and implemented developmentally appropriate curriculum focusing on oral communication skills.
- Managed class sizes of one to 12 students, from junior high school students to adults.

Business Related Experience

Export Sales Coordinator   7/1992–2/1993
Tokyo Pens, Inc.—Tokyo, Japan

- Coordinated order fulfillment for China sales representative.
- Interpreted on behalf of company's English-speaking foreign visitors.

Assistant to Vice-President (Internship)   Spring 1992
U.S. East Bank, Asian Division—Miami, Florida

- Performed data organization using IBM PC.
- Translated annual reports from Japanese to English.

Assistant to Director (Internship)   Summer 1990
Sister State Program, International Division—Miami, Florida

- Conducted data analysis and research on various tour programs in Florida.
- Planned, developed, and arranged tour itineraries for Japanese tourists.

Additional Skills

Computer: Word, Excel, Internet Explorer, Outlook/Entourage, SPSS

Certified Interpreter of Japanese and English, Japan Interpreters Association

• • •

Elizabeth M. Randolph

Profile

* Solid foundation in Reading Education, Reading Recovery, and Balanced Literacy.
* Experience training teachers in balanced literacy, MLPP, and other literacy-based programs.
* Strive to provide intellectually stimulating classroom environment which encourages students' growth into lifelong learners.

Education

University of Michigan • Ann Arbor, Michigan
Postgraduate courses in **Early Literacy**
M.A.T. with Honors—Reading (1983)

Alma College • Alma, Michigan
Elementary Teaching Endorsement (1985)
B.A. with Honors—Language Arts (1978)

Continuing Education

* Michigan Literacy Progress Profile (MLPP)—Regional Trainer
* MLPP—completed 35-hour course and 100+ application hours

Certifications

State of Michigan Continuing Teaching Certificate
  * K–8 All Subjects
  * K–12 Reading
  * 9–12 English and Art Education

University of Michigan
  * Certified Reading Recovery Teacher

Affiliations & Activities

* Reading Recovery Councils of North America and Michigan
* Oakland County Literacy Coaches—Member
* Pontiac Area Reading Council—Board Member (2003–2004)
* International and Michigan Reading Associations
* "ASAP Lap Grant," 3rd Annual Oakland County Early Literacy Conference—Panel Member

Relevant Experience

Pontiac Schools • Pontiac, Michigan
Reading Recovery Teacher and
K–2 Literacy Coach (2000–Present)
  * Teach daily individual literacy lessons for lowest-level first graders following the Reading Recovery early intervention program design.
  * Model and consult on balanced literacy approaches to support teachers in their development as balanced literacy instructors.
  * Organize, conduct, and participate in ongoing staff development. Designed and facilitated three-part workshop on comprehension strategies for K–5 staff. Trained K–3 staff in MLPP.

Pine Knob Elementary—Clarkston Community Schools • Clarkston, Michigan
LD Categorical Resource Special Education
Long-Term Substitute (2000)
  * Provided supplemental reading and writing instruction to students with varying abilities in grades 1–4 and middle school.
  * Adapted curriculum and teaching style to students' individual levels to maximize comprehension and improvement.

Belle Ann Elementary School—Brandon School District • Ortonville, Michigan
Title I Instructional Assistant (1998–1999)
  * Assisted students functioning below grade level in all subjects, especially reading.
  * Worked with students in whole groups, during teacher-directed activities, in small groups, and individually.
Volunteer (1995–1998)

Waterford School District • Waterford, Michigan
Reading Laboratory Teacher (1983–1990)
  * Hired to organize, coordinate, implement, and administer middle-school reading program.
  * Tested and placed students in individualized reading programs.

Oxford Area Community Schools • Oxford, Michigan
Teacher (1978–1983)
  * Taught junior high English, Remedial Math, Social Studies, and Science.
  * Managed elementary Reading Lab.

References and portfolio available on request

4520 Park Lake Drive ✶ Clarkston, Michigan 48346 ✶ 248-555-8216 ✶ e_randolph@isp.net

A creative two-column format is used to present lots of relevant information on one easy-to-read page. The unique design makes the resume memorable.

RESUME 41: BY EVA MULLEN, CPRW

ELIZABETH BEYER

8576 Reed Avenue
San Diego, California 92109

(858) 447-5873
ebeyer@hotmail.com

ESL EDUCATOR

Dedicated professional with a teaching philosophy that facilitates discovery of each child's potential through support, honor, and a positive learning atmosphere. Successful in communicating with ESL students in diverse environments. Receive excellent feedback from students and teachers. Taught ESL and attended two graduate classes in Ensenada, Mexico. Completed three semesters of university Spanish. Plan to continue Spanish education. Experienced in team teaching and Montessori methods.

EDUCATION / CERTIFICATION

M.A. in Education, Equity, and Cultural Diversity, University of California, San Diego, CA   2004
B.S. in Elementary Education, Minor in Sociology, Reno State College, Reno, NV   2000

- ESL Teacher Certification, State of California, 2004
- California Teacher Certification (K–6), 2004, Type VI Authorization—Temporary, 2002
- First Aid Certification, American Red Cross, 2003
- Nevada Teacher Certification (PreK–6), Provisional, 2001

PROFESSIONAL EXPERIENCE

Outdoor Education Teacher, River Hill Ranch School, Alpine, CA   2003
Implemented weekly lessons on farm life, natives, and the earth for 20 students ages 7–15.

K–6 Substitute Teacher, San Diego County School District, San Diego, CA   2002–2003
Taught art, language arts, math, music, reading, science, and social studies. Worked with ESL 3rd and 4th graders, autistic Kindergarten class, and Montessori students.

Preschool Long-Term Substitute Teacher, The Center for Children, Reno, NV   2002
Taught challenged students for University of Reno nonprofit organization. Prepared children for public schools. Encouraged emotional growth and interpersonal relations.

1–2 Teacher/Tutor, Journey School for Technology and Science, Reno, NV   2001–2002
Instructed *Education for All* literacy program. Designed individualized learning strategies.

K–6 Substitute Teacher, Reno City School District, Reno, NV   2001–2002
Taught students in diverse environments including rural areas, suburbs, and cities. Maintained learning productivity by creating positive, comfortable atmosphere.

Other Experience: Camp Counselor, Jewelry Instructor, Group Counselor, and Coach.

STUDENT TEACHING EXPERIENCE

- Fuerte Elementary School, ESL and Experiential Classes, La Jolla, CA, 2003–2004
- Emerald Middle School, 5th Grade, Reno, NV, 2000–2001
- Reno Elementary School, Kindergarten, Reno, NV, 2000

VOLUNTEER EXPERIENCE

- Fuerte Elementary School, Dual-Language Program, 2nd Grade, La Jolla, CA, 2003
- Habitat for Humanity, Reno, NV, 2001

Teaching philosophy is included in the profile; the rest of the resume is concise and well-organized.

RESUME 42: BY LINDA MATIAS, CEIP, JCTC

WANDA ORTIZ-RIVERA
265 Furlough Drive
Smithtown, NY 11787
(631) 382-2425
wrivera@net.com

ESL TEACHER

Experienced bilingual educator dedicated to fostering education by creating a stimulating, nurturing, and culturally friendly environment for bilingual students. Keen understanding of the importance of student assimilation and the need for respect of their native upbringing. Adhere to new procedures and commissioner regulations for LEP and adequately incorporate these methodologies in a classroom setting to enhance learning.

Highlights of Qualifications:

- **Motivator:** Create a powerful, committed, and sensitive learning environment for bilingual students that promotes personal growth and achievement.
- **Team Contributor:** Natural talent to effectively build administrative and teacher relationships that consistently meet the immediate and long-term needs of the students.
- **Parental Educator:** Keen ability to engage caregivers in the learning process and decrease the learning curve.

EDUCATION AND CERTIFICATION

COLUMBIA UNIVERSITY, Teachers College, New York, NY
M.Ed. in Spanish, Emphasis in Bilingual/Bicultural Education   2002

DOWLING COLLEGE, Oakdale, NY
Master of Business Administration   1996
Bachelor of Art, Natural Science, and Math; Minor: Spanish Literature   1995

New York State Certification, N-6 with an Extension in Bilingual Education
ESL Teaching Certification

TEACHING EXPERIENCE

Bilingual Resource Teacher, John F. Kennedy, Portchester School District, New York, NY   **2002-Present**

- Designed, created, and implemented innovative teaching curricula for kindergarten through fourth grade that successfully mainstreamed bilingual students.
- Encourage parental involvement in their children's education by facilitating interactive workshops.
- Perform, document, and review evaluations and assessments for student referral and mainstreaming with central staff and parents.
- Integrate reading, math, science, and social studies into learning curricula geared to facilitate mainstream topics and ideas.
- Actively interact with Title I teachers to create individualized educational plans.
- Utilize knowledge of CALPs and BICS to proactively engage students in the learning process.
- Administer school-wide ESL testing, properly distinguishing students with language barriers.

Bilingual First Grade Teacher, Pine Park, Brentwood School District, New York, NY   **1998-2002**

- Designed unique lesson plans geared to pique students' interests and promote active learning.
- Respected individual learning styles and modified assignments to meet individual objectives.
- Initiated a reading program integrating different reading methodologies and parental workshops.
- Collaborated with parents/guardians through regular telephone communication, workshops, and parent-teacher conferences.

Adjunct Professor, Bilingual Department, Teachers College, Columbia University, New York, NY   **1999-2001**

- Presented new methodologies to graduate students on how to properly teach first and second language acquisition to bilingual students.

continued...

This is a classic resume for a teacher of English as a Second Language: chronological, accomplishment-focused, and with a strong introduction. The "ABCD" graphic is a nice enhancement.

RESUME 42, CONTINUED

WANDA ORTIZ-RIVERA
Page 2

TEACHING EXPERIENCE CONTINUED

Researcher and Tutor, Spanish Bilingual/Bicultural Education Department, Teachers College, Columbia University, New York, NY — 1998-2001

Student Advisor, Bilingual Department, Teachers College, Columbia University, New York, NY — 1998-2001

Bilingual Elementary Teacher, P.S. 46, Bronx, NY — 1996-1998

Bilingual Math Instructor, Kingsborough Community College, Brooklyn, NY — Summer 1997

Elementary Teacher, South Country Summer Program, Bayshore, NY — Summer 1996

TEACHING METHODOLOGIES & ASSESSMENTS

- Woodcok Munoz
- LAB
- BICS
- Supera
- TPR
- CALP
- Terranova
- Gouins
- Brigance
- ESL assessments
- National Approach (Tracy Terrell)

COMMITTEES

- Served on Committee of Special Education (CSE) to determine the future status of bilingual students.
- Assisted in writing grants and proposals for state and federal funding.

HONORS

Fellowship Award, Multicultural Studies, Emphasis Bilingual/Education, 1998

Honor Student, National Dean's List, 1991-1993

Awarded by Columbia University and Fundacion Jose Ortega Y Gasset—Madrid
Presented Methodologies of Teaching Reading to Bilingual Students

Selected by college President and faculty to represent student body at Mediterranean XIII Conference in Barcelona, Spain, 1994

Selected as a Language Translator and Interpreter, Dowling College Symposium, for Dr. Camilo Jose Cela, 1989 Nobel Prize Winner In Literature, 1994

RESEARCH

Bilingual/Bicultural Classroom—Teacher's Reflective Practice

PRESENTATIONS

How to Help Your Child with Homework
How to Teach Your Child to Love Reading
How to Help Your Child with Test-Taking
Home and School Connection

PROFESSIONAL AFFILIATIONS

Member, Kappa Delta Pi, 1999-Present
Member, State Association of Bilingual Education (SABE), 1999-Present
Member, National Association of Bilingual Education (NABE), 1999-Present
Member, Statewide School Program, 2003-2004

Jason Lipman

192-37 35th Avenue
Flushing, NY 11351
718-555-9003

Physical Education Teacher (K-12)

- Eager to bring students into the twenty-first century using a unique combination of high-caliber physical education experience and athletic achievement. Will utilize teaching knowledge and more than fifteen years' background as a successful business owner to parallel the development of athletic abilities with the understanding of real-life skills.

- Dedicated to enthusiastic and dynamic teaching as a means of creating a lifelong love of sports and learning in children and young adults. Create an energizing educational experience that motivates students to enjoy physical, academic, and personal accomplishment.

- Trained for a teaching career, but in response to family need, reluctantly put plans aside and joined family business after college (worked in business from age of five). To stay in teaching, took substitute teaching assignments while running business. After fifteen years of profitable business management, have sold business to teach full-time.

Education and Certification

Post-Graduate Coursework
Currently attending Master's in Elementary Education program
St. Joseph's College, Brooklyn, NY

Three-credit Education Course
State University of New York at Stony Brook

Bachelor of Science in Health and Physical Education
Tennessee State University, Yarrow, TN 1983
(attended on full football scholarship)

Undergraduate Coursework
Jefferson Rangle College, Lincoln City, MD
(attended on full football scholarship)

Certification (Provisional, pending renewal)
NY State Physical Education K–12

Key Qualifications

- Experienced college-level coach; worked for five years as defensive line and strength training coach at Hofstra University. Experienced substitute teacher with ability to motivate students in difficult situations.

- As coach and teacher, incorporate learning modality principles into group and individual instruction. Plan, prepare, and instruct in each skills area using wide variety of motivational and implementation strategies to engage students in active learning and accomplishment.

- Possess unique ability to break down components of athletic training into easily assimilated units. Students struggling with techniques become successful after this instructional coaching.

Athletic Achievements

Played two years of semi-pro football for the Elkin Eagles

Tried out for the Giants and the Buffalo Bills

Defensive Line Coach for Hofstra University Bengals Football Team

Hofstra University Strength Training Coach

College Football:

_Azalea Bowl MVP
NAIA National Playoffs
Senior Year Team Captain
First Team, All-American
First Team, All-District_

High School Football:

_All-American
All-State
All-County
All-Long Island
All-League_

This resume incorporates numerous design elements with a high degree of originality. Because it is well written and well organized, it is easy to skim despite being fairly text-heavy.

Jason Lipman   2

Employment in Education

Substitute Teacher (grades 1–12), New York, NY   **1989 to present**

- **New York City Schools**
- **Sewhanaka School District**
- **St. Kevin's Elementary School, Elmont, NY**

Teach academic subjects and all physical education activities including indoor baseball, wiffle ball, basketball, and volleyball. Handle difficult assignments by developing a mutual respect with students and deflecting natural aggression towards substitutes. Utilize personal style of instruction that enhances motivation and reduces opportunities for student disruption. Create an energized atmosphere that generates interest and participation.

Defensive Line Coach for Hofstra Bengals Football Team
Weight Lifting Coach
Hofstra University, Hempstead, NY   **1983 to 1988**

As Defensive Line Coach, taught techniques and form; made up daily practice schedules and routines; set up film appointments for players and graded players by films. Reviewed game plans, incorporating defense and offense. Handled scouting and recruiting for New York and New Jersey teams; wrote scouting reports and attended team meetings. Taught visualization techniques for instinctive, reactive play.

As Weight Lifting Coach, attended NSCA convention; learned and incorporated cutting-edge conditioning strategies into workouts that encouraged college athletes to do total-body conditioning between sets. Developed jump-rope program that dramatically increased athletes' agility.

Student Teaching

Health and Physical Education (grades 7–12)
Johnstown Middle School and High School, Raleigh, ND   **1983**

Offered permanent position; declined due to family responsibilities. As student teacher, instructed students in football, weight training, and track. Used motivation and skills coaching to develop shot put ability in student struggling with technique; student qualified for state championship.

Health and Physical Education (grades K–12)
Hopewell School, Hopewell, TN   **1983**

Business Ownership

Owner/Partner/Operator
All-State Carting, Maspeth, NY   **1983 to 2001**

Recently sold business to a major public company in waste management. All-State was a six-partner waste management company with its own transfer station facility and was aggressively involved in the management/disposal of recycling, municipal solid waste, and construction/demolition debris.

CYNTHIA M. PEREZ

4 Myerson Way
Seattle, WA 82520   perezcm@aol.com

Day: (307) 449-1401
Eve: (307) 776-1511

PROFILE

Seasoned educational professional and noted expert from MIPS, the largest and most reputable American outdoor leadership school. Expertise in curriculum and program development and education administration. Experienced in creating and executing complex field rationing programs, managing staff, and directing participants.

EMPLOYMENT

MIPS Outdoor Leadership School, Seattle, WA

Chief Rationing Instructor   **1986 to Present**

Direct all facets of the educational program concerning backcountry expedition food planning. Provide instruction to 1,255 students annually on planning rations, ordering rations, and ensuring correct distribution. Conduct extensive training and direction for staff. Process 95,000 pounds of food annually. Manage food intake, labeling, packaging, and storage. Administer a $215K annual budget.

- Coordinate the logistics of providing rations to students and instructors. Conceptualize detailed rationing programs, accounting for smooth operations, variety and versatility of foods, nutritional standards, and budgeting.

- Collaborate with technical experts to design and execute food rationing protocol. The spreadsheet programs compute number of participants, number of cook groups, ration periods, and ration poundages. Direct students and staff in activities including packaging food and planning food for expeditions.

- Conduct public speaking, providing clear, specific, highly detailed, and articulate directions to participants in order to facilitate effective rations preparation within a short time frame.

MIPS PROFESSIONAL TRAINING

- Summer Wilderness Course
- Winter Ski Course
- Wilderness First Responder
- Management
- Supervision
- Communications

INDUSTRY PUBLICATIONS

- The MIPS Food Guide: Editor, 1st edition (1998); Co-author, 2nd edition (2002); Co-author, 3rd edition (2004).
- Subject of an article in *Camping America* magazine, "Cooking with Cynthia," August 2002.

EDUCATION

B.S., Outdoor Recreation, The University of Washington, Seattle, WA, 1985

This resume clearly communicates the expertise that is necessary to stand out in the highly specialized field of outdoor leadership instruction.

RESUME 45: BY LAURA A. DECARLO, CCM, CERW, JCTC, CCMC, CECC

TRAVIS A. JONES
1908 Irish Avenue
Atlanta, GA 30067
(770) 494-1005
jazzman@cc.rr.com

COMPUTER (MCSE) INSTRUCTOR ~ MCT
Microsoft Certified Systems Engineer & MCP + Internet / Certified Network Engineer

SUMMARY OF QUALIFICATIONS

Computer Technology Instructor with extensive experience in Network Administration, Project Management and Quality Management. Consistently recognized and awarded for performance. Key areas of expertise include

Instruction:

- Technical Instruction
- Curriculum Development
- MS Curriculum
- Lecture Techniques
- Student Assessment
- Lesson Plans

Computers:

- Microsoft Operating System
- Network Administration
- Windows 95
- Peripheral Equipment
- Novell Operating System
- Hardware Configuration
- Windows NT
- Proxy Server
- Internet Technology
- Software Configuration
- TCP / IP
- MS Office Professional

PROFESSIONAL EXPERIENCE

- **MCSE Instructor & MCT,** Computer Information Technology, Atlanta, GA, 2003–Present
- **Computer Instructor,** Adult Ed. Program, Marietta Community School, Marietta, GA, 2002
- **Software Instructor,** Hillsborough Community College, Tampa, FL, 1994–2001
- **Teacher,** Garden District High School, Tampa, FL, 1986–1993

Technical Instructor / Trainer

- Developed curricula; assembled training materials; prepared goals and objectives; created lesson plans; and taught college-level classes in computer applications, data processing, operating systems, and Microsoft Network Engineering.
  - Demonstrated ability to prepare goals and teach a diverse adult student body.
  - Provided innovative lecture techniques and teaching strategies for students.

Network Administration

- Provided complete knowledge of Novell and Microsoft network administration as a MCSE / CNE / A+ Certification and as instructor of the MCSE Program at CIT.
  - Performed course instruction in Networking Essentials ... NT 4.0 Core ... NT 4.0 Administration ... NT 4.0 Enterprise.
- Skilled in troubleshooting to the board level; excellent ability to facilitate, diagnose and troubleshoot networking and configuration problems of both hardware and software.

EDUCATION & TRAINING

- **B.S. in Education,** Marietta State College, Marietta, GA—GPA: 3.8
- **Computer Science Teaching Certification,** State of Georgia Education Program
- **MCSE, CNE and A+,** Valley Technical Institute, Atlanta, GA

For this technology instructor, the list of computer knowledge is as important as instructional expertise and work experience. The headline, centered between a double-line border, makes the job seeker's objective and expertise crystal clear.

Fred Fiero

1449 Jackson Court		(334) 891-7325 (Office)
Montgomery, Alabama 36116	ffiero@coolspring.com	(334) 864-0074 (Home)

WHAT I CAN BRING TO **BMS** AS A **DISTANCE LEARNING PROFESSIONAL** _____

❏ The **vision and experience** to guide strategic e-learning programs from concept to tangible results that serve your customers quickly,

❏ The **leadership** to transform groups of diverse employees into impassioned stakeholders, and

❏ The **skill** to manage risk well enough to help build your productivity faster than your competition.

RELEVANT WORK HISTORY WITH SELECTED EXAMPLES OF SUCCESS _____

More than 18 years in increasingly responsible positions as commissioned Air Force officer, including these recent assignments:

❏ *Promoted to* **Chief Learning Officer,** Air Force Doctrine Center, Cranston Air Force Base, Alabama, August 1999–Present
The Center provides the basic corporate vision guiding the professional efforts of 371,000 employees worldwide.

> Turned around a new organization that was swamped with urgent, unfocused tasks for two years. Guided a corporate-level needs analysis that integrated every level of proficiency in twelve major learning areas into our first master training plan. *Payoffs:* Our credibility—**our stock in trade—rose fast,** as did our **productivity.**

❏ *Promoted to* **Director of Curriculum,** Air Force Extension Correspondence Institute, Cranston Air Force Base, Marboro Annex, Alabama, November 1997–August 1999
The Institute was recognized as the educational institution with the most number of students in the world. With its $5.5 million budget, it serves learners in hundreds of disciplines at locations around the world.

> Served as direct reporting official for senior- and mid-level managers; indirectly supervised 35 curriculum editors and writers.

> Reignited an organization that had four CEOs in as many years, saw its staffing cut 36% in eight years, and suffered with stagnant budgets for four years. *Payoffs:* Skilled, but **"burned out," employees revoked** their **retirement** papers. **Productivity rose** dramatically. **Conflicts** that had festered for years were **resolved.**

> Did what others had tried, and failed, to do for years: convinced senior corporate levels of our true **value to our customers.** Guided our team to make a powerful presentation in just eight weeks. *Payoffs:* **Management increased our budget** by **$1 million at once.** Previously discouraged employees became convinced there was **no problem they couldn't tackle.**

More indicators of performance ⟶

This resume for the up-and-coming field of distance learning is an excellent example of how to transition military experience to the private sector.

Fred Fiero   **Distance Learning Professional**   (334) 891-7325 (Office)

Enlisted my team to teach me every aspect of their jobs. Then led these top-notch professionals to change from an outdated—but highly praised—development system to much more responsive methods. *Payoffs:* Typical course **development time dropped** from 22 days to 10 days. **Quality** remained **high.**

Restored responsiveness to thousands of customers when demand threatened to outstrip our resources and cause our customers' missions to fail. *Payoffs:* **My proposal documented savings of $1 million** by delivering formerly mailed material electronically.

❑ *Promoted to* **Chief of Distance Learning Policy,** Headquarters, Doctrine University, Cranston Air Force Base, Alabama, April 1994–November 1997

Our office served as the single point of contact for researching, employing, and delivering distance learning technologies.

Went beyond the obvious fix to help our customers who had high-tech distance learning technologies but not the training to use them. Found and removed potential roadblocks from every level. *Payoffs:* Our combination users' handbook, strategy document, and "priority-setter" was in the field in just six months. **Customers very pleased.**

❑ *Promoted to* **Director of Training and Development,** Headquarters, North American Command, Marly Air Force Base, Wyoming, June 1992–April 1994

Designed, developed, produced, delivered, evaluated, and validated "soft skills" training curricula serving some 1,700 people.

Overhauled a system that left new team members feeling left out of our organization for their first six months. Based my new program on a detailed needs analysis. *Payoffs:* **Spin-up time cut by a third.** Everybody won—from workers to managers.

Built a training program that helped our staff serve senior decision makers better and faster than ever. *Payoffs:* After we trained 600 professionals, production **error rate fell from 84% to 15%.**

❑ *Promoted to* **Training Instructor Developer,** Headquarters, Air Force Near Earth Command, Grizzly Air Force Base, Colorado, June 1989–June 1992

Managed traditional and distance learning programs covering 120 contact hours of highly technical skills training to customers across the United States.

Selected by a senior executive vice president **over hundreds of eligibles** for this position.

Salvaged a mission-critical program that had cost $2 million, but wasn't doing the job. Enlisted our experts to help streamline our methods. *Payoffs:* **Cut workload by a factor of 17.** The new system's quality was so high a foreign government asked to copy the methods.

❑ *Promoted to* **Training Branch Chief;** *promoted to* **Training Division Chief,** 91st Missile Wing, Frank Air Force Base, North Dakota, October 1986–June 1989

Guided highly technical programs that delivered training to 400 skilled professionals each month.

Page 2 of 3

Fred Fiero **Distance Learning Professional** (334) 891-7325 (Office)

COMPUTER SKILLS

- ❑ Expert in **Web page design, evaluation of distance learning software,** Internet search protocols, **PowerPoint,** Word, proprietary event reporting software
- ❑ Proficient in Excel, Outlook, Quicken
- ❑ Working knowledge of Access

EDUCATION AND PROFESSIONAL DEVELOPMENT

- ❑ Pursuing **Evaluator** Certificate Program, **Distance Education and Training Council**
- ❑ Pursuing **Certified Distance Educator Credential,** University of Wisconsin at Madison
- ❑ MA, **Organizational Communication,** University of Northern Colorado at Greeley, 1989
  Earned this degree while working 45 hours a week and attending classes on weekends.
- ❑ BA, Grove City College, Grove City, Pennsylvania, 1982
- ❑ Certified Toastmaster, 1985
  This credential is shared by the top 12% of all Toastmaster members and is awarded based on evaluated presentations.

RELEVANT PROFESSIONAL AFFILIATIONS

- ❑ President, Central Alabama Chapter, ASTD, 2001–2005
- ❑ Vice-President for Professional Development, Pike's Peak Chapter, ASTD, 2000
- ❑ President, Cheyenne Toastmasters, 1986

SELECTED PUBLICATIONS IN THE FIELD OF E-LEARNING

- ❑ With H. Kottler, J. Parsons, and S. Wardenburg, "Knowledge Objects: Definition, Development Initiatives, and Potential Impact," Learning Issues and Trends Report, Alexandria, Virginia, 2002–2003
- ❑ Distance Learning Resource Handbook, Air Force Distance Learning Office, Cranston Air Force Base, Alabama, October 2002
- ❑ Distance Learning Site Managers' Handbook, Air Force Distance Learning Office, Cranston Air Force Base, Alabama, July 2002

Page 3 of 3

PAMELA L. WHITFIELD

260 Haverstick Road, Apt. 14 • New Castle, DE 19700

Residence: (302) 326-3980   Office: (302) 297-4661

COMMUNITY HEALTH EDUCATOR

PROFESSIONAL PROFILE

Talented health educator with excellent academic and professional credentials and experience dealing with sensitive healthcare issues. Strong analytical, research, and project management skills combined with expertise in planning community outreach programs. Experienced counselor of at-risk populations. Extensive focus on train-the-trainer development, seminar/workshop design, and creation of educational materials related to STDs and AIDS/HIV. Committed to promote wellness and prevent disease. Strong written and verbal communications, interpersonal relations, needs assessment, and presentation skills. Proficient PC-based computer skills and knowledge of word processing, spreadsheet, and presentation applications. Internet research.

EDUCATION AND PROFESSIONAL DEVELOPMENT & TRAINING

HIV/STD Educator/Trainer Network, Atlanta, GA—1999–2000

Bachelor of Science, Community Health, INDIANA UNIVERSITY, Bloomington, IN—2003
• Internship: Student Health Promotion
• Vice President, Education, ETA ETA GAMMA National Honorary Society—2002–2003

Co-op and Internship Accomplishments

➤ Created and developed pamphlets for college campus student health promotions.
➤ Spearheaded marketing campaign on STD awareness, signs, and symptoms and distribution to nearly 13,000 collegians advising of safe-sex techniques and health awareness programs and services.
➤ Evaluated grant proposal targeting eligible women to receive free mammograms.
➤ Researched and created presentation for county health department targeting junior-high-school students on the dangers of unprotected sex, STDs, and pregnancy. Presentation adopted for use within the countywide school systems.

PROFESSIONAL EXPERIENCE

Public Health Educator (10/03 to present)
HEALTH & SOCIAL SERVICES, DIVISION OF PUBLIC HEALTH, Delaware

Recruited to serve as a specialist in preventive education measures, coordinating and implementing health education/risk reduction programs, presentations, and curricula to a variety of populations.
➤ Coordinate and implement health education/risk reduction programs for youth programs and schools, community-based organizations, and counseling and testing sites within the state. Co-facilitate programs at a variety of correctional facilities in collaboration with women's, men's, and youth correctional facilities.
➤ Create public information bulletins that include resource information and prevention messages.

Selecting a different font for the name is a simple yet effective way to enhance the appearance of this neat, well-organized resume for an individual in the community health education field.

Pamela L. Whitfield, Page 2

Professional Experience – *continued*

➤ Collect and analyze data for future assessment and approval of education projects; document completed tasks and contacts with constituents.
➤ Develop training brochures, pamphlets, training manuals, and resource guides.
➤ Implement established procedures and standards to ensure compliance with state public health policies.
➤ Trained and certified more than 400 volunteers in the train-the-trainer program.
➤ Assisted with reformatting HIV/AIDS Instructor Certification Course curriculum.
➤ Co-created community outreach survey that targets communication education needs for HIV/AIDS trainings and presentations.

Medical Secretary (6/03 to 9/03)
OCCUPATIONAL HEALTH CENTERS, Indianapolis, IN

Fast-track promotions from Physical Therapy Aide to Medical Secretary for an emergency, immediate-care health facility. Daily contact with outpatient population referred for workmen's compensation emergencies. Accurately annotated patient records. Scheduled physical and occupational therapy sessions with appropriate medical professionals and therapists.

Other work experience: 5 years of experience in customer service and consumer sales.

———————————— **PROFESSIONAL CERTIFICATIONS** ————————————

➤ Certified HIV/AIDS Instructor/Trainer—American Red Cross
➤ Certified HIV/AIDS Preventive Programming and Counseling and Testing Instructor/Trainer—DE Division of Public Health
➤ Elementary Student *No Smoking Campaign* Instructor—American Red Cross

RESUME 48: BY ROSS MACPHERSON, MA, CPRW, JCTC, CEIP

Giovanna Marina

55 Pheasant Run Drive
Markham, Ontario A2B 3C4
905-349-8899   giovanna@yahoo.com

OBJECTIVE: EDUCATIONAL ASSISTANT / SUPPLY TEACHER

SPECIALIZING IN PROVIDING SUPPORT AND EDUCATIONAL ASSISTANCE TO CHILDREN OF ALL AGES AND ABILITIES

Patient, caring, energetic, personable, and organized with outstanding interpersonal and communication skills. Recognized for ability to develop effective plans and programs for children. Extensive experience in community support and programming, infant and childhood care, and community outreach. **B.A. in Psychology.**

PERSONAL STRENGTHS

PLANNING / PROGRAM DEVELOPMENT:

- Experience designing, developing, and implementing comprehensive children's programs and activities for daycare and community programs.
- Proven ability to plan and coordinate large community events, designing agendas and coordinating all resources.
- Proficient working independently and developing programs from inception to implementation.

COMMUNITY SUPPORT & OUTREACH:

- 10 years of experience in community involvement, including daycare, public school, church, and Girl Guides.
- Extensive volunteer experience working with both children and adults, including developmental and special needs cases.
- Recognized for naturally caring and supportive demeanour, with a reputation for "going the extra mile".

LEADERSHIP AND PERSONAL INTERACTION:

- Held a variety of executive and leadership positions within community, liaising with individuals, parents, and public officials.
- Supervisory and leadership experience, overseeing and developing junior employees and volunteers.

COMPUTER PROFICIENCY:

- Experience working with Excel, Lotus, Internet, and email applications.
- Demonstrated ability to quickly gain proficiency with new and proprietary software programs.

ADMINISTRATION:

- Organized, efficient, and thorough with an ability to manage multiple tasks, work under deadlines, and adapt as situations arise.
- Additional skills include marketing, fundraising, event planning, and bookkeeping.

Note how work and volunteer experience are combined on the second page of this educational assistant's resume. The functional grouping of Personal Strengths on page 1 highlights what she has to offer.

GIOVANNA MARINA   905-349-8899   Page 2

WORK / VOLUNTEER EXPERIENCE

Owner / Operator—*Home-Base Community Daycare, Markham, Ontario*
- Created and marketed a highly successful home-based community daycare—overwhelming community response quickly resulted in waiting lists.
- Developed a comprehensive and child-oriented daycare program designed to provide a healthy, fun, and educational environment for children aged 6 months to 10 years.
- Designed creative activities, crafts, and excursions structured around weekly themes, augmenting activities with materials acquired from local libraries and services.
- Coordinated with parents to provide appropriate support for children with behavioural issues.

Vice-Chair, School Community Council—*Randall Wayne Public School, Markham, Ontario*
- Currently sitting on Executive Board for new school, responsible for defining roles and responsibilities and liaising between school and community at regular public meetings.

Brownie Leader—*Girl Guides of Canada, Markham, Ontario*
- Developed entire annual program for local troupe, including all weekly meetings, development activities, fundraising, and outdoor excursions.
- Organized annual Christmas trip to local Senior Citizens residence, organizing shared crafts activities and sing-alongs.
- Oversaw two Junior Leaders and completed all administrative and bookkeeping functions.

Sunday School Teacher—*All Saints Anglican Church, Markham, Ontario*
- Led weekly 75-minute lessons to 5–15 children aged 3 to 6, following pre-set program guidelines and encouraging participation among children.

Annual Picnic Coordinator—*All Saints Anglican Church, Markham, Ontario*
- Organized annual picnic for 100 attendees, planning activities and coordinating all resources and six adult volunteers.

Fundraising Committee—*Randall Wayne Public School, Markham, Ontario*
- Currently contributing to the development and implementation of school fundraising activities.

EDUCATION / TRAINING

Bachelor of Arts (Psychology)—*York University, Toronto, Ontario*   1993

Sexual Misconduct & Harassment Awareness Workshop—*Anglican Church of Canada*   2004

PERSONAL INTERESTS

Outdoor activities including canoeing, hiking, and camping.

References available upon request.

CHAPTER **8**

Resumes for Educational Support Professionals

- Librarians/Interactive Media Directors
- Media Educators
- Substitute Teachers
- School Social Workers
- Admissions Counselors
- Guidance Counselors
- School Psychologists
- School Volunteer Leaders
- Technology Coordinators
- Aides

MICHAEL MILLER

458 North Western Avenue, Salt Lake City, UT 84117 • Phone (801) 277-5555
E-mail: mmiller237@hotlink.com

INFORMATION SERVICES LIBRARIAN

PROFILE

Articulate, organized Librarian with more than 10 years of experience in all facets of Library Science–related work. Expertise in utilizing the World Wide Web as a tool for research and analysis. Skilled instructor of various workshops including The World Wide Web, The Internet, Electronic Databases, and Bibliographic Software. Excellent presentation skills. Advanced computer literacy.

TECHNICAL SKILLS

- Microsoft Office (Word, Excel, and PowerPoint) • WordPerfect, Lotus Notes
- NOTIS Library System • Arc View, Photoshop, FrontPage, UNIX, HTML
- Internet • Voyager Library System • Verity Search Engine
- LEXIS/NEXIS, OCLC

EDUCATION

Master of Library Science, University of Utah (1999)
Graduate coursework in Sociology, University of Phoenix (1997–1998)
Bachelor of Science in Sociology, Utah College (1996)
  - Dean's List
  - Received Dawson Scholarship (1989)
School of Library & Information Science, Catholic University (1993)

SPECIAL PROJECTS AND ACCOMPLISHMENTS

- Achieved Above and Beyond Peer Recognition Award for Library Service (1997).
- Presenter at Utah State Library Conference for University of Utah College faculty (2000). Topic: Integrating Technology into the Classroom via the Internet.
- Presenter at Utah Educational Research Association Annual Conference (1999).
- Spearheaded retrospective conversion of U.S. government documents for University of Utah Acquisitions Department.
- Pioneered Rio Grande Learning Center for homeless mothers. Managed and directed resource selection, furniture, and computer needs, and gathered potential funding resources for materials.

A clever graphic combining a large initial with a book is an eye-catching introduction to this librarian resume. The large headline and brief profile clearly communicate his expertise and career interests.

MICHAEL MILLER   Page 2

PROFESSIONAL EXPERIENCE

Salt Lake City Main Library, Salt Lake City, UT   1999–2005
INTERNET LIBRARIAN
- Collaborated with instructors in teaching specialized topics. Prepared and delivered workshops.
- Coordinated reference queries via phone and e-mail.
- Managed and directed website development for several websites including creation of intellectual content of SLC Library web pages.
- Wrote documentation for Rio Grande Learning Center and facilitated operation.
- Oversaw support staff in departmental area.

Alderman Library, University of Utah, Salt Lake City, UT   1998–1999
REFERENCE LIBRARIAN
- Administered direction and answers to reference questions.
- Created Alderman Library website and consulted on development of web-based tutorials.
- Prepared study aids and bibliographies.

Huntsman Library, Provo University, Provo, UT   1996–1998
REFERENCE LIBRARIAN
- Maintained e-mail inquiries in reference to cancer.
- Updated and coordinated cancer reference materials and catalog files.
- Troubleshot and maintained library equipment.

Science/Engineering Library, University of Utah, Salt Lake City, UT   1994–1995
REFERENCE PRACTICUM
- Utilized print, electronic medium, and online resources to assist patrons with reference questions.
- Conducted on-site instruction for use of various reference resources.
- Oversaw archives, periodicals, and circulation.

Cabal Library, Virginia Commonwealth University, Richmond, VA   1993–1994
REFERENCE LIBRARIAN/WEEKEND COORDINATOR
- Trained and supervised student employees in Circulation/Reserve Department.
- Coordinated workflow, shelving, and circulation.
- Handled billing procedures.

PROFESSIONAL AFFILIATIONS

- American Library Association
- Utah Library Association
- Task Force member, Salt Lake City Library and Information Network (2001)

Education

Master of Library Science, 1990
MICHIGAN STATE UNIVERSITY, East Lansing, Michigan

Bachelor of Arts in English, 1988
ADAMS COLLEGE, Adams, Michigan

Experience

ADAMS COLLEGE, Adams, Michigan
Chief Librarian, 1993–Present
Reference Librarian, 1989–1993

Direct the daily operations of campus library with 66,000 volumes, 300+ periodical titles, and seven staff members. Administer $235,000 annual budget. Determine policies and procedures, and plan goals and objectives for the library. Train and direct workers to receive, shelf, and sort materials, and to assist library patrons in locating materials.

Professional Achievements

- Converted from manual to electronic catalog system. Patrons and students now have quick access to all publications in the Adams County Library System, as well as the college library. Additionally, this technology reduced staffing requirements, saving approximately $28,000 annually.

- Developed and implemented seminars, "Study Smarter, Not Harder" and "Ace That Research Paper," to help students with their study skills and research techniques. These seminars were so successful that the syllabus is being used as a model to develop similar programs at high schools in Adams County.

- Chairman, Committee for Literacy, 1999–2000 term. Spoke to local television and radio stations on behalf of the committee, enhancing community awareness of illiteracy.

- Established a Reading Tutor Program, which allows English and Education majors to earn credits by tutoring high school students who are behind in their reading skills.

- Coordinated cultural workshops presented by the library on subjects such as Classical Guitar, Blues Guitar, Modern Poetry, and Michigan History.

- Coordinator/editor of <u>Adams College Poetry Anthology</u>, 1992–Present.

Joan M. Sullivan

121 College Drive

Adams, MI 48000

(734) 555-6412

jsullivan@tdi.net

This resume shows the dramatic impact of an unusual typestyle and graphic. Other than these elements, the resume is simply formatted in Times New Roman. Note the emphasis on achievements that will set her apart from other candidates.

Children's Media Education: Host ~ Educator ~ Presenter/Friend

Madonna Brown

Motivational educator/presenter. Inspire children's creativity and love for learning through dance and movement, the freedom of expression, the making of friends, and most importantly—by having fun.

Career Roles

- Classroom Teacher ~ Preschool to Age 8
- Drama Teacher ~ Ages 6 to 12
- Arts Coordinator (Art, Music, Drama, Media)

- Technical Advisor (Christian Television Program—*Footprints*)
- Assistant to Principal

- Stimulated whole school participation, producing video for the *Burke's Backyard* competition; inspired and encouraged students to demonstrate their talents.
- Technical Advisor for TV program— *Footprints*. Completed 26 episodes.

- Produced video of Year 4 students for appearance in a Vegemite™ commercial; conceptualised and choreographed dance, drama, and music.
- Accomplished choreographer/dancer.

Credentials

DIPLOMA OF TEACHING, *Jackson Teaching College*

BACHELOR OF EDUCATION, *Mt. Bookham Campus, Sydney University*, Expected late 2005
Early Childhood Contemporary Programs—**Credit**. Early Childhood Curriculum 1—**High Distinction**. Dramatic Form— **Distinction**. Drama in Schools—**Credit**. Creative Studies in Visual Arts—**Distinction**.

RADIO & TV PRESENTING, COPY WRITING & PRODUCTION, *Advanced TV*

What the Critics Are Saying

"Your delightful sense of serious play and installation of your process was enjoyed by all!... A witty response to the task and its presentation made most effective—Excellent Work!" Extract Course Evaluator

"Her initiative and creativity... clearly shone through... An honest and trustworthy person of the most reputable character. The list of her involvement is impressive." Parish Priest

Prime-Time Work

ST. JOHN'S SCHOOL, *Music Teacher Pre-School–Year 3, Drama Teacher Year 1–Year 7* 2001–2003

ST. MATTHEW'S PRIMARY SCHOOL AND ST. LUKE'S PRIMARY SCHOOL, *Relief Teacher* 1995–2000

ST. MARK'S PRIMARY SCHOOL, *Part-Time Assistant to the Principal—Religious Education* 1994

Rounds of Applause From:

Fred Smith, School Principal, Catholic Education (08) 5555-5555

Bev Jones, Pre-School Teacher, Catholic Education (08) 5555-0742

MADONNA BROWN: 544 EUNICE STREET, PERTH, WA 6000 • TELEPHONE: (08) 5555-1007

This creative resume, written to help a primary school teacher break into children's multimedia education, "marries" the essence of being a performer (dancing, movement, and expression) with television terms such as "prime time" and "what the critics are saying."

RESUME 52: BY DEBBIE ELLIS, MRW, CPRW

Barbara L. Baeker

109 Bonaventure Blvd.
DeLand, Florida 32724
(904) 236-9573
blbaek@mis.net

MISSION

To create, support, and continue a cooperative, stimulating environment that will encourage all children to learn, develop, and succeed.

PROFILE

An enthusiastic and caring educator skilled in building a positive rapport and mutual respect with students. Creates an engaging learning environment featuring thematic units with integrated curriculum, hands-on interactive lessons, and multimedia technology. Structures whole group, small group, and individual instruction to accommodate individual academic levels and learning styles. Encourages parental involvement in the form of home reinforcement and volunteerism.

- Degreed educator with four years of experience teaching children pre-school to grade 12.
- Recognized for superior classroom management techniques.
- Past Director of the Rebecca Caudill Public Library Story Hour program.
- Valuable experience in broad-based, interdisciplinary instruction.
- Contributed to feature article published in Florida's Department Libraries titled *Children's Interactive Program Design.*
- Successfully completed long-term assignment as substitute Librarian assisting pre-school and elementary school students.
- Highly developed written and oral communication skills.
- Self-directed professional, able to work independently or as part of a team.
- Computer literacy includes all popular Microsoft applications and Internet navigation.

EDUCATION

Florida State University—Tallassee, Florida—Dean's List, Magna Cum Laude
Degree awarded—Bachelor of Arts in Education, 1994

State of Florida, Middle School Certification Grades 5–8
Social Studies, Language Arts, and Reading, 1994–1998

TEACHING EXPERIENCE

1998–2002   **DeLand Board of Education**
Substitute Teacher. Assigned to replace staff for both long and short terms. Gained recognition for flexibility, dependability, and organization resulting in much higher than average rate of calls to work. Successfully implemented existing and original lesson plans both inside and outside areas of specialization including library science, language arts, social studies, math, algebra, reading, and art.

COMMUNITY SERVICE

Parent Volunteer, Hendricks Avenue Middle School 2002–2004
Volunteer, DeLand Humane Society 2003–2004
Den Leader, Boy Scouts of America 1998–2002
Volunteer, Salvation Army 1997
Parent Volunteer, Brookview Elementary School 1996–1997
Director, Rebecca Caudill Public Library Story Hour Program 1993–1995

ADDITIONAL EXPERIENCE

1995–1997   **Dexter Real Estate and Insurance Company**
1993–1995   **Creech Insurance Agency**
1985–1990   **Frazier Insurance Agency**

REFERENCES

Comprehensive portfolio and excellent professional references available on request.

After sending in this resume for a children's librarian position, this individual was called and interviewed the very same week. Printed in color, the book graphic looks particularly attractive.

Laura Negrete

23373 Moosewood Circle
Deerfield Beach, FL 33433

Phone: (954) 224-2020
Email: Lnegrete@aol.com

Clinical & School Social Worker (LCSW)
Psychotherapist

Adults • Children • Couples • Families • Elderly • Special Ed & Emotionally Disturbed

- Individual & Group Counseling
- Multidisciplinary Staffings & Conferences
- Crisis Intervention
- Family & Teacher Consultation
- Community Resourcing
- Medicare & Medicaid Reporting

- Case Study Coordination
- Social Development Studies
- Child Interviewing
- Psycho-Educational Support Group Leader
- Behavioral Contracting
- Diagnostic Assessment Using DSMIV

PC proficient in Microsoft Word, Lotus, and ClarisWorks (used in schools).

Professional Experience

PSYCHOTHERAPIST   2002–Present
Self-employed, Deerfield Beach, FL

Private social work practitioner serving adults, children, couples, and families in local metro area. Conduct individual therapy sessions with clients. Consult with families to assist emotionally and behaviorally disturbed children. Make service and alternative school placement recommendations to families. Regularly create behavioral contracts for families and children.

- Instrumental in making successful alternative school placement for recent special needs and emotionally disturbed child. Worked extensively with family to ensure child's needs were met within parent's financial constraints.
- Worked successfully with family to place Alzheimer's patient in appropriate nursing facility.
- Provided extensive individual and joint therapy for terminally ill patient and family.
- Currently volunteering on panel to place social workers in the South Florida County schools for *South Florida's Promise – The Alliance for Youth.*

SCHOOL SOCIAL WORKER   1999–2002
School District A, Chicago, IL

Recruited to serve entire school population (650 students) K–8. Conducted group and individual counseling and provided crisis intervention. Served as consultant to teachers and families. Conducted screenings, referrals, and evaluations on regular and special education students. Provided treatment seminars for parents and staff. Developed behavioral plans and developed social developmental studies. Conducted home visits.

- Granted tenure in 2001 for outstanding contributions.
- Developed the following highly successful programs and support groups:
  - *Self-Esteem Program* for 2nd and 3rd grade students – Used puppets, stories, and songs to engage students. Program was ultimately duplicated for EMH students.
  - *Peer Mediation Program* – Selected and trained panel of 4–5 students on managing inter-student conflict and delivering consequences.
  - *Divorce Support Group* – Trained teachers to lead student support groups.
  - *Grief Support Group* – Designed program to support children with ill or dying family members.

This effective resume uses keywords to emphasize areas of expertise and a combination of paragraph/bullet styles to distinguish accomplishments from responsibilities. The formatting is clean and classic.

Laura Negrete   Page 2 of 2

Field Experience & Internships

EXTERNSHIP   1998–1999
Maple Elementary School and Apollo Middle School, Chicago, IL

Provided individual treatment for K–6 students with behavior disorders and learning disabilities. Created and facilitated groups with special and regular education students. Collaborated with multi-disciplinary diagnostic team in screening and staffing. Prepared social developmental histories and individualized education plans. Administered pre-school screenings and Adaptive Behavior Scales.

SECOND YEAR FIELD PLACEMENT   1997–1998
Family and Community Services, Chicago, IL

Conducted long- and short-term individual, couple, and family therapy. Co-led a single-parent/child support group. Provided crisis intervention, financial counseling, and casework.

FIRST YEAR FIELD PLACEMENT   1995–1997
Appalachia Mental Health Center, Chicago, IL

Provided long- and short-term treatment to individuals and couples. Established and co-led weekly support group for after-care clients. Completed psychosocial assessments.

Education/Certifications/Licenses

Completed Post-Graduate Studies in Social Work
Loyola University, Chicago, IL, 1999, Concentration and Certification in School Social Work

MSW
Loyola University School of Social Work, Chicago, IL, 1998

BA Education (Early Childhood Education Major)
Northeastern Illinois University, Chicago, IL

Licensed Clinical Social Worker (LCSW) in Florida and Illinois

Current Teaching Certificate, K through 9

Type 73 Social Work Certified, Illinois

Continuing Education

Divorce Mediation Institute, 2001 — 40-hour divorce mediation certification program

Loyola University of Chicago Medical Center, Sexual Dysfunction Clinic, 2000
Completed 9-week certification program

Regularly complete 30 hours of continuing education units (CEUs) every 2 years in Florida and Illinois to maintain LCSW status.

Professional Memberships

- National Association of Social Workers (NASW) — National and Florida Member
- Illinois Association of School Social Workers (IASSW)
- Illinois Society for Clinical Social Work (ISCSW)

Greta Johannsen, M.S.

11815 Junction Lake Boulevard
Eden Prairie, MN 55344 — 320.555.7010

> "Greta is an educational 'welcome wagon'—out in the field or within the academic halls. Her love for education is contagious among all ages and people. She shines as an educator."
> Dr. Gerald Spovin
> MASSCCO President

HIRING ASSETS:

Twelve years of combined experience in college / secondary counseling and admissions roles, complemented by a teaching/coaching background. Sincere commitment to the welfare of the student. Special talent for assessing individual needs. Work cooperatively with students and families, colleagues, and the community.

Competencies: Individual Counseling, Group Counseling, Career Development, Educational Counseling, Measurement and Evaluation, Coordinator of Resources. Admissions. Liaison.

EDUCATION

UNIVERSITY OF MINNESOTA—Minneapolis, MN
M.S. Degree, Applied Psychology; Secondary School Counseling emphasis, 1998
B.E.S. Degree, Emphases: Special Education, Communications, Coaching, 1993

PROFESSIONAL EXPERIENCE

COUNSELING & MENTORSHIP

- Counseled students regarding career, college, and personal choices.
- Guided and implemented career classes for students in grades 9–12.
- Set up and administered standardized testing and advanced placement testing.
- Advised a successful TARGET program.
- Served as Advisor for student IEPs.
- Taught students (K–12) with special needs; coached numerous athletic teams.
- Facilitated groups for career, education, self-esteem, and other personal issues.
- Guided freshmen advisees, mentored advising team, and coordinated orientation activities.

ADMISSIONS, PUBLIC SPEAKING & RELATIONSHIP BUILDING

- Recruited students for several colleges through school presentations, informational sessions, and on-campus interviews. Represented collegiate institutions at college fairs.
- Conducted on-site presentations at up to 100 high schools per year regarding postsecondary options.
- MSU Advisory Board; Admissions Student Ambassadors; interviewed, trained / supervised interns.
- Represented the technical and college system on statewide panels.
- Partnered with college marketing teams; assisted with orientation programs.

CAREER PATH

ANOKA HENNEPIN TECHNICAL COLLEGE—St. Cloud, MN	2002–present
Admissions Representative	
RIDGEWATER COLLEGE—Hutchinson / Willmar, MN	2001–2002
Admissions Representative	
EDEN PRAIRIE HIGH SCHOOL—Eden Prairie, MN	1999–2001
Guidance Counselor	
MANKATO STATE UNIVERSITY—Mankato, MN	1993–2000
Admissions Representative	
BRECK SCHOOL—Minneapolis, MN	1997–1998
Guidance Counselor (Internship)	
MINNEAPOLIS PUBLIC SCHOOLS—Minneapolis, MN	1989–1992
Coach / Advisor / Instructor	

PROFESSIONAL LEADERSHIP

- MASSCCO, Minnesota Association of Secondary School Counselors and College Admissions Officers
- NASAA, National Association of Student Activity Advisors
- NACAC, National Association of College Admissions Counselors
- Minnesota School Counselors Association

A strong testimonial, placed prominently in the top-right corner, does a good job of "selling" this individual. Note that her experience is grouped in a functional style, followed by a brief listing of the positions she's held.

RESUME 55: BY TEENA ROSE, CPRW, CEIP, CCM

S B Steven J. Baker

5836 Woolery Lane
Dayton, OH 45415
Phone: (937) 264-0909

Email: sbaker@prosnet.net

SUMMARY

Seasoned elementary and intermediate school guidance counselor skilled at providing positive direction for students' academic, social, and emotional well being.

- Leader of curriculum tutoring and guidance programs to help students having academic difficulties.
- Creator of new reward, award, and recognition programs as student confidence-builders, subsequently inflating staff morale and promoting a positive atmosphere.
- Active, involved individual participating in numerous student training programs, contributing to academic associations, and upholding high standards of continued education and discipline with students and self.

CAREER SKILLS / KNOWLEDGE

- ❖ Social Block Tutoring
- ❖ Academic Advisement
- ❖ Public Speaking
- ❖ Program Creation / Implementation
- ❖ Testing Standards / Administration
- ❖ Career Counseling

EMPLOYMENT

INSTRUCTOR / OWNER
Dayton Learning Academy, Dayton, OH   2004–present
Provide educational programs for children: Schedule, administer, and review diagnostic and achievement testing; prepare and design curricula to address specific areas of academic deficiency as well as enhance strengths for personal educational growth; deliver tutoring services for specific subject areas. Monitor and address staffing needs to ensure that qualified, certified tutors are available to meet the academic needs of the learning center and the students.

GUIDANCE COUNSELOR
Monty County Educational Facility, Dayton, OH   1996–2004
Addressed academic progress, family dynamic issues, and postsecondary educational student concerns. Provided materials and supplemental resources to students.

- **Plan creation** —
  - ❖ School-Wide Professional Development Plan, Students' Individualized Educational Plans, School Safety Plan, New Student Eligibility Guidelines.
  - ❖ Served on the Building Leadership Team.
- Secured funds for Honor Roll and Birthday ribbons, notified the local press of top student performers, and assisted with Student of the Month Celebrations.
- Scheduled and coordinated in-service critiquing and conferences for administrators, special education staff, teachers, parents, and students; served as an advocate for the benefit of all students.
- Counseled hundreds of elementary students, providing daily guidance and counseling for individuals and groups; testing coordination and implementation for grade-level achievement; and intervention, writing, and assessment testing.

An eye-catching monogram and diamond-shaped bullets liven up this traditionally formatted resume. Note the keywords highlighted in the Career Skills/Knowledge section.

Steven J. Baker   Page Two

FOURTH GRADE TEACHER
Monty County Board of Education, Dayton, OH   1990–1996
Taught Basic Social Block (Math, Science, Social Studies, Ohio History) and reading programs. Implemented grade-level curriculum through basal text with trade books; met and exceeded county and state reading guidelines.

- Established a mentoring program, Indian Days, enabling fourth graders to teach and assist kindergarten classes on the academic knowledge gained from the curriculum.
  - ❖ Secured donations and materials for an authentic Indian Tribal as a permanently placed structure on school campus.
- **Committee Participation** —
  - ❖ Textbook selection committee, HASP Science Training.
  - ❖ Served on BLT, BBST.

MEMBERSHIPS / HONORS

Ohio and National Education Associations, *since 1992*
Monty County Reading Association
Ohio Counselor's Association, *since 1999*
Dean's List Auburn University and Troy State University
Monty Area Chamber of Commerce

TRAINING PROGRAMS

Reading Renaissance Training
After-School Tutoring and Discipline Program
Stephen Covey's Seven Habits of Highly Effective People
Play Therapy Training AUM / HASP Training, Monty University
Professional Development Training, Counseling / Education Related Fields
(300+ hrs, 1994–1999 cycle; 900+ hrs, 1999–2005 cycle)

EDUCATION

EDUCATIONAL SPECIALIST
Ohio State University (expected Fall 2006)

MASTER'S, COUNSELING, School Guidance Counseling Certification
Ohio State University, 1998

MASTER'S, EDUCATION
Monty University, 1996

B.S., ELEMENTARY EDUCATION
University of Dayton, 1990

THOMAS C. LANIER

tlanier86@aol.com

1104 East Bel Air Circle
Fox Point, Wisconsin 53112

Cellular: (414) 609-4679
Residence: (414) 353-9854

EDUCATIONAL PSYCHOLOGY PROFILE

A dedicated and creative educational psychologist with professional focus developing and facilitating individual and group sessions for community-based organizations and within school environments. Master of Educational Psychology and completion of comprehensive examination. Proficient using Microsoft Word and Excel, and the Internet. Demonstrated experience in the following areas:

- Program Development
- Classroom Presentations
- Individual & Group Counseling
- Conflict Resolution & Anger Management

- Solution-Based Therapy
- Crisis Intervention & Grief Management
- Family Dynamics
- Multicultural, Diverse Populations

PROFESSIONAL EXPERIENCE

Fox Point Elementary School, Fox Point, Wisconsin   Oct 2004 to Present

Educational Psychologist (Independent Consultant)
Design and implement a new program targeted toward 3rd and 4th grade students: "The Achievers Program." Small groups, meeting twice per week, focus on developing life skills such as motivation, resilience, resourcefulness, goal setting, time management, and decision-making. Mastery of skills evidenced by academic and behavioral improvement.

The Counseling Center of Ozaukee Co., Inc., Mequon, Wisconsin   Oct 2003 to Oct 2004

Prevention Education Coordinator
Developed, organized, and implemented prevention education presentations/activities designed to provide students with information and skills to cultivate and maintain healthy, happy lives. Classroom lessons included self-esteem, decision-making, stress, peer pressure, communication skills, and alcohol/drug avoidance.

YMCA, Milwaukee, Wisconsin   2002

Educational Psychology Intern
Provided individual, family, and children's group counseling to diverse, multicultural population. Developed and facilitated a large group program—Group Works—for children ages 7 through 14. Practiced and strengthened professional counseling skills and increased knowledge and sensitivity in areas of multicultural counseling, dynamics of diverse family compositions, referral networks for community resources, and clinical assessment techniques.

Congress Elementary School, Milwaukee, Wisconsin   1998

Guidance Counseling Intern
Provided individual and small-group counseling sessions and large-group counseling presentations within classroom and guidance office environments. Participated in parent/teacher meetings to discuss and develop emotional and behavioral strategies for students with physical, mental, and emotional challenges.

This is an extremely well-written resume that clearly presents the individual's expertise and broad background in counseling children.

Thomas Lanier Résumé   (414) 353-9854   tlanier86@aol.com   Page 2 of 2

PROFESSIONAL EXPERIENCE (CONTINUED)

Congress Elementary School, Milwaukee, Wisconsin   2002

Volunteer Support Staff
Facilitated in-classroom guidance program (3rd through 5th grade) consisting of anger and grief management, conflict resolution, empathy, and relaxation techniques. Developed program independently using individual creativity and resource materials.

Educational Policy & Community Studies, UW-Milwaukee, Milwaukee, Wisconsin   2000

Program Development Independent Study
Designed an after-school program called "Group Works" that provided an alternative to existing after-school care and incorporated community-mentoring components. Presented program to Boys' and Girls' Club of Ozaukee County, where it was received very positively.

Milwaukee Crisis Center, Milwaukee, Wisconsin   2000

Community Education Intern
Addressed self-esteem, aggression, and anger management issues to preschool and elementary children of cocaine-addicted mothers enrolled in the center's mental health program.

Family After-School Program, Mequon, Wisconsin   1999

Community Education Intern
Observed, participated in, developed, and presented developmentally age-appropriate activities for kindergarten and elementary school.

OTHER EXPERIENCE

Ozaukee Building Products, Inc., Mequon, Wisconsin   1990 to 1999

General Manager
Assisted owner with supervision of employees and business operations of a building supply distributor.

EDUCATION

Master of Educational Psychology, Marquette University—Milwaukee, Wisconsin
- Emphasis: Community Counseling   - GPA: 3.87/4.00

Bachelor of Science, Cardinal Stritch University—Milwaukee, Wisconsin
- Emphasis: Educational Policies & Community Studies   - GPA: 3.925/4.00

PROFESSIONAL AFFILIATIONS

American Psychological Association, Member

COMMUNITY INVOLVEMENT

- Children in Transition Support Group, Facilitator
- Fox Point School, Classroom Volunteer
- Area Community Center, Parent Education Program Committee Member
- Area Community Center, Campus Management Committee

DIANE A. SMITH

1212 Hacienda Place
Sherman Oaks, CA 91403
818-555-2470 — dianesmith@nownet

Parent Involvement and Volunteer Service Specialist

QUALIFICATIONS:

Parent Involvement:

- Recruited, oriented and encouraged parents to participate in child development programs.
- Assisted in facilitating parent participation in program planning, implementation and evaluation.
- Coordinated, scheduled and wrote materials for parent training in health, mental health, dental and nutrition education.
- Participated with teachers in individual parent conferences to discuss the child's physical, social/emotional and intellectual progress.
- Worked cooperatively with social services, health and handicap component staff to identify and inform parents of available community resources.

Volunteer Services:

- Consulted with administrators and staff to determine the program's need for volunteer services and plans for recruitment.
- Communicated effectively with other community organizations, explaining the Head Start program's activities and role of volunteers.
- Planned, organized and conducted volunteer orientation and training.
- Served as liaison between administration, staff and volunteers.
- Assisted in preparing statistical reports regarding volunteer services.

Management:

- Assisted in planning, organizing and conducting a variety of procedures and activities designed to assess and complete handicap component goals and objectives.
- Organized and established priorities and schedules.
- Established and maintained effective working relationships with adults from diverse ethnic groups.
- Coordinated, scheduled and maintained a staff training calendar.
- Assisted in planning and implementing a cost-effective budget utilizing donated goods and services.

PAGE 1 OF 2

Using a functional format to group qualifications under key areas, this resume presents a strong and cohesive picture of diverse volunteer experience.

DIANE A. SMITH

EDUCATION:

2003   M.A., Education
Pacific Baptist Theological Seminary, Encino, CA

1996   B.S., Family Relations and Child Development/Early Childhood Education
University of California at Los Angeles, CA

CERTIFICATION:

California: Preliminary Multiple Subject Credential

Nevada: General Provisional Teacher of Young Children

Provisional Kindergarten and General Provisional Elementary

RELATED PROFESSIONAL HISTORY:

1997–1998   Educational Consultant, Child Study Center, Culver City, CA

1997–1998   Nutritionist Aide, Culver Health Department, Culver City, CA

1995–1997   Kindergarten Teacher, Encino Independent School District, Encino, CA

HONORS:

Scholarships: ESTARL/California; WMU/California; ABWA/Nevada.

MEMBERSHIPS:

American Association of University Women

Yearbook Chairman/Family Life Education Chairman

National Association for the Education of Young Children

International Association for Childhood Education

PAGE 2 OF 2

RESUME 58: BY MARCY JOHNSON, NCRW, CPRW, CEIP

Melissa Ballentine

2316 Diamond Drive ▪ Ames, IA 50010 ▪ (515) 233-9874 ▪ melib@aol.com

OBJECTIVE: DISTRICT TECHNOLOGY COORDINATOR

PROFILE

Qualified technology instructor with desire to use advanced education in Curriculum and Instructional Technology to promote excellence in the classroom. Proven problem-solving abilities with both students and faculty. Passion for continuing education in the area of technology motivates and excites others.

- Recognized for technological instruction and mentoring.
- Solicited textbooks, software, and supplies to supplement tight budget constraints.
- Wrote successful grant applications for funding.
- Interacted with and developed rapport with diverse population from multicultural backgrounds.

EDUCATION

Ph.D., Curriculum and Instructional Technology, Iowa State University, Ames, IA, 5/05 (anticipated)

M.S., Curriculum and Instructional Technology, Iowa State University, Ames, IA, 5/02
- GPA: 3.69/4.0
- Thesis: *Student usage and perceptions of portable computers: The portable computer learning project*
- Worked full-time to finance education

B.S., Elementary Education, Iowa State University, Ames, IA, 5/99
- Dean's List

EXPERIENCE

Mentoring Program, Iowa State University, Ames, IA, 2/04–Present
- Tutor faculty members on computer literacy and specific software programs depending on their ever-changing needs.

Teaching Assistant/Research Assistant, Iowa State University, Ames, IA, 8/00–Present
- Teach computer lab for undergraduate pre-service teachers.
- Install software for Technology in Learning and Teaching Center.
- Provide mentoring, instruction, and computer problem-solving to faculty and students.
- Instruct pre-service teachers on computer incorporation in the classroom.

Tutor, Educational Resources, Ames, IA, 5/00–Present
- Tutor students of various ages with extended educational needs.

Science Teacher (6th and 8th Grades), Clear Creek Independent School District, Clear Lake, TX, 10/99–5/03
- Successfully solicited textbooks, software, and supplies from various vendors; wrote grants for additional funding.

Student Teacher (3rd and 5th Grades), Aldine Independent School District, Houston, TX, 1/99–5/99

COMPUTER PROFICIENCY

IBM and Macintosh platforms: Adobe Photoshop; Microsoft Word, Excel, PowerPoint;
FileMaker Pro; Claris HomePage; Hypertext applications; AVI

This resume, for a young woman with lots of education and enthusiasm but very little experience, uses a shadowed box to showcase her passion for educating others in the area of technology.

LAURA VICARRO

298 Temple Street • Orlando, FL 33221 • 407-555-7070

PROFILE

- Extensive experience gained working with children in private child care and volunteer settings, creating and leading activities that enhance and enrich their lives.
- Background in Social Services that has included department and case management of Public Assistance, Medicaid and Food Stamp programs.
- Management of staff and restaurant operations.
- Diverse skill base that includes exceptional competency in

▪ Organization	▪ Patience	▪ Customer Service
▪ Interpersonal Relations	▪ Tactfulness & Diplomacy	▪ Dedication
▪ Communication	▪ Confidentiality	▪ Project Management

WORK HISTORY

Cafeteria Aide: GENEVA ELEMENTARY SCHOOL—Geneva, FL   *2000-2005*
- Prepared and served lunch to students, teachers and staff—approximately 500 meals daily. Participated in annual health and nutrition seminars. Trained in all cafeteria functions.

Child Caregiver: SELF-EMPLOYED—Orlando, FL   *1994-1999*
- Provided care in my home to children ages 8 weeks to 10 years on a year-round basis. Led children in organized activities, including art and music. Prepared meals.

Senior Social Welfare Examiner: ORANGE COUNTY, DEPARTMENT OF SOCIAL SERVICES—Orlando, FL
- *[1990-1993]* Promoted to this position reporting directly to the Principal Welfare Examiner. Supervised six welfare examiners and support staff of two with an approximate caseload of 900. Maintained a working understanding of and interpreted state regulations in the management of Public Assistance, Medicaid and Food Stamp programs. Verified accuracy of case documentation. Approved/denied welfare requests. Attended training sessions specific to each program and trained staff.

Social Welfare Examiner
- *[1983-1989]* Managed a caseload of 80+. Determined Medicaid eligibility for individuals requiring long-term care in skilled nursing or health-related facilities through interviews with patients and their family members. Interacted with Health Department professionals to monitor care and determine methods of meeting other needs. Visited health facilities to ascertain level of care for recertification. Participated in various training sessions, including abuse identification and awareness.

Manager: CREPES 'N THINGS—Orlando, FL   *1983-1984*
- Oversaw restaurant operations including staff scheduling and supervision, food purchasing, weekly payroll and food preparation. Assisted with food preparation.

Stocks & Securities Assistant: PEOPLES STATE BANK—Groveland, FL   *1981-1983*
- Provided administrative support to the Trader. Produced purchase orders, communicated with security advisors and liaised with stockbrokers in an environment requiring high levels of timeliness and accuracy.

COMMUNITY INVOLVEMENT

Camp Counselor • Cub Scout Den Mother • Sunday School Teacher • Vacation Bible School Coordinator/Teacher
Organized/Hosted Young Mothers' Program • PTA Member & Parent Volunteer • Youth Group Leader
Church Elder • Church Financial Receipts Secretary • Chaperone, Children's Choir

EDUCATION

Coursework in Sociology and Social Work: University of Central Florida; 1984-1986
Liberal Arts Coursework: University of Orlando; 1979-1983
80 hours earned towards Bachelor's Degree

This individual used an expansive profile to pull together her diverse work and volunteer experience. Note the inclusion of "soft skills" (such as patience, tactfulness & diplomacy, confidentiality, and dedication) that are important though not easily measured.

RESUME 60: BY LORETTA HECK

Christine A. Corrigan

1400 East Greenwood Drive
Mount Prospect, Illinois 60056
Home: (847) 398-5021
Work: (847) 718-7044

— PROFESSIONAL PROFILE —

- Assist teaching staff of public schools by performing any combination of tasks in classroom.
- Hold Bachelor's Degree in Elementary Education.
- Specialize in Upper Elementary and Junior High Language Arts and Social Studies.
- Possess strong skills in identifying educational requirements.
- Dedicated to enthusiastic and dynamic teaching as a means of creating and nurturing a lifelong love of knowledge in children.
- Knowledgeable in Macintosh software, Microsoft Word, ClarisWorks, spreadsheet, database, and word processing.

— EDUCATIONAL EXPERIENCE —

Wheeling High School, Wheeling, Illinois
Writing Lab Supervisor — August 2002–Present
Tutor and assist students in the development of writing assignments by checking for grammar, organization, and proper mechanics using computer software programs. Also train faculty in the use of new software computer programs.

District 214, Arlington Heights, Illinois
Summer School Coordinator — June–August 2002
Communicated and trained school personnel on summer school procedures, data entry, and word processing.

John Hersey High School, Arlington Heights, Illinois
Summer School Clerk — May–August 2000
Registered students; processed attendance; and communicated with staff, administrators, and parents.

Barrington Middle School, Barrington, Illinois
Student Teacher — August–December 2000
Developed thematic unit, used Reading / Writing Workshop Program, participated in staff meetings to assess students, participated in Parent / Teacher conferences, involved in team teaching, attended school board meetings, and supervised field trips.

Olympia Middle School, Stanford, Illinois
Intern — March–April 2000
Worked with 30 students in eighth grade classroom. Developed and taught Language Arts unit, observed students' behavior, and assisted students individually.

This individual is qualified for a broad variety of education-related jobs and uses a Professional Profile to detail her relevant qualifications. The pencil-shaped bullets and informal headline font give this resume an appropriate playfulness.

CHAPTER 9

Resumes for University Educators

- College and University Faculty
- Adjunct Faculty
- Clinical Instructors
- University Education Coordinators

RESUME 61: BY LOUISE GARVER, JCTC, MCDP, CEIP, CMP

ELENA S. JUAREZ, MUS.A.D. Professor — Bassoon

3378 Park Avenue • New York, New York 05590
Home: 212.968.6744 • Mobile: 212.968.7433 • musicprofessor@abcx.com

CAREER PROFILE

*Distinguished career as a **bassoonist, international performer,** and **music educator** with
15 years of experience in universities, private school, private studio, and orchestras. Demonstrated talent in
motivating students and aspiring musicians, guiding them to realize their professional talents.
Mus.A.D. in Woodwind Performance. Trilingual in English, Spanish, and French.*

EDUCATION

NEW YORK UNIVERSITY, COLLEGE OF FINE ARTS, NEW YORK, NEW YORK   2000
Doctoral of Musical Arts: Woodwind Performance; GPA: 3.89
♫ Graduation with Distinction for "distinguished work beyond the scope of the degree"
♫ Awarded full University School of Music Scholarship and Dean's Scholarship

UNIVERSITY OF NORTH CAROLINA, CHAPEL HILL, NORTH CAROLINA   1995
Master of Music with High Honors: Bassoon Performance; GPA: 3.84
♫ Recipient of full-tuition scholarship under Professor Lorenzo Lamas

ACADEMY OF MUSIC, LONDON, ENGLAND   1990
Certificate of Advanced Studies in Bassoon and Bassoon Education
♫ Studied under direction of Professor Leonard Newton

CONSERVATORY OF MUSIC, PARIS, FRANCE   1989
Music Degree with High Honors: Bassoon Educator

ADDITIONAL STUDY

INTERNATIONAL SOMERS ACADEMY, COLOGNE, GERMANY   1991
Certificate in Bassoon
♫ Studied under direction of Professor Claudius Thurneman

TEACHING EXPERIENCE

FAIRFIELD UNIVERSITY, COLLEGE OF FINE ARTS, FAIRFIELD, CONNECTICUT   2000 to present
Assistant Professor—Woodwinds Department
♫ Teach bassoon to graduate and undergraduate students as well as to non-music majors with various
   musical backgrounds. Provide lessons in musicianship skills, theory, improvisation, and performance
   techniques.

NEW YORK UNIVERSITY, COLLEGE OF FINE ARTS, NEW YORK, NEW YORK
Graduate Teaching Assistant   1996 to 2000
♫ As assistant to Professor Alfredo Patini, provided coaching and conducted Chamber Music Groups.
   Guided students in defining their career goals. Designed course curriculum and coordinated lab
   instruction in reed making.

A Career Profile enhances what is essentially a traditional CV format for a college educator. The music-related graphics add interest.

ELENA S. JUAREZ, MUS.A.D. — PAGE 2

LOOMIS PRIVATE ACADEMY, NEW YORK, NEW YORK
Instructor   1997
♪ Provided classroom and individual instruction in bassoon, oboe, and clarinet to all woodwind
students and marching band members. Substituted for conductor during his absence.

Private Bassoon Instructor, CHAPEL HILL, NORTH CAROLINA
♪ Provided individual lessons in bassoon for private clients.   1993 to 1995

ORQUESTRA SINFONICA AND CONSERVATORIO DI MUSICA, FLORENCE, ITALY   1989 and 1991
Bassoon Instructor
♪ Taught bassoon and promoted the study of bassoon to new performers. Provided instruction in
techniques, music theory, history, and other aspects.

PROFESSIONAL EXPERIENCE — BASSOON PERFORMER

Highland Symphony Orchestra, New York, New York
2005: Music by Mozart, Strauss, Offenbach, Gershwin, Tchaikovsky, Sousa
2005: Music by Vanhal, Wagner, Beethoven
2005: Chamber music performances
2004: Peter and the Wolf & Instrument Showcase
2004: Music by Respighi, Tchaikovsky, Anderson
2004: Music by Beethoven, Martin, Nielsen
2003: Music at Sunset at the Abbey Jazz & Classical Concerts
2003: Music by Vivaldi, Strauss, Rachmaninoff, Barber, Williams, Tchaikovsky
2003: Music by Adams, Smetana, Ives
2002: Music by Beethoven, Mackey, Mendelssohn
2002: Music by Kapilow, Kabalevsky
2001: Music by Worlock, Handel, Finzi
2001: Music by Mozart, Copland, Brahms

South Coast Community Chorale, Boston, Massachusetts
2004: Music from Mozart's Requiem & Rutter's Magnificat

Boston University Wind Ensemble, Boston, Massachusetts
2003: Music by American Composers

Nantucket Symphony Orchestra, Nantucket, Massachusetts
2003: Various Pops Pieces

Boston University Symphony Orchestra, Boston, Massachusetts
2002: Chorale—Variationen über das Weihnachtslied, "Vom himmel hoch da
kommich her" by J.S. Bach; Symphony No. 1 (1986) by Christopher Rouse (b. 1949); Symphony No.
8 in C major and Op. 88 by Antonin Dvorak

Miami Symphony, Miami, Florida
2000: Music by Stravinsky, Rachmaninoff, Bernstein, Vaughan Williams, George Gershwin
2000: Music by Strauss, Lehar, Kalman, Von Suppe

Atlantic Classical Orchestra, Stuart, Florida
1999: Vivaldi Sinfonia No. 3 in G Major, RV 149; J.S. Bach Symphony No. 6 in G minor, Op. 6; Holst
St. Paul's Suite, Op. 29; Fauré Pavanne
1999: Telemann Overture in D Major; Strauss Oboe Concerto in D Major; Beethoven Symphony
No. 1 in C Major, Op. 21

RESUME 61, CONTINUED

ELENA S. JUAREZ, MUS.A.D. — PAGE 3

SOLOIST PERFORMANCES — BASSOON

New York University, New York, New York
2000: Soloist—Doctoral Recital for Bassoon and Piano, music by Telemann, Etler, Schumann
1999: Soloist—Doctoral Recital for Bassoon and Piano, music by Vivaldi, Danzi, Glinka, Poulenc
1998: Soloist—Doctoral Recital for Bassoon, Harpsichord, and Piano, music by Bertoli, Lauro

University of North Carolina, Chapel Hill, North Carolina
1995: Soloist—Master's Recital for Bassoon, music by Fasch, Devienne, Saint-Säens, Poulenc

Orquesta Sinfonica, Florence, Italy
1994: Soloist—Concerto for Bassoon, Johann Nepomuk Hummel
1993: Soloist—Concerto for Bassoon and Orchestra K491, Wolfgang Amadeus Mozart
1986–1992: Performed as bassoonist on international tours to several cities in Europe, Japan, South America, and United States (Tanglewood, MA) under the direction of world-renowned conductors Eduardo Mata, Tsutsumi Shunsaky, Manuel Galduf, Akira Endo, and many others.

Academy of Music Orchestra, London, England
1998: Soloist—Concerto for Bassoon and String Orchestra in A Minor, Antonio Vivaldi
1997: Soloist—Concerto for Bassoon and Orchestra K491, Wolfgang Amadeus Mozart
1996: Soloist—Recital for Bassoon and Piano, music by Jolivet, Rachmaninoff, Grovlez

Orchestra of Spain, Barcelona, Spain
1989: Soloist—Concerto for Bassoon and Orchestra, Carl Maria Von Weber
1988: Soloist—Concerto for Oboe, Bassoon, and Chamber Orchestra in G Major, Antonio Vivaldi

REFEREED CONFERENCES

Attended the International Double Reed Society Conferences:
England—1999; Germany—1992; England—1989

AFFILIATIONS

American Federation of Musicians
Musicians Association Local 4-666
International Double Reed Society

RESUME 62: BY ELONA HARKINS, MOS

KAREN A. OLSEN
18 Glenside Drive
Fanwood, NJ 07023

Home: (908) 322-0771   kolsen723@aol.com

PROFESSIONAL OBJECTIVE
A tenured teaching or adjunct position providing the opportunity to make a strong contribution within a college setting by utilizing and expanding upon related education, skills, and capabilities.

OVERVIEW
- ✓ Strong academic preparation; graduated with high honors and currently completing graduate studies.
- ✓ Highly motivated and energetic; worked full time while attending college.
- ✓ Experienced in training employees and teaching children of differing abilities.

EDUCATION
RUTGERS UNIVERSITY, Newark, NJ
Master of Arts, English/Writing Program, 2005

KEAN UNIVERSITY, Union, NJ
Bachelor of Arts, History; Minor, English/Writing, G.P.A.: 3.87/4.0, President's Honors List, 2001

UNION COUNTY COLLEGE, Cranford, NJ
Associate of Arts, Education, 1997

Awards:
Teacher's Education Award for Outstanding Academic Excellence, 1994 & 1995
Received Alumni General Scholarship, 1994

QUALIFICATIONS PROFILE
Related qualifying skills and practicum include the following:

- ♦ **Coursework** (Selected):

Creative Writing Courses and Basic Skills	Adolescent Psychology
American Literature	Psychology in Education
Freshman Composition	Writing Prose
Journalism & Advanced Journalism	Short Stories, Fiction & Non-Fiction

- ♦ **Leadership Skills:**

  Training and instructing employees one-on-one as well as in group settings.
  Organizing teams to complete assignments/projects within set goals.
  Motivating, encouraging, and building rapport with people of all backgrounds.

- ♦ **Communication Skills:**

  Developing effective lessons and teaching strategies on short notice.
  Providing individual tutoring to ensure comprehension of material content.
  Demonstrating excellent writing, speaking, and presenting skills.

INSTRUCTIONAL EXPERIENCE
CRANFORD BOARD OF EDUCATION, Cranford, NJ   2002–Present
Substitute Teacher

Teach 7th through 12th grade students in Math, English, Science, Social Studies, and Reading. Effectively present subject matter in creative and innovative context to stimulate interest and enthusiasm. Able to remain calm and maintain an objective viewpoint under duress. Evaluate student progress.

For this teacher, who has only limited experience, a strong Qualifications Profile is a good way to convey her capabilities.

KAREN A. OLSEN

Page 2

ADDITIONAL WORK EXPERIENCE

FIRE AND WIND HEALING INSTITUTE, Tappan, NY   1998–2002
Secretary/Receptionist
Coordinated and scheduled appointments. Administered new student registration. Directed phone messages to the appropriate departments and mailed brochures with upcoming course offerings.

HONORS

Member—Lamba Alpha Sigma, Liberal Arts
Member—Science Honors Society, Phi Kappa Phi
Member—Honors Society, Phi Alpha Theta Honors Society

RESUME 63: BY ARNOLD BOLDT, CPRW, JCTC

Melanie E. Powers, CFM
5 Redleaf Lane
Birmingham, Alabama 35222
(205) 591-9807
E-mail: mpowerscfm@msn.com

Objective: An adjunct faculty position teaching business-related topics to traditional and continuing education students.

Summary: *Top-performing business executive with extensive experience training, recruiting, and mentoring employees. Exceptional track record of outstanding sales and marketing performance, based on excellent ability to develop and maintain long-term client relationships and strategic business alliances.*

Education:

Master of Arts, Sociology
University of Alabama; Birmingham, AL

Bachelor of Arts, Sociology
University of Alabama; Birmingham, AL

Associate of Arts, Social Science
Smith County Community College; Midville, AL

Professional Development:

Certified Financial Manager
Certified Financial Planner (In-Process)

NASD Series 7 & 8; Series 3, 63, 65 & 68

Professional Experience:

HOWELL AND LOVELL

1992–Present   **Financial Consultant / Certified Financial Manager**
Provide financial services to more than 600 individual and small-business clients, managing assets in excess of $70 million.
- Build client base through diligent prospecting and follow-up.
- Develop new business through seminars, referrals, and networking.
- Perennial incentive trip winner and Chairman's Club member.

1999–2003   **Resident Manager; Birmingham, AL**
In addition to servicing a substantial account base, fulfilled managerial and administrative responsibilities for branch office operations.
- Supervised financial consultants and office staff.
- Reviewed performance and motivated sales force.
- Coordinated professional development activities for team members.

1996–2001   **Manager—Professional Development; Birmingham, AL**
Administered two-year professional training program for newly hired representatives. Maintained client base and regular sales duties while fulfilling the responsibilities of this position.
- Conducted seminars in prospecting and client development at National Training Center in Baltimore, MD.
- Implemented training programs for up to 20 interns.
- Delivered weekly two-hour training sessions for interns on topics including maintaining relationships and servicing clients, making sales presentations, and prospecting/client development.
- Mentored interns, offering advice on setting goals and developing marketing plans.

This successful businessperson wanted to pursue part-time teaching positions at local community colleges, focusing on areas where her business career would add value.

Melanie E. Powers, CFM
Résumé – Page Two

Additional Experience:

TRI-STATE STRUCTURES; Tuscaloosa, AL
1985–1992   **Vice President, Sales & Marketing**
Developed/implemented marketing plan and managed sales force for firm manufacturing and erecting wood and metal buildings in Alabama, Georgia, and Mississippi.
- **Increased sales volume by 330% over three-year period.**
- Designed and executed print and electronic advertising campaigns.
- Developed direct-mail marketing campaign and collateral materials.
- Established strategic relationships with lending institutions to assist customers in obtaining financing.
- Prospected for individual and small business accounts through diligent cold calling.
- Hired, trained, and supervised staff of twelve sales representatives in three branch offices.

Computer Literacy:

Microsoft Office (Word, Excel, PowerPoint)
Internet, IP telephony, electronic books, DVD, multimedia applications

Community Involvement:

Birmingham Area Foundation
St. Mary's School of the Holy Childhood
Birmingham Rotary
United Way

References Available Upon Request

SHARON C. BRAXTON

sharoncbraxton@aol.com

2501 West Summit Avenue
Milwaukee, Wisconsin 54443

Home (414) 563-2341
Facsimile (414) 563-3242

OBJECTIVE: To Obtain an Adjunct Faculty Position Teaching Criminal Justice

A highly organized and capable teacher and facilitator with several years of experience developing and implementing instructional programs. Extensive background presenting within multi-cultural, inclusionary, and regular classrooms. Excellent interpersonal and written communication skills. MA in Public Service with undergraduate degrees in Criminal Justice and Education. Demonstrated expertise in the following areas:

- Curriculum Design & Development
- Instructional Materials
- Research, Analysis & Presentation
- Teacher Training & Leadership
- Interdisciplinary Teams

- Classroom Management
- Interactive & Multimedia Instruction
- Diagnostic Evaluation & Program Planning
- Educational Administration
- Special Events Planning & Management

PROFESSIONAL EXPERIENCE

Milwaukee Public Schools — Milwaukee, Wisconsin   1989 to Present

SPECIAL EDUCATION TEACHER

Develop curricula and lesson plans for multicultural learning-disabled, behaviorally disabled, or cognitively disabled children within an inclusionary setting. Adapt materials to meet individual needs, and teach split classes in language arts and reading. Create and implement Individualized Education Plans (IEPs) providing interpersonal and written counsel to students and parents/guardians. Consult with psychologists, social workers, parents/guardians, and students to establish behavior plans including techniques for improvements and appropriate consequences for repeated misbehavior. Direct referrals to alternative educational programs. Review and analyze ADA regulations to ensure programs comply with current laws.

Accomplishments
- Recognized by staff, faculty, and students as an exceptionally competent professional who mentors new staff and cares deeply about the students.
- Selected to participate on curriculum/program analysis and development teams for educational programs at all age levels.
- Selected to evaluate and apply new, assistive learning programs within the classroom, including specialized computers with speech synthesis and interactive software.

The strengths of this resume are its attractive, highly readable format, comprehensive list of keywords, and emphasis on accomplishments as well as responsibilities.

SHARON C. BRAXTON résumé	sharoncbraxton@aol.com	Page 2 of 2

PROFESSIONAL EXPERIENCE (continued)

University of Wisconsin Milwaukee—Milwaukee, Wisconsin   1999 to Present

EDITORIAL ADMINISTRATIVE ASSISTANT

Assist editor (Professor John Kindberg) of the *Teaching Special Education Professional Journal* with pre- and post-publication activities. Solicit throughout professional community for articles. Receive articles and submit manuscripts for peer review. Prepare journal for publication.

EDUCATION

MASTER OF ARTS IN PUBLIC SERVICE (specialty Administration of Justice) 2004
Marquette University—Milwaukee, Wisconsin

BACHELOR OF SCIENCE IN CRIMINAL JUSTICE (National Dean's List 1995) 1999
University of Wisconsin—Milwaukee, Wisconsin

BACHELOR OF ARTS IN EDUCATION 1982
Mississippi State University, Jackson, Mississippi

TECHNOLOGY SKILLS

Proficient with Microsoft Word, Excel, and PowerPoint—Windows and Macintosh

COMMUNITY ACTIVITIES

Black Women's Network—Co-Chair & Committee Head for Annual Recognition Award Dinner
Miss Black Wisconsin Scholarship Pageant—Recruiter & Mentor for program participants
St. Cecilia's-Lakeside—Tutor & Mentor for underprivileged children

PUBLICATIONS AND RESEARCH PROJECTS

- "The Impact of the Use of Advanced Technology in the Criminal Justice System," August 2004. Independent Research Project.
- "Pseudofamilies in Prison: Advantages and Disadvantages," June 2004. Correctional Management and Policy Analysis.
- "Project S.T.O.R. (Schools Teaching Options for Reconciliation) Proposed Evaluation," May 2004. Research, Program Planning, and Evaluation in Criminal Justice.
- "The State of Incarceration: Where We Are Today," July 2003. Independent Research Project.

Michael J. Smith

4321 Storm Barn Way
Morgantown, WV 26501
(304) 555-5512
Email: mjsmith@hotmail.com

Career Profile

University-Level Telecommunications Instructor / Distance Education Coordinator

**Media Relations ◈ Radio/Studio Production ◈ Project Management
Computers ◈ State-of-the-Art Telecommunications Equipment**

Results-oriented telecommunications instructor able to orchestrate and manage challenging projects—providing quality instruction and training. Chaired major projects on campus introducing the university to the benefits of distance education, web-based learning, and a radio station.

Professional Experience

Distance Education Coordinator & Telecommunications/Journalism Instructor
West Virginia University, Morgantown, West Virginia   1996 to 2005

Distance Education Coordinator—Title III Distance & Continuing Education Program
- Successfully implemented a Distance Education Learning program from the ground floor. Created a marketing initiative to convince teachers that distance education would greatly enhance their work using cutting-edge technology.
- Consulted with faculty and staff to develop web and video-based curriculum. Guided development of web and video-based courses and programs.
- Effectively trained faculty on techniques and methodologies of web-based curriculum development and telecourse video instruction. Operated high-tech equipment to tape/transmit courses.
- Reviewed and recommended current off-the-shelf web development products and telecourses.
- Co-chaired the Campus Information Technology Committee.

Full-Time Instructor
- Taught 12 credits a semester to sophomores, juniors, and seniors: News Writing and Reporting, Broadcast Management, Television Production and Programming, Introduction to Radio Production and Programming, and Television Performance. Developed curriculum and class syllabi and administered tests.
- Academic advisor for 12 assigned students each semester.
- Editor of the departmental newsletter *Views,* 1998 to 2003.
- Faculty Coordinator of the campus closed-circuit Media Center. Faculty Advisor to campus media organization. Supervised the campus television weekly newscast.

Because this individual was most interested in distance education, he emphasized this in the profile and led off the Professional Experience section with the most relevant of his activities and accomplishments.

Michael J. Smith   **Page 2**

Project Manager/Student Radio Station

- Envisioned, created, built, equipped, and completed the first-ever university campus radio station (WHWK-AM) to serve the student population.

- Received a budget of $160K and coordinated all phases of the project including initial planning, design, building renovation, equipment procurement, and installation. The project took 10 months to complete and the radio station is fully operational with three studios—one digital and two analog. Trained student programmers and announcers.

Media Arts Instructor

Ohio State University, Columbus, Ohio   Summer 2004

- Faculty liaison for the Ohio State University Committee for the Olympic Games. Taught courses and directed media-based instruction for student participants in the OSU-Host Broadcast Training Program—designed to employ student workers in fulfilling the International Broadcast of the 2004 Summer Olympic Games.

Technical Skills

Adult Learning Programs/Development & Delivery	PowerPoint	Multimedia Distance
Web Course Development Software	WebCT	Education Tools
Closed-Circuit Cable Transmission	HTML	Microsoft FrontPage 98
Windows NT System	T1 Lines	Microwave Link Satellite
Microsoft Word	CUseeMe	Picture-Tel

Education

Master of Arts in Broadcast Journalism, University of California, 1995
Internship: Assistant Photographer, Gary News Service
Bachelor of Arts in Communications, Ohio State University, 1992

Notable Awards

Outstanding Man of the Year, Men in Communications, 1998

RESUME 66: BY CAROL ROSSI, CPRW

ZACHARY FELDHART

212 Mannington Street
St. Louis, MO 63122

Home: 314-984-4321
E-mail: zfeldhart@aol.com

COLLEGE INSTRUCTOR & HEAD ATHLETIC TRAINER
Exercise Science / Sports Medicine / Health & Human Performance

Extensive experience in simultaneously lecturing for college-level courses, operating a college athletic training program, and managing a commercial fitness facility. Very strong ability to teach theory as well as practical applications. Developed experience and skills in the following areas:

- Course & Program Proposals
- Curriculum Development
- Expense Reductions

- Student Instruction
- Injury Prevention
- Enrollment Increases

- Committee Participation
- Community Involvement
- Affiliation Agreements

EDUCATION & TRAINING

Master of Science in Sports Medicine • Truman State University, Kirksville, Missouri
Bachelor of Science in Health & Physical Education • Truman State University, Kirksville, Missouri

Additional Training in Previous 5 Years:
- Upper Extremity Injury Treatments
- Pediatric Sports Medicine Concepts
- Cervical Spine Injuries

- Clinical Instructors Seminars
- Football Injury Prevention
- Sports Medicine Conference

- Baseball Injury Prevention
- Strength & Power Instruction
- Knee Rehabilitation

PROFESSIONAL EXPERIENCE

ST. LOUIS COMMUNITY COLLEGE AT MERAMEC, St. Louis, MO — Fall 1992 to Present

Lecturer • Fall 1994–Present (10 years, concurrent with Head Athletic Trainer position)

Lecture groups of 16–22 students 3–5 days a week in 6 different exercise science and sports medicine classes. Research articles on which to base class readings and questions. Develop new methods to deliver materials through Socratic and cooperative lesson planning. Create all quizzes and exams. Instruct classes in APA format for term paper procedures and documentation styles. Serve as approved facilities supervisor.

Curriculum Revisions
- Authored curriculum for three existing courses after previous instructors left without providing course materials or notes: Fitness Measurement, Athletic Training Skills, and Physical Activity in Modern Living.

Program Development for Two-Year Liberal Arts Degree in Exercise Science & Sports Medicine
- Co-developed a proposal for a new two-year liberal arts degree in exercise science & sports medicine with curriculum committee approval obtained May 2004.

- Developed a cohesive program with credits transferable into four-year degree programs elsewhere. Wrote curriculums for two new classes to be implemented in the degree program: Care & Prevention of Athletic Injuries and Kinesiology.

Affiliation Agreement Development
- Developed an affiliation agreement in 2002 between Meramec and Truman State University that established Meramec as a clinical facility providing hands-on training of practical applications in sports medicine for an intern from the Truman State School of Graduate Medical Education.

- Created protocol for new student interns in collaboration with Truman State University, and will personally serve as the Meramec clinical site instructor providing internship training in addition to regular duties.

Page 1 of 2

Subheadings are used to divide lengthy experience and thus improve the readability of this resume.

ZACHARY FELDHART   314-984-4321 • zfeldhart@aol.com   **Page 2 of 2**

PROFESSIONAL EXPERIENCE continued...

ST. LOUIS COMMUNITY COLLEGE AT MERAMEC (continued)

Program Development for One-Year Exercise Science Certificate
- Co-developed a one-year exercise science certificate program to provide a fast track for employment in the fitness industry and student readiness to sit for the American Council on Exercise (ACE) certification exam; completed prerequisites for a two-year degree and transferable credits. New program resulted in expanded Health & Physical Education Department as well as new faculty positions and greater positioning for justification of improved facilities and grant money.
- Created course proposals, obtained approval, and authored curriculum for 12 of the 22 credits for the new one-year certificate program, including Strength & Conditioning Physiology, Management & Rehabilitation of Athletic Injuries, and Exercise Physiology.
- Researched and located a national certification organization to endorse the one-year program. Collaborated with the director of certification for ACE to create a written agreement allowing Meramec to use the ACE name in marketing efforts.

Honors & Committees
- Awarded grade advancements in 1994, 1997, and 2000 based on three years of accomplishments each time.
- Current member of newly formed National Health & Physical Education Hall of Fame Committee to develop nomination criteria, create list of nominees, and coordinate awards banquet.

Head Athletic Trainer • Fall 1992–Present (12 years)
Manage prevention, care, and rehabilitation of athletic injuries for 10–12 different sports teams every year. Coordinate pre-season and in-season medical examinations. Attend home games 2–3 times a week and provide medical supervision. Establish and enforce policies/procedures for the college athletic training room.

- Formulated and implemented a volunteer team physician position. Located and negotiated with a local orthopedic doctor to provide physicals as well as comprehensive medical treatment for all 10–12 teams at no cost to the college.

ST. LOUIS FITNESS CENTER, St. Louis, MO — Fall 1995 to Present (9 years, concurrent with Meramec)

General Manager

Manage staff of 25 and 10,000 sq. ft. of operational space. Educate personal trainers and fitness instructors in proper exercise protocols and techniques. Prepare weekly employee schedules. Maintain member appointment book for facility orientations and personal training sessions.

- Established general business, accounting, and payroll procedures. Developed fitness testing and health screening methods.
- Increased annual revenues 450% and membership enrollments 362% since 1993 through direct marketing, advertising, and community involvement efforts. Quarterly revenues have grown from $30K to $165K.
- Initiated community involvement by sponsoring youth teams and church functions as well as developing business relationships with 15 different local businesses. Efforts resulted in greater name recognition, increased referrals, and expanded revenues.

AFFILIATIONS & CREDENTIALS

Current Memberships: National Athletic Trainers Association, Athletic Trainers Society of Missouri, and Midwest Conference Athletic Trainers Society

Credentials: Missouri Athletic Trainer License and current American Red Cross CPR Certification

EVELYN A. REYER

5300 Spring Mountain Road
Las Vegas, Nevada 89146

(702) 222-9411
evelynreyer@aol.com

PHYSICAL EDUCATION TEACHER
with special expertise in Adaptive Physical Education (APE)

PROFILE

✓ Graduate degree, ten years of experience, and demonstrated competencies in Curricula Development ... Course Evaluation ... Program Design/Implementation ... Student Advocacy and Counseling ... Marketing/Networking/Community Resourcing ... Recruiting and Supervising Program Volunteers ... Sports Team Coaching.

✓ Outstanding facilitation, presentation, research, needs assessment, and organizational skills; effectively interact with and support faculty, administration, and students.

PROFESSIONAL EXPERIENCE

1998–2004   RED MOUNTAIN UNIVERSITY, REDLANDS, CALIFORNIA
Physical Education Instructor

Taught Beginner, Intermediate, and Super Circuit Weight Training as well as Adaptive Physical Education (APE) courses, i.e., Adaptive Fitness and Sports Education.

✓ Developed course descriptions, curricula, written exams, and schedules.

✓ Taught, motivated, and evaluated students; prepared IEPs; arranged for additional assistance and intervention as deemed necessary.

✓ Liaised with local rehabilitation centers, advocacy groups, and community organizations to increase APE program awareness.
— Successfully cultivated and recruited new students.
— Designed educational literature and marketing materials.

✓ Wrote and implemented the APE peer tutor training manual; recruited, scheduled, trained, and supervised 30+ volunteer peer tutors.

✓ As member of the Disabled Student Services Committee:
— Served as an APE Program Liaison and Student Advocate.
— Delivered presentations to the college administration regarding program results and augmentation.

✓ As member of the Physical Education Committee:
— Participated in developing and improving physical education curriculum.
— Researched, reviewed, and incorporated federal funding regulations and the latest APE information into programs and procedures.

Page 1 of 2

This resume for a college-level physical education instructor is extremely readable, thanks to a large, clear typeface and well-organized layout.

EVELYN A. REYER

Page 2 of 2

1994–1997   GRAMBLE COMMUNITY COLLEGE, REDLANDS, CALIFORNIA
Assistant Coach — Women's Basketball Team

- ✓ Coordinated game schedules, developed strategies, and monitored students' academics.
- ✓ Counseled students in academic and personal issues.

EDUCATION

FRESNO STATE UNIVERSITY, FRESNO, CALIFORNIA
Master of Arts: Physical Education; Adaptive Phys. Ed. Specialty — 1997

RED MOUNTAIN UNIVERSITY, REDLANDS, CALIFORNIA
Bachelor of Arts: Physical Education; Adaptive Phys. Ed. Specialty — 1994

VOLUNTEER ACTIVITIES

FRESNO STINGRAYS, FRESNO, CALIFORNIA
Head Coach — Wheelchair Basketball Team, 1994 to 1996

- ✓ Instructed and motivated team members.
- ✓ Scheduled season practices, games, and transportation.

ROBERT PARISI

540 Hawthorne Street, Apt. 5C, Tarrytown, NY 10591
rparisi@westnet.com

(914) 555-1234
fax (914) 777-4321

SUMMARY

- Goal: A challenging teaching position utilizing my advanced education and 13 years of experience contributing to a liberal arts college setting.
- Qualified by demonstrated competencies in teaching, writing, research, customer service, and international relations.
- Specialize in the influence of international politics on commerce and finance. Strong interest in Middle Eastern studies and oil politics.
- Conversant in Spanish. Ability to read Spanish, Italian, Romanian, Portuguese, and French.
- Formal diversity/multicultural training.

EDUCATION

Master of Arts, History   2004
New York University, New York, NY
GPA: 3.9, President's List Honors

Certificate in International Affairs   2004
New York University, New York, NY

Bachelor of Arts, Education/Social Studies   1986
Marymount College, Tarrytown, NY

RELATED EXPERIENCE

Adjunct Professor of History   2005–Present
Iona College, New Rochelle, NY

- Teach a weekly class in American History.

Guest Lecturer   2000–2002
Marymount College, Tarrytown, NY

- Delivered class lectures in West European and Middle Eastern History. Consistently invited by colleagues because of graduate studies and known interest in these subjects.
- Authored prospectus for History 254, "Geopolitics of the Modern Middle East."
- Advised History Department on new classes upon request.

Teacher   1989
Carnegie High School, New York, NY

- Taught five classes of Economics and Honors History (Western Civilization and American). Prepared students to pass Regents examinations.

Note the Related Experience section on page 1 that allows this individual to put his strongest experience front-and-center while relegating less-relevant experience to page 2.

ROBERT PARISI   PAGE TWO

ADDITIONAL PROFESSIONAL EXPERIENCE

Bursar   1992–2004
Marymount College, Tarrytown, NY

- Managed 1000+ accounts averaging $7,000,000 USD annually. Accounts tripled during tenure.
- Expanded billing program to accommodate increased enrollment, new academic offerings, and the addition of summer and music programs for the community at-large.
- Fostered an environment where students and families could discuss educational financing, payment plans, and options.
- Introduced processes and systems to improve service: Coordinated pro-rated billing for ESL students and streamlined registration for the returning education program.
- Served as the primary liaison among the college, students, and their sponsors. This often required communication with embassies, consulates, international banks, and corporate sponsors.
- Supervised and trained student workers in the practices of the business office.
- Facilitated communication among the administration, registrar, and financial aid. Ensured seamless transitions during Business Office staff changes. Prepared and delivered presentations as required.
- Initiated increased involvement in campus life as member of committees for new academic programs. Contributed understanding of the impact of program changes on billing.
- Edited the college catalog annually and the staff handbook as needed.

Account Manager   1990–1992
Marine Midland Bank, White Plains, NY (now HSBC)

- Managed international purchases and cardholder accounts. Management implemented suggestion that these accounts be treated separately for improved customer service.
- Investigated and analyzed cardholder queries to provide resolution of issues.
- Researched account histories for the security department.
- Composed internal and external correspondence for the department.

Researcher   1989–1990
Citibank, N.A., New York, NY

- Prepared Letters of Credit based on research using the department's microfilm library.
- Researched transactions and queries on Letters of Credit and Foreign Exchange.
- Communicated with banks in Europe and Africa to document and process drafts/checks to be cleared by the Federal Reserve Bank of New York.

CURRENT MEMBERSHIPS

Celtic League American Branch   1993–Present
West Hampton Historical Society   2000–Present

Susan T. Shields, M.S.N., D.A.C.B.F.N.

90 Merriam Drive • Fairfield, CT 06430
Phone: 203-975-2009 • Email: susan@shields.net

NURSING MANAGEMENT PROFESSIONAL

Nursing Instruction & Teaching • Program Management • HR & Administration

Master's-prepared genetics/perinatal nurse offering 20+ years of clinical management experience and extensive qualifications for a teaching/nursing faculty, health services program management, or human resources/administrative position. Team-based leader with proven ability to drive forward process improvement and organizational change to achieve common goals. Extraordinary communication and listening skills; highly self-motivated and tenacious in completing projects. Demonstrated expertise in:

- Nursing Management/Administration
- Pediatric, Obstetrical & Neonatal Nursing
- Family Advocacy & Bereavement Counseling
- Nursing Instruction, Teaching & Mentoring
- Program Development & Management
- Health Promotion & Preventative Health Issues

EDUCATION & CREDENTIALS

M.S.N., Perinatology and Genetics, Summa Cum Laude
University of New York – New York, NY – 1996

B.S.N., Nursing, Magna Cum Laude
University of Connecticut – Hartford, CT – 1983

A.S., Nursing
Webster Community College – Chicago, IL – 1978

B.S., Sociology/Psychology/Social Work
Central Illinois University – Deerfield, IL – 1975

Certifications & Licensing

Clinical Nurse Specialist (CNS), Perinatology and Genetics
Certification and Diplomate, American College Board of Forensic Nursing (DACBFN)
Certified Basic Life Support Instructor (BLSI) • Certified Bereavement Counselor and Coordinator
Connecticut Nursing License #098765 • New York Nursing License #256430

PROFESSIONAL HIGHLIGHTS

Teaching & Nursing Instruction/Patient & Staff Education

- Instructed nurse interns in a classroom setting for the past 12 years, teaching courses and lecturing on neonatal genetics, maternity unit care, and neonatal grief counseling. Facilitated nursing students' learning and coordinated patient-care activities in collaboration with nursing faculty members.
- Spearheaded funding and development of an in-service training program covering issues involved in supporting parents coping with death of an infant or birth of a severely physically challenged infant.
- Performed pre-JCAHO inspection of educational programs; isolated areas for improvement and recommended changes that enhanced quality of staff orientation and patient educational counseling.
- Served as educational staff development officer; exceeded goals and achieved 95% compliance in an in-service and skill verification program for medical staff at an internal medicine clinic. Researched and briefed nurse educators on disease management and preventative clinical care strategies.
- Fielded thousands of urgent care and triage telephone calls on a medical triage line serving a population of 30,000+. Instructed patients in appropriate self-care techniques; measurably improved resource management and decreased patient care costs $50,000 in just 7 months.

This resume for an experienced nurse/educator includes teaching experience on page 1 because that is her career target. If she were interested in a nurse manager position, she could easily swap the order of her experience.

RESUME *69*, CONTINUED

Susan T. Shields, M.S.N., D.A.C.B.F.N.   Page 2

Nursing Management & Administration

- Led a 30-person staff of RNs and technicians in a regional referral, high-risk neonatal intensive-care/ newborn nursery serving 80–100 infants each month. Attained recognized status as a level III NICU. Oversaw 18 nurses/providers in an internal medicine clinic with 2,500 outpatients each month.

- Directed, supervised, and evaluated medical technician/nursing staffs composed of up to 22 medical professionals on obstetrical units with up to 5 labor rooms, 33 postpartum beds, and 20 cribs, handling an average 2,000 deliveries annually and coordinating care with 12 providers.

- Cost-effectively managed budgets exceeding $160,000 annually and state-of-the-art medical equipment valued at more than $490,000. Investigated and devised cost-saving initiatives, including a low-tech infant security system that saved $68,000 by eliminating the need for specialized equipment.

- Planned, implemented, evaluated, and directed delivery of high-quality, cost-effective nursing services for 1,200 pediatric patients monthly. Executed quality improvement initiatives and developed comprehensive operating guidelines for all patient care, ensuring focus on preventative care.

- Initiated and headed development of cutting-edge programs, including a grief support and outreach program, breast cancer awareness luncheon, and a working group concerned with Advanced Directives and Durable Power of Attorney for patients. Led development of associated policies and procedures.

- Contributed to the development and implementation of process and quality improvement initiatives based on quantitative and qualitative data collected as a member of several multidisciplinary committees, including the Utilization/Quality Management, Infection Control, and Health Promotion Committees.

- Coordinated the smooth relocation of an obstetrical unit and the subsequent assimilation of a second obstetrical/infant care and neonatal intensive care unit. Developed policies to meet quality of care standards. Created a staff orientation program that eased the transition and improved morale.

CAREER HISTORY

U.S.A.F. Adams Medical Facility, Adams A.F.B., MI, 2000–Present
Medical Telephone Triage Nurse (Feb 2004–Present)
Facilitator/Coordinator, Women's Health Initiative (Dec 2002–Feb 2004)
Nurse Manager, Primary Care Management Clinic (Mar 2002–Dec 2002)
Nurse Manager, Pediatric Clinic (Sep 2001–Mar 2002)
Newborn Nursery Nurse Manager, Obstetrical Unit, Labor & Delivery (Aug 2000–Sep 2001)

Baker Hall Medical Center, Corona A.F.B., CA, 1996–2000
Nurse Manager, Maternity Unit/Newborn Nursery—Mother/Infant Recovery

Armistead Medical Center, Armistead A.F.B., NY, 1988–1996
Nurse Manager/Asst. Nurse Manager, Internal Medicine Clinic (Nov 1994–Jul 1996)
Nurse Manager/Asst. Nurse Manager/Staff Nurse, Neonatal Intensive Care (Feb 1988–Nov 1994)

Berlane Regional Medical Center, Berlane A.F.B., IL, 1983–1988
Nurse Manager/Staff Nurse/Flight Nurse

PROFESSIONAL AFFILIATIONS

Member, American Association of University Women (AAUW)
Member, Association of Women's Health, Obstetrical and Neonatal Nurses (AWHONN)
Former Chairperson and current Member, AWHONN Research Review Committee
Diplomate, American College of Forensic Nurses (DACFN)
Member, International Society of Nurses in Genetics (ISONG)
Member, National Association of Neonatal Nurses (NANN)
Member, National Bereavement Alliance—known as Resolve Through Sharing (RTS)
Member and Adams State University Nominating Board, Sigma Theta Tau—national nursing honor society

CHAPTER 10

CVs (Curriculum Vitae)

- Secondary and University Educators
- International Educators

EDMUND J. SCIBILIA

P.O. Box 110, Middletown, CT 06457
(860) 347-0011 • fax (860) 347-0012
escibilia@snet.net

PROFESSIONAL SUMMARY

- Highly motivated and accomplished teaching professional with more than 20 years of exemplary experience; outstanding command of the general science curriculum with special expertise in developing and implementing comprehensive curriculum enhancements.
- Utilize dynamic, synergistic style in collaborating with other educators in a team-teaching approach; considered a catalyst with keen strategic planning skills and a pragmatic, resourceful approach to responsibilities.
- Lifelong advocate of continued learning and advancement; very effective in influencing the grasp of knowledge and love of learning in others.
- High energy level complemented by demonstrated ability to reach learners at all levels and incite them with a thirst for learning to the maximum extent possible.
- Dedicated and involved community volunteer with demonstrated leadership; Vice Chair, Board of Education.

EDUCATION

SOUTHERN CONNECTICUT STATE UNIVERSITY • New Haven, CT
- *Sixth-Year Professional Diploma of Advanced Studies as Secondary Science Specialist* (1992)

SOUTHERN CONNECTICUT STATE UNIVERSITY / YALE UNIVERSITY / MIT
- *Fellowship through Institute for Science Instruction and Study* (1989)

EASTERN CONNECTICUT STATE COLLEGE • Willimantic, CT
- *Master of Science, Elementary Science Education* (1982); Dean's List Standing

CENTRAL CONNECTICUT STATE COLLEGE • New Britain, CT
- *Bachelor of Science, Education* (1975); Dean's List Standing

PROFESSIONAL EXPERIENCE

1976–Present **NORTH BRANFORD MIDDLE SCHOOL** • North Branford, CT
Grade 6 Science and Reading Teacher (Science, 1979–Present; Reading, 2002–Present)
Utilize well-honed skills in planning, preparing, delivering, and assessing. Promote a positive environment for in-classroom learning complemented by ability to bring real-life examples to instruction, both in science and reading. Teaching style reflects a continual effort to innovate and excite students. Consistently complement curriculum through nontraditional methods in teaching; incorporated team-teaching concepts working with students identified as learning disabled a full decade before the inclusion approach was embraced. Implemented variety of hands-on modeling techniques for reading students in absence of curriculum; created rubrics designed to foster performance-based assessment. Provide exposure to examples of excellence in literature, adult nonfiction, historical accounts, and classics as catalyst for creative discussions and response journal writings.

Salient Accomplishments ...
- Appointed to serve as Chairman of Curriculum Development Committee, fully rewriting science curriculum at all grade levels consistent with the Connecticut State Department of Education's Science Curriculum Framework (1998–Present); previously contributed extensively to two comprehensive rewrites of science curriculum between 1976 and 1994.
- Macintosh consultant, presenting workshops for CEUs to professional staff and educators; expertise in Microsoft Word, Claris, Lotus, Quicken, FileMaker Pro, and MacSchool grading programs (1991–Present).
- BEST Mentor (1994); certified by State of Connecticut as cooperating teacher and mentor for new and beginning teachers; mentor to teacher on performance review (2003).

This CV starts off with a strong summary. After page 1, it follows a standard format of simply listing activities, credentials, memberships, and so on.

RESUME *70*, CONTINUED

EDMUND J. SCIBILIA   Page Two

PROFESSIONAL EXPERIENCE *(cont'd.)*

NORTH BRANFORD MIDDLE SCHOOL • North Branford, CT
Grade 6 Science and Reading Teacher (Science, 1979–Present; Reading, 2002–Present)
• Member, Middle School Building Committee (1999); preparing specifications for new 5–6 Middle School addition.
Grade 6 Honors Science Teacher (1992)
Grade 6 Social Studies Teacher (1995–1999)
Grades 6 and 7 Science Teacher (1977–1979)
Grade 6 Science and Math Teacher; Grade 7 Science Teacher (1976–1977)

1975   **FARM HILL SCHOOL** • Middletown, CT
Grade 4 Classroom Teacher

1973–1974   **MIDDLESEX COMMUNITY COLLEGE** • Middletown, CT
Lab Assistant and Teaching Assistant / Purchasing Agent

PROFESSIONAL AFFILIATIONS

• **National Science Teachers Association (NSTA)** • Member
• **National Education Association Representative Assembly Delegate** (Orlando, FL, 2003)
• **NSTA Convention Participant** (New Orleans, LA, 1997; Portland, ME, 1992; Hartford, CT, 1976; Providence, RI, 1974)
• **Connecticut Science Teachers Association (CSTA)** • Member
• **Connecticut Association of Boards of Education** • Member
• **National Education Association, Connecticut Education Association, North Branford Education Association** • Member
• **Connecticut Education Foundation, Inc.** • Volunteer

DISTINCTIONS

• **Who's Who in America** (2004)
• **Who's Who in Science and Technology** (2003)
• **Who's Who in the East** (2003, 2002)
• **Who's Who Among American Teachers** (2000)
• **Nominee, Presidential Award for Excellence in Secondary School Science and Mathematics Teaching** (1995)

CONTINUING PROFESSIONAL DEVELOPMENT

• Strategic Planning Core Values & Expectations Committee (2003)
• Strategic Planning Renewal and Action Team Member in Association with Cambridge Associates (2001)
• Core Institute for Support Teachers (1991); Mentor, newly certified first-year teacher (2001–Present)
• Connecticut Association of Boards of Education; Public School Policy Development (2000)
• Project Learn A Time For A Change; Alternative Scheduling (2000)
• Investigation of a Middle School Model; Education of the Blind (2000)
• Educator's Role in Helping Children with Grief; Suicide Prevention, Referral Process & Procedure (2000)
• Connecticut College Regional Inservice Enhancement Center for Science / Physics Refresher (1999)

EDMUND J. SCIBILIA
Page Three

CIVIC/COMMUNITY INVOLVEMENT

- **Middletown Board of Education** (2000–Present)
    - Vice-Chair/Secretary (2001–Present)
    - Member (2000–Present)
    - Chairman, Policy Committee
    - Chairman, Tolerance Committee
    - Member, Curriculum Committee
    - Member, Transportation Committee
    - Member, Building and Grounds Committee
    - Member, Communications Committee

- **North Branford Education Association** • Vice President (1998–Present)
    - Middlesex County Council (2003–Present)
    - CEA Summer Leadership (2002)

- **Association of Connecticut Fairs** (1985–Present)
    - Delegate
    - Chairman, Scholarship Committee
    - Premium Book Chairman

- **Guilford Fair Foundation, Inc.** (1982–Present)
    - Founder
    - Treasurer (2001–Present)
    - Secretary (1999–2001)

- **Mt. Ascutney Property Owners Association** (1991–Present)
    - Member, Executive Committee (1993–Present)
    - President (2004–2005)

- **Guilford Agricultural Fair Association, Inc.** (1987–Present)
    - Honorary Member (1997) • Awarded for exemplary voluntary service
    - Treasurer/Coordinator of Exhibits
    - Advance Sales
    - Superintendent of Gates
    - Chairman, Scholarship Committee
    - Member, Constitution Committee

- **Middletown Town Committee** • Treasurer (1997–Present); Member (1986–Present)
- **Church of the Epiphany** • Treasurer/Vestry Member/Junior Warden (1989–1998)
- **Middletown Zoning Board of Appeals** • Vice-Chairman (1987–1993; elected position)
- **Connecticut Public Television Volunteer** (1990–2001)
- **North Branford Community Television** • Board of Directors/Founder (1978–1984)

Curriculum Vitae

William Allan

26 Fairfield Crescent
Hillsborough
Auckland

Phone (09) 625 7588 (home)
Phone (025) 156 291 (cellular)

This CV, for a client in New Zealand, conforms to the expected style and length for an education professional's CV in that country. The layout allows the interviewing panel to make annotations in the margins.

Curriculum Vitae, page 2

William Allan

Personal Details

Name: William Alexander Allan
Address: 26 Fairfield Crescent, Hillsborough, Auckland
Telephones: (09) 625 7588 (home), (09) 621 9780 (work), (025) 156 291 (cellular)
Email: wil.al@xtra.co.nz

Interests: Golf, running, tennis, swimming, family time, sporting activities, gardening, reading, studying, and computers

Presentations: Keynote speaking engagement at Technology Conference, 2003

Publications: Papers on the development of technology and technology education

Career Objective

To continue my career as a Lecturer specialising in technology within a higher education establishment, where I can utilise my core competencies and experience to add value and make a measurable contribution.

Personal Attributes

Extracts from references:
- "William is **hardworking, extremely focused,** and very **task oriented.** His work has been characterised by **thoroughness,** effective use of a variety of media, and planned down to the last detail. William is very **creative** and **professional** in his approach, and the materials he produces for workshops and presentations are of high quality. He is **innovative** and experimental and highly skilled in the use of a variety of media… Feedback from his schools has invariably been positive and full of praise for his approach and professionalism."

- "William is a **dynamic** and **effective leader.**…I would wish to place most emphasis on his staff direction, his **inspirational dynamism,** his ability to think laterally in the solving of problems.…The credit for all (William's) achievements…I believe…(are) two outstanding characteristics: his **prodigious work effort** and **drive,** and his total **professionalism.**…William's work is characterised by **careful** and **thoughtful** planning. He has the rare ability to look ahead as well as to attend to the day-to-day detail.…His immediate staff are inspired by his depth of knowledge and his **perceptive leadership.**…He is an **exceptional man,** a real professional whose skills and standards never fall below a level that most craftsmen find unattainable. With that goes an **unusual warmth** and **kindness,** a **dedication** to this job and the welfare of students, and an **unsurpassed measure of integrity.**"

These references may be cited in an interview.

Curriculum Vitae, page 3

William Allan

Core Competencies

DESIGN AND TECHNOLOGY
- Strong in the use of computer technologies for design.
- Impressive imaginative flair and creativity.
- Excellent background in the use of visual media and marketing (graphic and design fields in both business and schools).
- Confident in using electronic and visual media equipment and programs; consistently use a wide range of visual presentation systems.

MULTIMEDIA
- Possess considerable multimedia skills especially in the development of Internet and LAN-based instructional and flexible learning-based materials—have reinforced and initiated learning programmes through the development of online resources and courses.
- Extremely skilled in web design, multimedia, and publishing on the Internet.

PEOPLE DEVELOPMENT
- Possess an innate talent for developing and coaching people.
- Sincere attitude to help and serve people.
- Ability to enhance the performance of others.

PROGRAMME MANAGEMENT
- Ability to mobilise people and resources to achieve planned objectives.
- Strong grasp of programme management methodologies.
- Ability to adapt and integrate different technical disciplines, methodologies, and industry knowledge to ensure best possible solutions.

PROJECT MANAGEMENT
- Confident in managing projects at all levels of education including primary, intermediate, secondary, and tertiary (evidenced in my contract work and Taranaki Polytechnic).
- Worked as a Contract Facilitator.
- Confident in the coordination of contract work—successfully led, coordinated, and managed one of the most successful "Information Technology for Teachers" programmes in the country for Telecom NZ.

TEACHING
- Demonstrated talent for motivating, encouraging, and leading students in a positive direction for better learning.
- Co-produced a very successful Internet website as a teacher resource (www.hasslefree.co.nz).

EDUCATION
- Experience in leveraging information technology to enhance education.
- Have a sound knowledge of the processes involved in curriculum development in schools.

Curriculum Vitae, page 4

William Allan

Career Profile

2003–2004   Dunedin College of Education
Senior Lecturer of Technology Education

- Developed and directed a video on technological practice and benefits of links with community resources.
- Wrote a resource on "Design" for the Ministry of Education.
- Organised and delivered professional development programmes for schools on computer graphics, multimedia, and web production techniques.
- Developed an Internet website and a programme of learning for a group of Manoia School students who come to DCE for their technology education.
- Developed graphic material which promoted and identified the technology education department.

2004–present   New Zealand Qualifications Authority
Member of the National Assessment Panel

- Meet with the National team of panel members to develop the style of assessment that can be expected in the year 2006.

2003–2004   Employed by a variety of schools
Consultant

- Advised on property design and development issues for technology education/creative environments.
- Liaised with school administration boards to establish needs.
- Provided information on professional development related to technology education.
- Developed concepts of spatial design possibilities to accommodate and deliver an effective technology education.
- Compiled a plan of action and brief for architectural firms to undertake the development of these facilities.
- Provided a service accommodating change management.

2002–2003   Christchurch Polytechnic
Tutor for the Commercial Computer Graphics Course

- Wrote and delivered units of work in Graphic Design, Time-Based Media, Digital Imaging, Visual Imaging, Computer Reprographics, and Web-Based Media.
- Assisted in preparing material for the application of a Course in Bachelor of Visual Arts.

2002   Ministry of Education
Contract

- Wrote the guidelines for Property Management in Schools for Technology Education. Contracted to various schools to provide advice for property development and work with architects in the creation of plans for technology blocks.

Curriculum Vitae, page 5

William Allan

Career Profile (continued)

2002   New Zealand Qualifications Authority
                        Regional Moderator

- Moderated Graphics and Design Unit Standards.
- Coordinated the moderation activities of allocated local moderators.
- Checked moderate samples of provider assessment material.
- Confirmed that judgements were consistent with National Moderation Standards.
- Reported on check moderation process and assessment material.
- Resolved disputes and undertook the process of mediation.

2000–2002   Albany University College of Education
                        Contract Facilitator of Technology

- Provided leadership in the professional development of teachers in technology education throughout Albany and Auckland areas.
- Provided guidance to principals and boards of trustees about the implementation of technology.
- Worked collaboratively with teachers and other advisers to develop positive teaching and learning environments for technology.
- Worked with schools on developing integrated programmes of work and negotiated the structure of curriculum policy statements.
- Regional coordinator for the National Technology Association.
- Maintained links and co-ordinated Technology Education in (over the two and a half years) 70 primary schools and 9 secondary schools.
- Developed strategies for the positive assessment and reporting of technology education.
- Developed a help line.
- Responded to milestone report requests

2000–2002   New Zealand Qualifications Authority
                        Writer

- Writer of Unit Standards, training manual, and assessment guide; moderator for Graphics and Design Unit.
- Coordinated Unit Standards information from a variety of sources.
- Wrote assessment guide material.
- Moderated schools' Unit Standard material.
- Provided professional development workshops.

1999   The University of Auckland
                        Consultant

- Organised, produced, and delivered design presentations for technology curriculum development.
- Created a full multimedia production to provide an historical and informative presentation on Design and how it fits into the technology curriculum.
- Delivered the presentation in three major areas of the Auckland Region.

Part II: Sample Resumes for Teachers and Educators

RESUME 71, CONTINUED

Curriculum Vitae, page 6

William Allan

Career Profile (continued)

1995–1999   Maree Campbell College, Auckland
HOD Information Technology and Applied Art and Design

HOD Information Technology:
- Developed learning activities based on computer applications.
- Coordinated access to computer resources.
- Ensured computer network and classroom resources were maintained and provided future analysis about direction the school should proceed when upgrading.
- Prepared and monitored a budget for computing.
- Evaluated the effectiveness of classroom programmes.
- Developed individualised in-service training programmes for teachers.

HOD Applied Art and Design:
- Ensured the schemes of work met the National Syllabus requirements.
- Ensured objectives met the local needs and the abilities of the students and that the necessary teachers' resources were managed with care.
- Ensured the budget was adhered to and funds wisely used.
- Provided a constant link with the updated technology involved in this area of study.
- Constantly consulted with teachers to advise and evaluate classroom activities.
- Teacher in charge of implementing technology.
- Provided information to staff and Board of Trustees about technology and the proposed implementation procedure.
- Ensured well-documented information on proposed expenditure and expected budget.
- Investigated the necessary resources required for implementation.

1992–1995   Hillsborough College, Auckland
Assistant Teacher in the Graphics and Technology Department

- Updated the Graphics and Design Technology Curriculum.
- Produced a series of Modules for future Senior Graphics and Technology education.
- Managed personnel and many departmental programmes.
- Taught Technology and Graphics in levels three to seven.
- Ran a peer support programme with the third form students.

1986–1992   New Terrace High School, Auckland
HOD Applied Art and Design

- Instrumental in developing the Technology and Graphics Departments from a low status in 1992 into one of the most sophisticated technology departments in the country.
- As a result of the above achievement:
"Air New Zealand, in the last two years, has employed more apprentices from this school than any other."
"Trainee Teachers in the Technology course at Auckland College of Education virtually queued to obtain an appointment here and lecturers now conduct tours of students through the workshops."
- Instrumental in developing electronics and robotics as secondary schools–based programme.

180

Curriculum Vitae, page 7

William Allan

Qualifications

Certificates and Diplomas

- Masters in Education Degree, 2002

- Higher Teachers Diploma, 1995

- Quality Management Certificate, 1997

- Trained Teacher Certificate, 1987

- Teacher Diploma, 1985

- Projectionist Certificate, 1985

Courses

- Graphic Presentation and Photography, 1983

- Computer Awareness (Mac), 1990

- Advanced Computer (Mac), 1992

- Photography, 1991

- Design, 1993

- Graphics and Technology, 1993

Referees

Verbal referees available at an interview.

RESUME 72: BY DON ORLANDO, MBA, CPRW, JCTC, CCM, CCMC

Curriculum vitæ tailored to the needs of Trinity Episcopal School

Mark C. Carver, M.A., B.S., B.A., A.A.

P.O. Box 555 (114 Shadeline Street) Raleigh, North Carolina 27604
☎ 704.555.5555 (home) – 704.555.6666 (cell) – mccarver1004@aol.com

"Mark Carver is everything that is right in today's educational system....He instills his students with a love of science and learning....I have never before come in contact with a teacher who so openly admits how much he loves his job, his students, and the school he teaches in...." Sharon Younger, Parent

Education:

❑ M.A., Paleobiology, Brooklyn College, Brooklyn, New York   1985
  Paid my own way to earn this degree by working 20 hours a week while carrying a full academic load.

❑ B.A. and B.S., Geology, Biology, and Pre-Med, Brooklyn College, Brooklyn, New York   1982
  Worked 12 hours a week while simultaneously pursuing two rigorous scientific majors.

❑ A.A., Liberal Arts, Bronx Community College, Bronx, New York   1974

Employment history with selected examples of qualifications in action:

❑ Teacher and Science Department Chair, Raleigh International Baccalaureate Middle School, Raleigh, North Carolina   1994–Present
  Our school serves some 250 students of which 20 percent are minority.

"The level of enthusiasm of his students is testimony to their enjoyment of his classes, and the results of their State Tests indicate their high level of achievement....We wouldn't be Raleigh International Baccalaureate Middle School without him."
Mina Harker, Principal

Transformed a program that had "covered the content" with a 15-year-old curriculum that bored our students and drove some of our best teachers away. Designed and fielded a Steps Toward Empowering Potential Scientists program using material I had presented at conferences. Then championed the idea to beat 12 finalists and win the $12,000 grant we needed to fund the program. ***Outcomes:*** Students tell me they can't wait to get to class. My program is now the county template for all middle schools.

Found, and improved upon, the best model I could find for interdisciplinary curricula that used real-life problems as teaching tools. ***Outcomes:*** Students feel they are learning as they grow. Nine of my 7th grade students who studied current FDA tests for carcinogens had their new recommendations in the field published. My students treat their textbook for this course with reverence and love the learning that takes place both inside and outside the classroom.

Tailored my instruction to lead every student to all the benefits that my approach to teaching offers. ***Outcomes:*** One student, who couldn't read above the third grade level, became so involved in the learning process that he began—for the first time—to read on his own. His reading rose four grade levels in only two and one-half years.

This detail-rich CV is outcome-based and clearly communicates extensive expertise and value. It enabled the job seeker to secure a position as a high school teacher and negotiate full reimbursement for a Ph.D. as well as a flexible schedule while he completed it.

RESUME 72, CONTINUED

Mark C. Carver   704.555.5555

Selected by the County Science Coordinator to mentor all 150 science instructors in our county's middle schools. Some of these have no background in education at all, some are new teachers with no classroom experience, some are seasoned veterans. I overhauled the mandatory, six-day in-service program. ***Outcomes:*** By replicating the classroom during in-service training, every teacher got the benefit of seeing their curriculum through their students' eyes. When I added a year of personal follow-ups, our teacher attrition dropped. Course evaluation instruments have shown remarkable support for this new approach.

> "Mr. Carver's three heterogeneous Biology Classes were the top three classes on the End of Grade Test in Raleigh... In addition, 100% of his students scored higher than the state average.... I am particularly intrigued by his teaching methods... making all the learning translate into a mural that never ends." Tom Lighter, Media Specialist

❑ *Sought out by the Professor of Gifted Education to serve as an* Adjunct Instructor, North Carolina State University, Raleigh, North Carolina   1998–Present
I teach some 25 students 3-hour graduate-level courses in Science and Math for Educators of Gifted and Talented Students and Science Curricula for Science Teachers.

Did some of the pioneering work in interdisciplinary teaching, combining social studies and science. Despite a busy schedule, made time to be an active member of the team that won a major grant in only 10 months. Contributed as a member of a three-person team to deliver 16 weeks of curriculum including all the supporting materials. ***Outcomes:*** Pilot program very successful when we tested it in one the poorest counties in the state. Now other schools seek to emulate our programs.

❑ Teacher and County Renaissance Coordinator, Port Lucie High School, Port Lucie, Florida   1989–1994
Taught classes for 9th through 12th grade students in Earth and Space Sciences and Leadership Skills Development. Also served as a Peer Teacher Trainer, Student Council Advisor, and County Coordinator of the Renaissance Student Incentive Program.

> "Mark Carver is without a doubt the best teacher I have ever had the pleasure of knowing and observing... I was taught motivation is intrinsic. Mark has proven that theory inaccurate... he has the rare gift of understanding, of emotionally connecting to all individuals...." Janice Collier, Guidance Counselor

Built, from the ground up, an entirely new course on leadership. Not only completed the traditional, educational needs analysis, but extended my research to what our community and faculty wanted. Used in-class instruction on public speaking and leadership to set the stage for community-centered activities that promised positive rewards beyond just letter grades. ***Outcomes:*** Built nearly 20 extracurricular clubs. Student enrollment for these electives went from 0 to 90 in 3 years.

> "Mark initiated a great new program this year called Renaissance, which has had an overwhelming response by community businesses, our students, and especially the faculty... school morale has improved dramatically." Jeffrey Miller, Guidance Counselor

Mark C. Carver   704.555.5555

❑ *Sought out by the Provost to serve as* **Adjunct Instructor**, Indian River Community College,
Fort Myers, Florida   1990–1994
Taught 30 diverse students in 4 to 6 geological and physical sciences courses a year.

❑ *Asked by the Principal to join the faculty as a* **Teacher**, Fort Myers Central High
School, Fort Myers, Florida   1988–1989
*Taught classes in Earth and Space Sciences to a diverse study body of about 2,000. Served as Key Club
Advisor.*

❑ **Teacher and Drop-Out Prevention Facilitator**, Esther Clarke Hunter Junior
High School, Brooklyn, New York   1985–1988
*This school had the highest number of weapon-related, violent crimes in the country and the highest
crime rate in the City of New York. I taught classes in Earth and Integrated Sciences and served as the
Drop-Out Prevention Program Coordinator for the 8th Grade.*

Met challenges that went beyond trying to educate gang members (most with arrest records)
who averaged three years older than the typical 8th grade student. Earned their trust in the
only way they could understand: not backing down to threats, but reaching out to help them
learn. They saw something completely new: a teacher offering boxing and weight lifting. But,
in the process, I taught them basic physics… and how to use real knowledge to lead better
lives. **Outcomes:** When they came to me, they had an average absentee rate of 30 percent;
when they left, that rate had dropped to 10 percent. Only 2 of the 40 I started with failed to
graduate—a rate feat in this setting.

❑ **Adjunct Instructor**, Lehman College, Bronx, New York   1982–1988
Taught courses in Geological, Physical, and Biological Sciences.

❑ **Adjunct Instructor**, Brooklyn College, Brooklyn, New York   1982–1985
Taught courses in Geological, Physical, and Biological Sciences.

Professional development:

❑ "Webmaster Training," Raleigh Professional Development Center   July 1997–June 1999
❑ "The Language of the Internet," University of North Carolina   July 1998
❑ "Family Living to Ethical Behavior to Human Sexuality," Raleigh Professional Development,
45 classroom hours   October 1995–April 1996
❑ "First Annual Conference for the Gifted Learner," William & Mary College   March 6–8, 1996
❑ "Middle Years Program—Teacher Training Workshop—Interdisciplinary Curriculum:
Design and Implementation," International Baccalaureate North America   March 27–30, 1996
❑ "Key Issues: Bringing Environmental Issues into the Classroom," Colorado School of Mines–
Keystone Science School   July 8–15, 1995
❑ "Exemplary Science Curriculum and Instruction for High Ability Learners" (K to 8), William
& Mary College   June 19–22, 1995

Page 3 of 5

Mark C. Carver   704.555.5555

❑ IBM Instructional Educational Program, Port Lucie Professional Development   August 1991

❑ Member, Florida Goals 2000 Committee, Writing Cooperative Learning Portion of the New
  Statewide Curriculum for Education   April 1994

❑ Chair, School Activities, Port Lucie High School, Southern Association of Colleges and
  Schools, initial accreditation   1990–1991

Service to my communities:

The Academic Community

❑ Coach and Mentor, Science Olympiad for Grades 6–12. More than 350 hours volunteer time
  per year, Carter County, North Carolina Coaches and Students   1996–Present

❑ Mentor and Teacher, The After School Scientist at Morton College — Current and Former
  Students, Students at Large   1997–2003

❑ School Leader, Paper Recycling Program to School and Community, Raleigh   1996–Present

❑ Co-author and Presenter, *Student Cancer Researchers Discover a New "Ames" Mutagenic
  Substances Test,* National Science Teachers Association Conference   March 2001

❑ Co-author, *A Low-cost Ames Spot Overlay Method,* Association for Biology Laboratory
  Education   October 2000

The Public Community

❑ Creator/Director, Raleigh Community Nature Trail and Outdoor Classroom   1994–Present

❑ Project Director, Morton College Community Service Project (Freshman students) 2002–2004

❑ Teacher Representative, Parent to Teacher to Student Association, Raleigh International
  Baccalaureate School   1998, 1999, 2003

Recognition in my field:

❑ Above and Beyond Award, Advisory Panel for Parents of Exceptional Learners   2002–2003
  Nominated by the families in the local school district to win this award.

> "The past two years I have been a co-worker... he was also my son's teacher last year.
> When I recently asked my son who was the best teacher he ever had, he replied, 'Mr.
> Carver.' He is one of those unique teachers who has the distinction of being the hardest
> and best-liked teachers at our school." Cheryl Lionn, Language Arts Teacher

❑ Raleigh International Baccalaureate Middle School Teacher of the Year   2001–2003

❑ Science Olympiad First Place Team Awards   1997–Present
  Led my student teams to victories in regional competitions seven times.

❑ Distinguished Service Award, North Carolina Association of Educators   June 1995

❑ CMS "Break the Mold" Award   January 1995
  *Recognized at the county level as an educator who goes beyond the classroom to help students become
  responsible citizens.*

> "Mr. Carver has indeed "Broken the Mold" and ventured well into the new era of teaching
> that beckons us all." David Carrley, PhD International Baccalaureate Counselor

Page 4 of 5

RESUME 72, CONTINUED

Mark C. Carver   704.555.5555

❑ St. Lucie County Teacher of the Year   1994
Successfully competed with teachers from 10 elementary, middle, and high schools to be the only winner in our district.

❑ Golden Apple Award   1993
Honored by the Fort Myers News. *I was the only teacher from 2 high, 6 middle, and 12 elementary schools to be selected.*

❑ Rotary Youth Leadership Award   1992
Selected by the community for this award.

❑ Florida State University's Honor and Scholar's Award   1992
Nominated by my former students who were then enrolled at Florida State.

❑ Principal's Award for Outstanding Service to School and Community   1989, 1990,
                                                                   1991, 1992, 1993
This award is given to the most outstanding faculty member and I am the only person to win this honor five times.

❑ Grant Recipient, $50K Grant for "Science Innovation in an Economically Depressed Community District," District 23, Brownsville, Brooklyn, New York   May–June 1986

Professional affiliations:

❑ Member, National Association of Biology Teachers   Since 1996
❑ Member, National Science Teachers' Association   Since 2000
❑ Former member and school representative, Classroom Teachers' Association   1994–1997

Contributions to my discipline—academic papers and workshops:

❑ Glover et al, Spot-Overlay Ames Test of Potential Mutagens, in *Tested Studies for Laboratory Teaching,* pp. 1 to 18 V. 22, S. J. Smythe, Editor, The Association of Biology Laboratory Education.   June 2000

Technology skills:

❑ Proficient in Word, Excel, Access, PowerPoint, Internet search protocols, and proprietary educational and administrative software suites.
❑ Working knowledge of financial software.

Page 5 of 5

TEDRA ORGAMANI

Curriculum Vitae

4702 Logan Court   (641) 461-9611
Kellerton, Iowa 50133   orgamani@aol.com

EDUCATION

Doctoral Candidate	University of Dublin, Dublin, Ireland	In progress
LLM	Iowa State University, Ames, Iowa	1997
MSW	Iowa State University, Ames, Iowa	1995
LL.B./JD	University of California, Northridge, California	1993
BBA	University of California, Northridge, California Management	1985

LICENSURE AND CERTIFICATION

Master of Social Work, Addiction Counselor   2003
National Board of Addiction Examiners, Des Moines, Iowa

Certified Criminal Justice Specialist   2003
National Board of Addiction Examiners, Des Moines, Iowa

Licensed Professional Counselor   2002
Board of Health, Des Moines, Iowa

TEACHING APPOINTMENTS

Iowa Children and Family Services Agency (CFSA), Des Moines, Iowa   2000–Present
Training Specialist
Train staff in family and child welfare practice. Develop curriculum in relevant
areas in field.

Missouri State University School of Social Work, Kansas City, Missouri   1998–2000
Assistant Professor/Instructor
Collaborated with Kansas City School System to bring drug awareness program to
primary schools. Partnered with MSU and community organizations to develop and manage
homeless coalition program to reduce effects of substance abuse in Kansas City.
Subjects taught:
- Social Welfare Policy
- Social Work Practice
- Human Behavior
- Social Work and the Law

Des Moines Community College, Des Moines, Iowa   1997–Present
Instructor
Subject taught:
- Business Law

University of Iowa, Training Resource Associates, Des Moines, Iowa   1997–Present
Instructor
Subjects taught:
- Human Behavior
- Ethics for Substance Abuse Counselors

(Continued on Page Two)

This concise, two-page CV details the qualifications for a college professor and training specialist in the field of social work.

TEDRA ORGAMANI
C.V. Page Two

TEACHING APPOINTMENTS (Continued)

University of Iowa, Ames, Iowa (Lamoni, Iowa Campus)   1997–Present
Instructor
Subjects taught:
- Ethics for Professionals
- Professional Development
- Constitutional Law
- Business Law

PROFESSIONAL EXPERIENCE

Iowa Children and Family Services Agency (CFSA), Des Moines, Iowa   2000–Present
Substance Abuse Specialist
Formulated substance abuse resources for CFSA. Originated pilot projects for
women and children.

City of Des Moines Human Resources Administration, Des Moines, Iowa   1989–1998
Social Work Supervisor/Social Worker Staff Analyst/Fair Hearing Officer
Initiated substance abuse treatment and prevention program for birth parents.
Provided individual, group, and family therapy in field. Created and enlisted
community substance abuse services providers in city.

HONORS AND AWARDS

Four-year Academic Scholarship for Undergraduate Study   2002
Social Work Award, AFL-CIO Local 563, Des Moines, Iowa   1995

PRESENTATIONS

Child Welfare System and the Impact of Substance Abuse   1994
Ahmed Rasheesh Foundation, Des Moines, Iowa
United Nations and the Convention of the Rights of the Child   1999
California State University, Northridge, California

COMMITTEES AND COMMUNITY INVOLVEMENT

Member	Des Moines, Iowa Drug Court Development Committee	2005–Present
Trainer	Train Superior Court Judges on substance abuse issues and community resources	2005–Present
Board Member	Fighting Back Initiative, *Substance Abuse Program* Roberts Wood Johnson Foundation	2003–Present
Member	Served on review panel to draft drug status report Drug Strategies, Inc., Des Moines, Iowa	2003
Trainer	Foster Parents and Drug-Exposed Infants	2002–Present

AFFILIATIONS

Member	The Association of Legal Writing Specialists	2002–Present
Member	Association of Trial Lawyers of America	2001–Present

CHAPTER 11

Resumes for Educational Administrators

- Assistant Principals
- Principals
- Athletic Directors
- University Student Activities Directors
- Public School Administrators
- Superintendents of Schools
- University Administrators
- Directors of Education
- Educational Materials Coordinators
- Daycare Licensing Administrators

George Themeles, CAGS, M.Ed.

62 Anderson Street
Cumberland, RI 02808

(401) 454-7854
gthemeles@worldnet.att.net

Objective: Key position in educational administration

PROFILE

- Strong academic background combined with graduate degree in education, advanced degree in administration, and a record of achievement in classroom teaching
- Massachusetts Certified Teacher, Social Studies, grades 5–9 and 9–12
- Massachusetts Certified Principal/Assistant Principal, grades 5–9 and 9–12
- Well-developed oral and written communication skills and interpersonal abilities
- Natural leader and team builder, with practical administrative-level experience
- Member, Phi Delta Kappa

EDUCATION

UNIVERSITY OF MASSACHUSETTS LOWELL, Lowell, MA
- Certificate of Advanced Graduate Study in Educational Administration, Planning, and Policy
- Master of Education in Curriculum and Instruction, June 1997

BOSTON UNIVERSITY, Boston, MA
- Bachelor of Arts in International Relations & Political Science (double major), January 1994

PROFESSIONAL EXPERIENCE

NORTH REGIONAL SCHOOL DISTRICT, Cumberland, RI   2002–Present
Assistant Principal – Nathan Hale Middle School
Provide general and specific program management assistance in support of an effective and productive learning environment for students and staff. Areas of focus include
- Special education: Schedule, coordinate, and chair all meetings. Oversee the implementation of IEPs.
- Staff development: Facilitate the evaluation, selection, and promotion of professional development activities, including courses and conferences. Evaluate teachers.
- Student support and management: Established a homework hotline to improve school/home communication. Handle all student disciplinary matters. Act as liaison between teachers and parents.
- Budgeting: In-depth support of the budgetary process with the school principal. Recommend programs and staffing provisions for the following year.
- Special programs: Established an "Odyssey of the Mind" team to foster participation in widely recognized competition designed to encourage and develop cooperative problem solving.

JEFFERSON MIDDLE SCHOOL, Groton, MA   1997–2002
Teacher, Grade Seven
Developed objectives and created age/ability-appropriate lessons in accordance with curriculum guidelines, employing a variety of methods to meet multiple intelligences and diverse learning styles. Monitored and evaluated performance and progress. Sections included social studies (3), math (1), and science (1). Completed 300-hour administrative practicum involving budgeting, staff evaluation, day-to-day administration, and leadership activities.

An unobtrusive yet appropriate apple border gives visual appeal to this resume for a middle school assistant principal. The resume is well organized and easy to skim, so the reader can quickly pick up important information.

George Themeles, CAGS, M.Ed.   Page Two

(Jefferson Middle School, continued)

Participated in a variety of leadership and administrative activities:
- Building-Based Support Teams: Trained in strategy and implementation of peer-based assistance designed to expand resources available, facilitate problem solving, and build relationships among staff.
- Social Studies Task Force: Reviewed state guidelines and curriculum in preparation for revisions and development. Suggested goals and curriculum standards.
- Professional Development Committee Co-chair: Oversaw the designing, planning, implementing, and evaluating of professional development courses and in-services system-wide.
- Student Government Advisor Co-chair (2000–2001): Coordinated student group designed to foster leadership through charitable community activities.

HUNTINGTON LEARNING CENTER, Andover, MA   1999–2000
Tutor
Designed individual programs in reading and math for students across the spectrum of ages, development, and abilities, including assistance with regular classwork as well as enrichment activities.

LAWRENCE HIGH SCHOOL, Lawrence, MA   Winter/Spring 1997
Student Teacher
Taught U.S. History (1877–Present), Government, and Sociology courses to junior and senior classes. Employed debates, role plays, and other action-centered methods to increase student interest. Provided one-on-one tutoring in the Transitional Learning Center.

JOHNSON MIDDLE SCHOOL, Tewksbury, MA   1994–1996
Moderate Special Needs Teacher
Taught all subjects to special needs students with both emotional and physical handicaps. Met regularly with other classroom teachers to support and contribute to individual educational plans. Coordinated closely with other special needs teachers, guidance counselors, and school psychologists to ensure that mainstreaming goals were met.

Substitute Teacher
Taught all subjects to middle school students. Also functioned as a permanent substitute teacher in life science, physical science, and pre-algebra classes.

References available upon request

Bonnie Gregg

1325 19th Street
Annwald, WA 98001
(360) 555-2727

Dedicated and successful **ELEMENTARY SCHOOL PRINCIPAL** with proven ability to:

- Advocate and sustain a school culture conducive to continuous improvement for students and staff.
- Develop and monitor procedures and practices that promote a safe school environment.
- Assist instructional staff in development and implementation of curriculum, instruction, and assessment aligned with state and local learning goals.
- Manage human and financial resources to accomplish student achievement goals.
- Communicate with colleagues, parents, and community members to promote student learning.

EXPERIENCE

Principal, Annwald Elementary School, Annwald, Washington   2000–present

- Supervise, hire, and direct staff of teachers, educational assistants, and administrative support—Provide fiscal management—Observe and evaluate Certified staff—Implemented Special Education Inclusion—Administer student discipline.
- Implemented student discipline program resulting in 50% reduction of student referrals for discipline.
- Implemented Interdisciplinary Team Organization—Site-Based Management—Curriculum Development.
- Implemented "Success for All" reading program—increase of 35% in students reading at grade level.

Principal, American Tribal School, Flower, Washington   1998–2000

- Selected and assigned personnel, providing orientation for new and returning employees—Provided in-service with input from staff—Participated in Curriculum Planning and Development—Implemented and maintained Curriculum—Established and maintained budget for all programs—Observed and evaluated Certified and Classified staff—Directed USDA food service, transportation, facilities, operation, and maintenance of school.
- Implemented Site-Based management—Work Sampling System, including Portfolio Assessment—"Reading Recovery" program.
- In response to needs, implemented All-Day Kindergarten.
- Served on Science Textbook Selection Committee, Cultural Planning Committee, and Discipline and Attendance Planning Committee—Attended conferences, including IASA, Goals 2000, NISBA, and NIEA.

Vice Principal, American Tribal School, Flower, Washington   1996–1998

- Oversaw student discipline and parent and community relations—Conducted school board meetings—Participated in teacher observations and evaluations—Set up and managed school budgets—Led self-esteem programs—Participated in selection and assignment of staff members.

"...one of the finest leaders in our school system today..."

"...instrumental in creating learning environments that allow every student to be both challenged and successful..."

"...works with teachers, students, and parents to achieve a climate of positive and appropriate behavior..."

"...an outstanding individual whose talents and efforts make her an admirable and respected principal."

Teachers,
Annwald Elementary

Continued next page...

This resume shows clear career progression and a solid list of achievements. The testimonials are unobtrusive yet highly effective.

Bonnie Gregg

Page 2

EXPERIENCE CONTINUED

Teacher, American Tribal School, Flower, Washington, 1993–1996

Taught all subjects to 4th, 5th, and 6th grade students—Taught 7th and 8th grade Math, Science, Social Studies, Art, Health, English, and P.E.

Student Teacher, Daly Elementary School, Flower, Washington, 1993

Observed, planned, and taught 5th grade class—Planned and taught units in Reading, Math, and P.E.—Participated in parent conferences and staff meetings—Participated in and used Cooperative Learning while teaching in the school for the 21st Century.

EDUCATION

M.Ed., School Administration, Western Washington University, 1999
B.A., Education, University of Northern Colorado, 1993
Initial Elementary Principal Certificate, 1999

CONTINUING EDUCATION

Seattle Pacific University, 30 hr, Spring 2003: CEU 1276 Management of Behavior Problem Children
Salish Kootenai College, 4 CEU, Spring 2000: CEN 180 The Heart of Leadership

PROFESSIONAL DEVELOPMENT

Enhancing Your Effectiveness as an Elementary School Principal	Bureau of Education and Research	Winter 2003
Using Discipline with Dignity	NBI, Inc., Otter Pond Institute	Winter 2003
Nonviolent Crisis Intervention	Annwald School District	Winter 2002
Processes and Practices of Staff Evaluations	Annwald School District	Fall 2002
Success for All Reading Program	Annwald School District	Fall 2002
Summer Reading Institute	Northwest ESD 189	Summer 2002
Incorporating Essential Learning	Northwest ESD 189	Spring 2002
Kinderroots Training	Annwald School District	Winter 2001
Family Support Team	Annwald School District	Fall 2001
Building Principal as Instructional Leader	Northwest ESD 189	Fall 2001
Success for All Reading Program	Annwald School District	Fall 2001
Special Education and the Law	U.W. Law Division	Fall 2001
School-Wide Positive Discipline	Northwest ESD 189	Spring 2001
Pre-employment Interviewing	WSPA Olympia ESD 114	Spring 2001
Working with High-Risk Kids	Recovery Foundation	Spring 2000
Staff and Community Relations	American Tribal School	Spring 1999
Assertive Discipline	American Tribal School	Fall 1998

PROFESSIONAL MEMBERSHIPS

National Association of Elementary School Principals (NAESP)
Association of Washington School Principals (AWSP)
American Association of School Administrators (AASA)
Association for Supervision and Curriculum Development (ASCD)
National Indian School Board Association (NISBA)
National Indian Education Association (NIEA)

SPECIAL INTERESTS

Reading—Golf—Skiing—Swimming—Aerobics—Music

RESUME 76: BY JENNIFER RUSHTON, CRW

SCOTT CREIGHTON JAMES

345 Evergreen Terrace,
Beaverton, OR 97007   ScottCJ@aol.com   Home: (503) 662-7177
    Fax: (503) 662-8901

PRINCIPAL – ELEMENTARY EDUCATION

Skilled educator and excellent communicator with a strong, decisive, and established teaching style. Extensive training and experience in education and administration, coupled with skills in coaching, observation, and supervision of education professionals.

Sound knowledge of elementary education and broad-based experience creating and implementing dynamic interactive programs to reach new goals. Ability to forge strong, sustainable relationships with parents, students, and faculty members. Solid track record of success and demonstrated expertise in the following areas:

- ☑ Multi-Age Education
- ☑ Multiple Intelligence
- ☑ Integrated Instruction
- ☑ Technology Integration
- ☑ Cognitive Coaching
- ☑ Cooperative Learning
- ☑ Classroom Management
- ☑ Collaborative Decision Making
- ☑ Individualized Instruction
- ☑ Leadership/Team Building
- ☑ Balanced Literacy Program
- ☑ Budgeting/Forecasting

QUALIFICATIONS

UNIVERSITY OF PHOENIX   **Master of Education** (1999)
Major: Education Administration

UNIVERSITY OF NORTHERN IOWA   **Bachelor of Arts** (1994)
Major: Elementary Education

PROFESSIONAL LICENSE: State of Oregon — Initial Administrator License ALL LVL; Basic Elementary Teacher License

State of Arizona — Standard Elementary Education, K–8; Principal

PROFESSIONAL EXPERIENCE

BRENTWOOD SCHOOL/CAHLAN LEARNING COMMUNITIES, INC. — Oregon   Feb 1999–PRESENT
Principal

Reporting directly to Southwest Executive Director for private schools while supervising a staff of 35. Specific areas of responsibility include all aspects of the educational program; staff hiring and evaluation; program development; extended day and summer camp program implementation; budgeting; payroll administration; financial management; school marketing campaign development; student recruitment and retention; accreditation; and state licensing.

Key Contributions:

➤ Instrumental in designing and implementing a school improvement model, resulting in **100% of 3rd and 5th grade students meeting the standards in all areas of the Oregon Statewide Test;** in mathematics the number of students exceeding the standards increased from 36% to 82% in 3rd grade and from 50% to 78% in 5th grade.

➤ Spearheaded accreditation process, resulting in **Brentwood School being awarded Accreditation With Merit** and a $500 grant award for outstanding student achievement.

➤ **Improved communications** through the development and establishment of Brentwood's first School Parent Organization. Provided parents with a framework for discussing issues and school programs, while offering support to teachers, administration, and children.

SCOTT CREIGHTON JAMES   CONFIDENTIAL   1

Solid achievements are shown for every position, from classroom teacher through elementary principal.

PROFESSIONAL EXPERIENCE, CONTINUED...

- ➢ **Implemented a budget reduction plan** following Oregon school experiencing budget shortfalls after the opening of a new building. Successfully reduced operating costs and froze salaries and wages **without negatively impacting classroom size, program materials, or teacher support.**
- ➢ **Introduced staff-development programs** to support the implementation of Dr Arthur Costa's "Habits of Mind" model, a theoretical model that continues to be a strong part of Brentwood's school improvement plan.
- ➢ **Led management and relocation of preschool program to new facility,** resulting in a successful modern facility with 5 classrooms, multipurpose room, library, and kitchen nearing enrollment capacity.

FORRESTER ELEMENTARY / ROYAL UNIFIED SCHOOL DISTRICT — Arizona   Mar 1997–Jan 1999
Coordinator of Student Management/Dean of Students

- ➢ Collaborated with Forrester's central office administration in **developing and training staff in an extensive Crisis Management Plan** to ensure school safety and security on campus.
- ➢ **Created fair and consistent behavior management plans,** placing responsibility for appropriate behavior on students. Worked directly with students, parents, and staff to assist in solving student issues, arrange for counseling, and follow district discipline protocols.
- ➢ **Established a 20-member Student Safety Patrol due to high levels of violent behavior.** Patrol provided upper elementary students with an opportunity to develop leadership skills, act as positive role models for younger students, and create a sense of school pride.

ASHLEY HILLS ELEMENTARY/ BEVERLEY SCHOOL DISTRICT — Oregon   Sept 1993–Mar 1997
2nd Grade Teacher/4th Grade Teacher

- ➢ **Appointed Building Representative on District Mathematics Review Committee,** responsible for the successful development of a revised mathematics curriculum and participation in the development of staff development models.
- ➢ **Served as member of Child Study Team,** responsible for working with teachers on the development of intervention programs for children, prior to special education evaluation.

PROFESSIONAL DEVELOPMENT

Early Literacy ◆ Leadership Lake Oswego ◆ Teaching With Love & Logic ◆ Teaching for Intelligent Behavior ◆ Habits of Mind ◆ Assisting At-Risk Students ◆ Creating Multiple Assessments for Multiple Intelligences ◆ Mediated Learning, Modifiable Intelligence & Mind States ◆ Holonomy: The Five States of Mind & Creating Dispositions for Learning ◆ Creating a Strategic Plan for the Mindful School ◆ Special Education Program Administration

PRESENTATIONS

Media & Technology in Schools — Touchstone School, Lake Oswego, Oregon	2003
Habits of Mind: An Introduction — Evergreen Academy, Bothel, Washington	2002
Is Your Child Developing Good Habits of Mind? — Touchstone School, Lake Oswego	2002

PROFESSIONAL AFFILIATIONS

Member, Association for Supervision & Curriculum Development	Current
Member, National Association for the Education of Young Children	Current

REFERENCES AVAILABLE UPON REQUEST

JAMES KLEIN
jmklein@aol.com

80-01 Queens Boulevard
Forest Hills, NY 11375

Home: (718) 275-6666
Cell: (917) 242-1111

PROFILE

Accomplished Elementary School Principal with 35+ years of comprehensive experience in the New York City Public School System. Proven ability to influence decision makers and secure annual grants totaling close to $1 million. Proactive leader and administrator with demonstrated success shaping and monitoring curriculum and boosting statewide test scores by as much as 20% over a three-year period. Areas of expertise include

- Special Education Populations
- Gifted and Talented Programs
- Community Partnerships
- Extended Day Programming
- Textbook Review

- Grant Writing
- Budgeting and Forecasting
- Staff Management and Development
- Recruitment and Retention
- Curriculum Development

PROFESSIONAL EXPERIENCE

Competitive Grants

Wish For Foundation School Library Grant, 2001–2004

Community School Programs Grant, NY State, 1992–2002

New York Cares Grant, 1992–2004

School Recognitions

Exemplary Elementary School in New York State, 2000

Improved Reading Scores, 1998

Administrator Recognitions

City Councilman's Award for Exemplary Leadership Services within the Community, 2001

P.S. 999, Queens, NY   **1988 to Present**
Principal for this 300-student elementary school with a 99% student enrollment at or below poverty level and the highest number of special education students in the district (26%). Supervise up to 30 classrooms at peak in eight grades from pre-kindergarten to sixth grade. Oversee a staff of 90, including 30 teachers; eight paraprofessionals; learning and development specialists; and administrative, cafeteria, and custodial staff. Manage annual budget of approximately $4 million.

Grants

- Negotiated and secured $850,000 library grant, one of 15 awards offered across 1,200 schools city-wide. Upgrades included the creation of a new library space, a computer multimedia center, and 7,500 new volumes of books selected by child literacy experts.

- Researched/received $110,000 annual school programs grant for ten consecutive years. Created after-school programs for seven grades using these funds.

A two-column format is used to draw attention to special activities, achievements, and recognition.

JAMES KLEIN, Page Two

- Lobbied for United Federation of Teachers Technology Center; school was selected to host one of five state-of-the-art centers city-wide dedicated to improving teacher/administrator computer-based skills.

- Competed for and awarded New York Cares Grant 12 years in a row; grant supported upgrade of school facilities and landscaping.

School Performance

- Led district in lowest percentage of level one (at risk for promotion) scores on state fourth grade reading test over a three-year period, despite having highest percentage of special education students in the district.

- Reduced number of level one fourth grade math test scores to 0%, representing a 20% shift from previous three years.

- Slashed student tardiness by approximately 20% by offering an early morning computer class incentive.

- Successfully counseled an at-risk transfer student with a previous history of multiple school infractions; reduced disciplinary action to 0%, marking a 40% decrease in total time spent on student interventions.

- Authored a comprehensive teacher instructional guide addressing five core subjects; trained 70 teachers using this tool.

- Consistently met Board of Education expectations for quality education with no occurrences of corrective action.

Community Building

- Spearheaded annual Career Day, recruiting 35–40 speakers per year for 14 consecutive years using various community outreach strategies.

Administrator Recognitions

School Guidance Award, 2000

Principal of the Year, 1997

Community School District Award for Leadership and Outstanding Parent Involvement, 1993

Teaching Recognitions

Dedicated Service to Gifted and Talented Students, 1988

Excellence in Teaching, 1988

Gifted and Talented Teacher Award, 1986

Public/Private Partnerships

A New Day Foundation

New York Cares

Smith-Jones Consulting

Queensplaza Securities Industry Corp.

Full Academic Scholarships

Columbia University, Leadership of Evolving Vision Summer Program

Harvard University, Child Development Summer Program

RESUME 77, CONTINUED

JAMES KLEIN, Page Three

<u>*Scholarships (continued)*</u>

Brooklyn College Psychological Institute, Ph.D. Program

New York University, M.Ed Administration Program

Queens College, M.Ed Program

<u>**Professional Affiliations**</u>

President, NYC Elementary School Principal's Association, 1995–Present

Vice President/Conventions Manager, NYC Elementary School Principal's Association, 1990–1995

Editor in Chief, Phi Delta Kappa Professional Newsletter, 1980–2000

Executive Board, Council of Educational Supervisors and Administrators, 1990–Present

- Built relationships with four Manhattan- and Queens-based organizations; initiated weekly mentoring and reading programs and an annual scholarship fund.

- Partnered with newly formed boutique high school with 100 students to share building space in exchange for access to program facilities and amenities.

- Selected to mentor principal of a failing school during a summer program hosted by Columbia University.

- Forged student exchange program with Mayor of Dublin, Ireland; pilot program scheduled for fall, 2005.

P.S. 888, Queens, NY   **1981 to 1988**
Sixth grade teacher for this 350-student school.
- Recipient of district-wide Gifted and Talented Program teaching award; selected from 12 applicants.

P.S. 777, Brooklyn, NY   **1975 to 1981**
Fourth grade teacher for this 305-student school.
- Selected by principal to teach the gifted and talented program students after first academic year.

P.S. 555, Bronx, NY   **1968 to 1975**
Third grade teacher for this 300-student school with a 30% population of English-as-a-second-language students.

EDUCATION

Doctoral Coursework, Psychology, *Brooklyn College Psychological Institute*
M.Ed., School Administration, *New York University*
M.Ed., Elementary School Education, *Long Island University*
B.A., Political Science, *Queens College*
Certificate, Leadership of Evolving Vision, *Columbia University*
Certificate, Child Development, *Harvard University*

Jacob D. Simmons

8118 Cresskill Road
Asheville, North Carolina 28804

Home: (828) 252-9569
Office: (828) 274-7264

Athletic Director—Higher Education or Preparatory School

Twenty-year career as collegiate and high school athletic administrator, coach, and recruiter. Consistently successful in introducing innovative administrative systems, athletic and recruitment programs, and student services. Strong leadership, communication, and student and institutional advocacy skills. Frequently conducted high school and college football clinics. Committed to holistic student development and learning. Core competencies include

- Departmental Leadership
- Player Recruitment & Admissions Support
- Budgeting & Fundraising

- Collegiate Athletic Operations
- Facility Renovation
- Hiring & Staff Development

Professional Experience

FLETCHER COUNTRY DAY SCHOOL—Asheville, North Carolina   1999–Present

Athletic Director

Direct interscholastic athletic program for this private school—grades 7 to 12—composed of 60 teams (16 sports, 700+ participants) and more than 60 coaches. Coordinate all scheduling, team travel and transportation, and procurement and care of uniforms and equipment. Recruit, hire, and develop coaching staff. Manage $750,000 in annual operating/administrative budgets and a $170,000 Booster Club budget.

Scope of responsibility encompasses operation and maintenance of 11 athletic fields, a 2,500-seat stadium with an eight-lane rubberized track, two gymnasiums, 10 tennis courts, weight room, wrestling room, and two training rooms. Supervise staff of 22, including 16 varsity head coaches and three certified athletic trainers. As Vice President of five-school conference, schedule all league contests.

❏ Won Wachovia Cup three consecutive years (2001–2003); recognized as the top private school athletic program in North Carolina.

❏ Spearheaded planning for new $16 million athletic facility. Focused department's mission and initiated allocation of resources (delivered formal group presentations and currently assist in fund-raising) to enhance program quality and increase student participation. Initiated architect search.

❏ Instituted a strength and conditioning program for all sports teams. Established strength/conditioning coach position.

❏ Created Hall of Honor, a recognition structure to acknowledge past students, coaches, and administrative staff who have contributed significantly to the school's athletic program. Established a 12-member selection committee and drafted selection criteria.

❏ Instituted a harmful substance abstinence pledge system—an education program—for all athletic team members.

❏ Established Sports Information Director position to coordinate dissemination of all athletic information to local media. Also developed a web page for the athletic program.

❏ Upgraded athletic department computer system providing an integrated network link with all departments.

❏ Directed the installation of an eight-lane rubberized track and a $170,000 renovation of a four-athletic-field complex. Also coordinated an $86,000 stadium lighting renovation project.

❏ Developed a leadership program including a 12-member Captain's Council (students) and a 10-member Athletic Advisory Council (senior coaches and athletic administrators) to promote student involvement, reduce management costs, and improve program efficiencies.

❏ Drafted a coaches' handbook and produced a parents' athletic department handbook.

Because much of a coach's success is proved by a winning record, this resume includes this important information. The keywords included in the summary show multiple areas of expertise.

RESUME 78, CONTINUED

Jacob D. Simmons   page 2

UNITED STATES NAVAL ACADEMY—Annapolis, Maryland   1978–1999

Assistant Football Coach (1982–1999)

Served initially as Junior Varsity Assistant Coach (12/82–12/86) and then as Varsity Assistant Coach (1/87–6/99). Traveled throughout New England and upstate New York to identify and recruit top talent within region. Coached Division I varsity and junior varsity running backs, place kickers, receivers, defensive backs, and special teams.

❑ During my tenure, Navy played in three Bowl games. Ground game ranked within the top five nationally, seven of eight years as running back coach.

Office Manager (12/80–6/97); **Recruiting Coordinator** (12/82–12/89)

Maintained broad-based organizational, administrative, and athletic office responsibilities for 16 years. Also directed staff of 16 (13 recruiters, three support) and managed a $250,000 annual budget. Managed nationwide recruiting activities, including coordination with admissions support program (1500 liaison/reserve officers) and an internal talent scout network. Maintained liaison between Navy Football Office and Annapolis Admissions Office, assisting in decision-making process. Planned and organized recruiting weekends for recruits and their families.

❑ Designed and launched a multi-faceted football recruitment program, including high school visitations, in-home presentations, 48-hour campus visitations, one-day open houses, and targeted direct mail. **Results:** Navy played in its first two Bowl (Cherry, 1987, and Peach, 1988) games.

❑ Directed conversion from manual to automated data management system for football office in 1986.

THE PEMBROKE SCHOOLS—Richmond, Virginia   Fall–Winter 1982

Physical Education Teacher/Senior English Assistant Teacher/Coach/Advisor

PREVIOUS EXPERIENCE:

Sales Representative, Procter and Gamble, Baltimore, Maryland   Spring 1982

Education

LONG ISLAND UNIVERSITY, C. W. Post College—Long Island, New York

❑ M.S., Counseling, 1985

UNITED STATES NAVAL ACADEMY—Annapolis, Maryland

❑ B.S., Engineering, 1976

Professional Affiliation

National Interscholastic Athletic Administrators Association

Community Activity

Member & Football Team Representative, Fellowship of Christian Athletes (1987–1999)

Professional Development

Independent School Management Athletic Director Workshop (40 hours), July 2000

Pat Sanderson

psanderson@snet.net

Home 203-488-0956 • Mobile 203-309-8909
89 Benson Drive, North Branford, CT 06471

SECONDARY EDUCATION ADMINISTRATOR

Accomplished professional with a track record of improving educational and operational performance through vision, leadership, and team building. Experience spans urban and rural school districts and includes 6 years' administrative experience complemented by 7 years' classroom teaching and extensive athletic coaching experience.

Strengths include defining goals, creating and enforcing policies, and accomplishing objectives by empowering staff. Advanced skills in scheduling classes and managing/manipulating EMIS data. Consistent record of building community and family connections. Proven ability to effect change and drive continuous improvement.

PROFESSIONAL EXPERIENCE

MILLVILLE REGIONAL JUNIOR-SENIOR HIGH SCHOOL, Millville, CT   2000–Present
Principal, 2002–Present • **Assistant Principal**, 2000–2002

Led a performance turnaround of 550-student junior-senior high school, recording substantial improvements in both measurable and intangible areas of evaluation: student attendance, test scores, state evaluations, morale, student participation, teacher engagement, and school population driven by the school's growing reputation for excellence.

Directly responsible for all personnel, curriculum, instruction, and daily operations of junior-senior high school (grades 7–12). Manage $220K budget for facilities and operations.

Challenges and Results

Lax discipline and substandard attendance (89%) were creating a poor educational environment and negatively affecting test scores. Recruited as Assistant Principal to improve these fundamentals.
- Set new discipline and attendance policies—and enforced them.
- Gained community support/culture shift through an intensive and ongoing communications campaign.
- Personally supervised after-school and Saturday detentions, becoming the visible face of the new culture.
- Encouraged attendance through meaningful incentives and recognition events.

In one year, improved attendance to state standard (93%); increased to 95.5% (highest building attendance in Essex County) by 2003–2004 school year.

School had been designated as "academic emergency" by state evaluation board. Upon promotion to Principal, designed and led multiple, aggressive initiatives to improve academic performance.
- Developed performance data on every student in the building and used data to customize tutoring and other support programs on an individual basis.
- Gained parental support through frequent personal communication.
- Implemented short-cycle assessments, aligning teaching and testing with mandated test standards and enforcing weekly reporting to allow early intervention.
- Reduced overcrowded classrooms through better scheduling and more proactive monitoring of student progress.
- Converted full-block schedule to semi-block, allowing greater freedom and flexibility for students.
- Empowered teachers, gained their support for changes, and percolated culture of performance excellence into every classroom in the building.

Delivered immediate and sustainable improvements in meeting building report-card standards:

00–01	01–02	02–03	03–04	04–05
3 of 12 (**25%**)	7 of 12 (**58%**)	11 of 12 (**92%**)	11 of 12 (**92%**)	7 of 7 (**100%**)

Improved proficiency test results—in 2003, 10th grade passed all 5 indicators with 85% and above; 9th grade passed all 5 indicators with 75% and above; 8th grade passed 4 of the 5 indicators with 75% and above.

Graduation rate improved from 75% to 86%. AP program participation grew by one-third. In open-enrollment district, student population grew from 490 to 550 students.

A Challenges and Results format is used to tell—in some detail—the story of a school turnaround. The table adds interest and gets attention.

RESUME 79, CONTINUED

Pat Sanderson   Home 203-488-0956 • Mobile 203-309-8909 • psanderson@snet.net

MILLVILLE REGIONAL HIGH SCHOOL   continued

In an era of shrinking resources, faced with managing facilities and operations on a tight budget.
- Created new system for supplies and materials—improved control and ensured equitable allocation.
- Focused attention on energy efficiency; eliminated substantial waste and saved $20K over prior year.

Came in under budget every year.

Athletic program had been operated by "seat-of-the-pants" standards and lacked proper accountability. Requested by School Board to take on concurrent position as Athletic Director (01–02 school year).
- Created new athletic policy and ensured it was followed.
- Ensured all coaching staff were properly trained and certified.
- Developed new processes for communicating athletic news to parents and the community.

Athletic participation increased by one-third.

EAST HAVEN CITY SCHOOLS, East Haven, CT   1996–2000
Site Base Manager, 1999–2000 • **Administrative Internship, Hyde Middle School,** 1999
Discipline Coordinator (7th and 8th Grades), Hyde Middle School, 1998–1999
Mathematics Instructor, Horace Mann Middle School, 1996–1998

NORTH BRANFORD SCHOOL DISTRICT, North Branford, CT   1995–1996
Elementary Teacher (4th Grade)

COGINCHAUG REGIONAL SCHOOL DISTRICT, Durham, CT   1990–1994
Mathematics and Computer Science Instructor

EDUCATION AND CERTIFICATION

UNIVERSITY OF CONNECTICUT, Storrs, CT: Master of Administrative Educational Leadership, 2005
SOUTHERN CONNECTICUT STATE UNIVERSITY, New Haven, CT: Bachelor of Science, Elementary Education

CERTIFICATIONS: Connecticut Superintendent Certificate • Connecticut Secondary Administrator Certificate

COMMITTEE PARTICIPATION

MILLVILLE REGIONAL HIGH SCHOOL: Site-Based Management Committee • Connecticut Special Education Review • Intervention Assistance Chair • Attendance Incentive Grant Committee Chair

EAST HAVEN CITY SCHOOLS: Discipline Committee Team • Nonviolent Crisis Intervention Team

NORTH BRANFORD SCHOOLS: Mentor Program • Mathematics Course of Study Revision Committee Chair

COACHING HISTORY

EAST HAVEN CITY SCHOOLS: Reserve Boys Basketball Coach • Reserve Boys Baseball Coach • Reserve Girls Softball Coach • Middle School Football Coach • Middle School Basketball Coach

EAST HAVEN CITY SCHOOLS: Varsity Boys Basketball Assistant Coach • Varsity Girls Volleyball Coach • Varsity Boys Basketball Coach—District Champions • Reserve Boys Basketball Coach

COGINCHAUG REGIONAL SCHOOL DISTRICT: Varsity Boys Basketball Assistant Coach • Reserve Boys Baseball Coach • Junior High Football Coach • Junior High Girls Basketball Coach

C O N F I D E N T I A L

CHARLOTTE KRONIG

8888 Norwood Drive
Collinsburg, Alabama 36100

334-555-5555 (Home—Central Time)
334-555-6666 (Office—Central Time)

WHAT I CAN BRING TO LAWRENCE COLLEGE AS YOUR NEWEST DIRECTOR OF STUDENT ACTIVITIES

- ❏ The **leadership** to develop and implement effective student life programs,
- ❏ The **wisdom** to guide, counsel, and support students, and
- ❏ The **integrity** to earn the trust of every constituency.

EDUCATION

- ❏ Pursuing M.S., **General Counseling,** Alabama State University, Montgomery, Alabama. *Expect graduation in the Fall of 2005.*

- ❏ B.S., **Social Work,** Tuskegee University, Tuskegee, Alabama, 1993. *Dean's List virtually every semester. Earned this degree while working up to 30 hours a week.* **Honors.**

RELEVANT WORK HISTORY WITH SELECTED EXAMPLES OF SUCCESS

- ❏ **Coordinator of Student Activities,** Green State University, Collinsburg, Alabama
  1996–Present
  GSU is an historically black university with approximately 1,600 students, 1,000 living on campus.

  Directly responsible for activities of up to 65 Greek, professional, and honor student organizations. Assistant coordinator of student activities reports directly to me.

  Transformed our underfunded, stagnant student activities program. Built strong staff, faculty, and student support campus-wide. Then expanded and integrated our programs as part of a rigorous curriculum. *Outcomes:* **More than doubled** the number of activities each academic year. **Student turnout soared** and stayed high.

  Sought out high-risk students others had tried, and failed, to integrate with our student body. Earned their trust by soliciting their ideas and then placing them in accountable leadership positions. *Outcomes:* All **improved academically and socially.** Nearly all graduated.

  Increased public relations impact of Miss ASU pageant by winning support of local businesses—a first. *Outcomes:* Winning **students** now **work confidently** with schools, churches, charities, and nursing homes. **Great payoff** for our university.

  Established my office's reputation as a place students can turn for help solving tough problems. *Outcomes:* Recently "rescued" a student who fell through the cracks of the financial aid system. Turned young person ready to quit into a successful graduate.

- ❏ **Independent Consultant,** Collinsburg, Alabama
  1987–1996

  Guided small, inward-looking, disorganized Student Government Association to improve the academic year's kickoff event. Led them to triple their representatives in the student body in just three days. Showed them how to cut planned expenses in half. *Outcomes:* **400** students **turned out**—a great start for all our students.

More indicators of performance ➲

The resume for this administrator shows capability in a support position with two constituencies: the school and its students.

RESUME 80, CONTINUED

CONFIDENTIAL

Charlotte Kronig   **Director of Student Activities**   334-555-6666 (Office)

Work history (continued):

❑ **Founder** and **Manager,** Keep Entertaining Everyday People (KEEP), Collinsburg, Alabama 1985–Present
KEEP is a non-profit organization that has established rotating partnerships with local schools. With its 28 volunteers, it provides leadership and personal development activities for up to 125 at-risk children at a time.

Built this organization with no money, no support, and no name recognition. Found and filled the needs of underprivileged children by asking them what they wanted. Then got high-visibility venues to showcase their talents. *Outcomes:* **Strong, continuing community support** lets us feature 140 community performers before standing-room-only audiences of 1,200 — **every year for 15 years.**

SELECTED CONTRIBUTIONS TO MY COMMUNITY _____

❑ List of audiences of at least 400 addressed in 2003 as a featured speaker:

D.A.R.E.	Black Caucus Conference	Urban League of Nebraska
National Tots and Teens Convention	African American Women's Conference	Black Awareness Observance, United States Air Force
Coalition of Alabamians Reforming Education	Alabama Young Authors' Conference	National Voting Rights Museum

❑ University coordinator for these key events:

Student Voter Registration Drive, 2000–2004

Student Organizations Leadership Workshops, 1998–2004

Campus and Community Black History Month Programs, 1994–2004

❑ Service on these academic support committees:

Fall Convocation, 1998–2003	Honor's Day, 1998–2003
Founder's Day, 1998–2003	Homecoming, 1998–2002
Graduation, 1998–2002	

❑ Advisorships:

Miss GSU and Court, 1998–2003	Voices of Praise Choir, 1998–2003
Founder, Office of Student Activities Assistance Team, 2001–2003	Student Government Association, 1999–2001

PROFESSIONAL ASSOCIATIONS _____

❑ Alabama Counseling Association

❑ Business and Professional Women's Club of Collinsburg

CONFIDENTIAL

Page two

JOHN BRYAN ATKINS

345 Evergreen Terrace
Milton Mills, NH 03852

jbatkins@aol.com

Home: (603) 292–7404
Home Fax: (603) 292–7405

PROGRAM SPECIALIST

Dedicated to the development and education of all students

Highly skilled professional dedicated to making a positive impact on students' lives by creating an atmosphere conducive to learning. Cater to diverse learning modalities to promote and enhance individual student strengths, instilling in youth a love of knowledge and the desire to meet and exceed expectations. Skilled in the use of positive reinforcement, communication, and problem-solving to establish outstanding rapport with students. Exceptional team-builder and leader, creating a strong sense of community for students and staff.

- ☑ Progress Monitoring
- ☑ Classroom Management
- ☑ Curriculum Design & Development
- ☑ Visual & Tactile Learning Methods
- ☑ Individual Educational Plans (IEPs)
- ☑ Budget Planning
- ☑ Student Motivation
- ☑ Parental Involvement
- ☑ Vocational Development
- ☑ Team Building Techniques

QUALIFICATIONS

Bachelor of Science, Special Education
UNIVERSITY OF MAINE, Orono, Maine

2003

EDUCATIONAL EXPERIENCE

GABE FOUNDATION SCHOOL — *Ogunquit, Maine*   1996 to PRESENT
Program Specialist
Report directly to Director of Special Education for this private school, developing educational programs; researching and developing curriculum; writing IEPs; attending meetings in accordance with IDEA; teaching integrated curriculum; interacting with school districts; and managing classrooms.

Program/Curriculum Development

- Initiated and implemented three educational programs for at-risk youth, actively engaging students and creating programs to satisfy the school's growing referral base.
- Independently developed curriculum for elk-farming program, enabling students to run the day-to-day operation of the elk herd, including TB testing, worming, and cutting velvet.
- Taught an integrated curriculum in all content areas by adapting curriculum to accommodate vastly diverse functioning levels, accelerating achievement of educational objectives.
- Expanded programs to serve more students and promote active learning; started new programs (aquaculture) and added new themes to current programs (scuba diving, boat building).

Student Learning/Interaction

- Collaborated with students in resolving Fish & Wildlife concerns about contamination of local fish populations with the importation of tilapia. After 2 years of fighting, students received permits to import and raise tilapia.
- Provided a more structured and intense reading program, increasing student interest and learning in reading.
- Encourage student involvement in their local community through the implementation of community projects. This year's project involved building offices in a community center. Past projects included developing a park, building a bandstand, and roofing town buildings.

To position a business professional for a career transition, this resume presents extensive and highly relevant volunteer experience ahead of actual paid work experience.

JOHN BRYAN ATKINS   Page 2

Educational Experience, Continued

- Directed the foundation's Fertile Farm Program, providing tutoring for up to 14 students diagnosed with ADHD, ADD, and Bipolar.

Communication/Relationship Building

- Collaborated with parents, fellow teachers, and school-based support team members to develop IEPs, enabling all students to progress towards individual goals.
- Develop and maintain professional business relationships with district administrators to ensure adherence to IDEA by attending meetings and interacting with Directors and Superintendents in 7 school districts in 2 states.

RIVERTON SCHOOL — *Wells, Maine*   1991 to 1996
Substitute Teacher — Special Education Aide — Shop Teacher

- Substituted all grades in art, music, and gym, creating and implementing lessons in the absence of lesson plans to support student academic, social, and personal development.
- Provided tutoring to behaviorally disordered special needs students to enhance student learning and understanding of subject matter. Ensured effective behavior management by incorporating motivational activities and positive reinforcement strategies.
- Instrumental in developing middle-school woodworking shop program, creating educational activities to make learning enjoyable and exciting.
- Transported students with handicapped conditions, ensuring the safety of all students.

PROFESSIONAL EXPERIENCE

ATKINS ELK FARM — *Milton Mills, New Hampshire*   1976 to PRESENT
Business Owner/Manager

- Engage special-needs students in educational activities to make learning enjoyable and exciting; transport students to and from the elk farm, allowing them to interact with animals.
- Manage and execute all operational processes for 20-head elk farm, including managing aquaculture hatching and grow out facility.
- Appointed as manager by the State of Maine to operate the abused farm animal facility, ensuring the proper care and well being of the animals.

CERTIFICATIONS

Vocational Special Needs

PROFESSIONAL AFFILIATIONS

Member, North American Riding for the Handicapped Association (NARHA)

REFERENCES AVAILABLE UPON REQUEST

RESUME 82: BY LORETTA HECK

JOHN P. NORTON

Route 5, Box 99, Sparta, Wisconsin 54656
Home (608) 269-1515 — Office (608) 269-3908 — E-mail: john-norton@one.net

SUPERINTENDENT: SPARTA AREA SCHOOL DISTRICT

PHILOSOPHY OF ADMINISTRATION

The primary purpose of educational administration is to provide an environment in which individuals can work together cooperatively to serve the needs of students through accomplishing the goals of the institution. Administration should be a democratically oriented process designed to foster an atmosphere in which staff members assist one another, plan together, and freely exchange ideas. A structure must be developed that allows people to participate in the decision-making process. People grow as they attempt to solve problems and seek answers to questions. Administrators should encourage staff participation to increase the possibility of many people being able to secure the kind of interaction through which they share and grow through the interchange of ideas. Relating to subordinates in a democratic manner fosters the development of high staff morale and creates the group cohesiveness necessary for the educational improvement of a school district.

CAREER HISTORY

Superintendent of Schools	Sparta Area School District, Sparta, WI	1994–Present
	Truman Community Schools, Truman, MN	1991–1994
	Winnebago Community Schools, Winnebago, MN	1985–1991
	East Greene Community Schools, Grand Junction, IA	1983–1985
	Ringsted Community Schools, Ringsted, IA	1982–1983
Principal	Des Moines Christian School, Des Moines, IA	1980–1982
Guidance Counselor	Calvert County Schools, Prince Frederick, MD	1978–1980
Teacher	Bradford Area Schools, Bradford, PA — Sixth Grade	1975–1978

EDUCATION

Doctor of Education	University of South Dakota, Vermillion, SD Major: Educational Administration	1990
Educational Administration	Iowa State University, Ames, IA Non-degree program	1982
Master of Science	Saint Bonaventure University, Saint Bonaventure, NY Major: Guidance and Counseling	1978
Bachelor of Science	Bryan College, Dayton, TN Major: Elementary Education	1975
Credentials are on file at:	Teacher Placement Office Saint Bonaventure University, Saint Bonaventure, NY	

Rather than detail job duties and accomplishments, this resume leads off with a Philosophy of Administration and follows with a CV-style listing of employment and experience.

RENE HARBOR

23515 Oak Tree Drive, Newhall, California 91321   661-259-7990

ASSISTANT PRINCIPAL / DEAN OF STUDENTS / COORDINATOR / EDUCATOR / TRAINER offering expertise in the development and teaching of educational programs designed to meet a broad cross-section of learner needs. Experience in teaching, project development, and behavioral management. Counseling and training abilities. Excellent administrative, interpersonal, and communication skills, as well as expertise in identifying instructional requirements and developing effective course curriculum. Positive motivator skilled in educating both student and adult learners. Conversational Spanish.

EDUCATION AND CREDENTIALS

Master of Arts, Educational Administration, University of Southern California
Bachelor of Arts, History, minor in Spanish, University of California, Los Angeles

Certifications: **Administrative Services**
                     Standard Supervision (Life)
                     General Secondary (Life)

ACCOMPLISHMENTS

- **Focus on Learning Pilot WASC Accreditation Process.** Interpreted guidelines set by the state of California; analyzed process; developed methodology and materials to implement these guidelines; and provided individualized training to staff, students, and parents. Currently providing training, guidance, and materials to a second district high school.

- **Coordinator for Categorical Programs** (Gifted and Talented Education/Advanced Placement/ESL). Guided programs successfully through a period of tremendous growth in quality, enrollment, and curriculum.

- **Expanded and refined school curricula.**

- **Directed significant increase in staff development activities,** including the concept of "teachers training teachers."

PROFESSIONAL EXPERIENCE

Assistant Principal — DALE HIGH SCHOOL, Dale United School District, Newhall, CA   1993–Present

Curriculum/
Instruction
- Supervise instructional goals and objectives. With staff, develop new course offerings in areas of foreign languages, science, math, social studies, ESL sheltered classes, and instructional teaming.
- Direct staff, manage operational budgets, and coordinate activities for GATE, ESL, SB 1882 Staff Development, Advanced Placement, Summer School, and SASI administrative computer system.
- Recently directed development of the Dale High *Vision, Beliefs,* and *Expected School-wide Learning Results.*
- Develop master schedule.
- Supervise Library Services.
- Actively interview, evaluate, and recruit instructional staff.
- Serve as committee member to select Dale District Mentor Teachers.

Given the lengthy listing of job duties needed to fully describe the scope of responsibility in each position, accomplishments are set off in a separate section to ensure that they aren't overlooked.

RENE HARBOR   Page Two

Staff Development

- Use site-based management principles to support teachers' participation in the decision-making process and assume ownership for school results.
- Work closely with teachers to instill the confidence necessary to perform effectively.
- Provide common planning time for staff to better coordinate curriculum.
- Conduct regularly scheduled performance reviews for certificated and classified staff.
- Supervise and coordinate work of chairpersons of staff development committees.

Plant Management/Daily Operations

- Supervise maintenance and custodial staff; redefined performance standards for custodial staff.
- Schedule all facility utilization.
- Handle all repair and maintenance requests and supervise plant manager in their implementation.
- Oversee school master calendar, key distribution, telephone system, daily bulletin, marquee, and printing.
- Regularly publish a newsletter to keep parents informed about school activities, events, and general information. Facilitated technological upgrade in presentation.

Guidance Services

- Supervise counseling staff.
- Manage all Registrar's office functions, ROP Program, and Career Center.
- Member, Crisis Intervention Team.
- Coordinate all school-site testing programs.

Instructor — UNIVERSITY OF LAVERNE, LaVerne, CA   1994–Present
Teach course entitled Field Work in Educational Administration.   (Concurrently)

Prior to 1994
Assistant Principal — Sierra Madre Junior High School, Wm. S. Dale U.S.D., Canyon Country
Dean of Students — Voyota High School, Dale United School District, Saugus
Dean of Girls — Dale High School, Dale United School District, Newhall
Dean of Girls — Grant High School, San Fernando Valley, Los Angeles Unified District
Social Studies Teacher — Grant High School, San Fernando Valley, Los Angeles Unified District
Social Worker — All Nations Neighborhood Center, East Los Angeles

PROFESSIONAL AFFILIATIONS

Phi Delta Kappa
Women in Educational Leadership
USC Educational Alumni
Association of California School Administrators,
    Santa Clarita Chapter — Staff Development Award
Dale District Management Association — Past President,
    Vice President, Secretary, Salary & Benefits Chairperson

Member, WASC High School Accreditation Teams
    Montebello High School, Montebello
    Troy High School, Fullerton
    Bishop School, La Jolla
    Granite Hills High School, San Diego

COMMUNITY ACTIVITIES

Assistance League, Santa Clarita Valley   UCLA Alumni Association

LAWRENCE S. COSTNER

Home: (407) 380-1654
Office: (407) 381-5413

2764 Gray Fox Lane
Orlando, Florida 32826

ACADEMIC ADMINISTRATOR

Accomplished professional with a diversified background in academic administration and secondary education. Consistently successful in introducing strategic marketing and operational plans, athletic programs, and student services to increase enrollment, enhance the student experience, and strengthen competitive market position. Strong leadership, communication, student, and institutional advocacy skills. Areas of expertise:

• Finance / Capital Development	• Enrollment	• Financial Aid
• Curriculum Development	• Student Affairs	• Team Development
• Fundraising	• Public Relations	• Foundation Management

PROFESSIONAL EXPERIENCE

SAINT PETER'S HIGH SCHOOL, Orlando, Florida   1995 to Present

Principal

Senior Academic Administrator with full autonomy and financial accountability for a private high school. Challenged to turn around this distressed school on the brink of closing. Scope of responsibility was diverse and included all phases of administration and management, strategic planning, capital and budget development and administration, foundation management, fundraising, staffing and personnel functions, curriculum development and implementation, and public relations. Direct a staff of 25 teachers, one business manager/bookkeeper, and four administrative staff. Led improvements within all areas returning school to financial stability.

Management / Finance
- Reversed a deficit budget within five years and currently manage a $2 million budget with a surplus.
- Improved discipline, morale, and the entire campus environment, elevating integrity and esteem.
- Established a collaborative administrative council to analyze and improve the curriculum and academic program.
- Led a capital campaign to establish two new science laboratories and numerous renovations throughout the school.
- Introduced new technology systems throughout the administrative offices and classrooms.

Curriculum
- Instituted a gifted program and eight Advanced Placement classes. Improved the foreign language and science programs.
- Established a Curriculum Development Committee to consistently review and upgrade course offerings.
  Results: 98% of the students now go on to higher education, and students consistently score above the state and national averages on standardized tests.

Athletics
- Led a complete upgrade of the Athletic Program and developed teams that now compete in state championships.
- Doubled the Co-curricular Athletic Program.

Admissions & Enrollment
- Built enrollment to record highs (from 230 to more than 350), producing the largest freshman and graduating classes ever. Increased enrollment by 33%.

Breaking down a long list of accomplishments into subsections is a good way to increase their impact and ensure nothing gets overlooked.

LAWRENCE S. COSTNER   Page 2

SAINT PETER'S HIGH SCHOOL (Continued):

Foundation Management / Financial Aid
- Restored shattered relationship with foundation donor and merited an additional $1 million in foundation funds.
- Increased financial aid from $70,000 to $130,000 annually.
- Elevated overall student education scores, attracting more than $2 million in scholarships for over half of the 60 graduating students (1998).

Fundraising
- Raised more than $250,000 annually, in a low-income community, to supplement the school's operating budget.

Public Relations
- Initiated articulation meetings with principals and teachers from feeder schools to better coordinate and improve total academic program.
- Established a Student Ambassador Program to assist with public relations and fundraising functions and represent the school throughout the community.

ORANGE CATHOLIC COLLEGE PREPARATORY, Princeton, New Jersey   1974 to 1995

Assistant Principal of Student Affairs (1992 to 1995)
Athletic Director (1976 to 1991) — **Teacher, Social Science** (1974 to 1991)

Transitioned through all phases of academic administration for this 650-student private college preparatory school. As Assistant Principal of Student Affairs:

- Held management positions including Dean of Students, Director of Student Activities, Student Government Moderator, and Core Administrator responsible for daily operations.
- Served on the Advisory Board and several committees, including Finance, Admissions, Planning, and Curriculum Development.
- Appointed Summer School Principal with full responsibility for academic program and curriculum.

As Athletic Director, held responsibility for the supervision of 35 interscholastic teams and 56 coaching personnel. Managed athletic budget and equipment, student eligibility, coach hiring and evaluations, and individual/team records.

- Elevated the total athletic program to one of the top programs in New Jersey.
- Doubled the size of the girls' program.

As Social Science Teacher, taught U.S. History, Civics (Mock Convention), World History, South East Asian History, Geography, Street Law (Mock Trial), Contemporary Issues, and Leadership.

EDUCATION

Masters, Educational Administration	Stetson University, DeLand, Florida, 1993
Administrative Services Credential	Stetson University, DeLand, Florida, 1989
Florida State Teaching Credential (Standard Lifetime)	State of Florida, 1979
History, Physical Education	
B.A., History	Princeton University, Princeton, New Jersey, 1974

PROFESSIONAL AFFILIATIONS

National Association of Secondary School Principals
Florida Association of School Administrators
Association for Supervision and Curriculum Development

Gwendoline J. Tober

Confidential Resume

442 Georgetown Drive, Lake Erie, Ohio 43460 • 419.667.9999
Email: gjt_eriehs@lakeerie.edu

SECONDARY ADMINISTRATOR / EDUCATOR

Education administrator with more than 20 years of experience leading faculty and students. Expertise in development and implementation of school improvement and curriculum programs that impact accomplishment of district-wide strategic planning goals. Lifetime commitment to quality education programs that emphasize the personal development of students. Ability to apply creative thinking skills toward short- and long-range goals.

AREAS OF ADMINISTRATIVE STRENGTH

Community Involvement & Leadership ~ Administrative & Board Relations ~ Block Scheduling
Curriculum & Program Development ~ Staff Training & Development ~ Outcomes Accreditation
Strategic Planning ~ Budget Analysis ~ Student Needs Assessment ~ Special Education Programs
Grant Writing ~ Continuous Education ~ Staff Development & Training ~ Contract Negotiations

CAREER PROFILE

ERIE HIGH SCHOOL (Lake Erie School District) – Lake Erie, Ohio   1992–Present
High School Principal

Located in NW Ohio, Lake Erie School District consists of 2,200 students with 725 enrolled in grades 9–12. The mission of the high school is based on a partnership with the community that emphasizes the personal development of each student through a unified academic program promoting life-long learning skills and enhancing social responsibility and employability.

Guide and direct all aspects of administration and instruction at the high-school level. Promote a team-building atmosphere and delegate through a staff comprising assistant principal, department chairs, 50 full-time certified instructors, guidance counselors, and education support staff. Work closely with school psychologist, food service, transportation, and building and maintenance staff. Charged with full budget responsibilities for high school and athletic complex.

- Gained marked improvement in student ACT scores with increases being recorded 6 years in a row. Currently scores are at their highest level.
- Direct strong curriculum and instruction programs resulting in increased student performance on state proficiency tests at an accelerated rate compared to similar schools in the state.
- Facilitated successful program development to achieve Outcomes Endorsement from North Central Association in 1997.
- Spearheaded development and implementation of a block-scheduling program that has been in successful operation since 1996.
- Oversee and monitor grant programs such as Pacesetter, Venture Capital, and Systemic Improvement.
- Coordinate and supervise student teachers in liaison with two local universities.

After retiring from the school district where she had spent 12 productive years, this administrator used this resume to land a senior administrative position with a school district in another state.

GWENDOLINE J. TOBER...continued

SCHOOL ACHIEVEMENTS & HIGHLIGHTS

- Erie High School was the first school in NW Ohio to pursue advanced accreditation status from North Central Association known as the Outcomes Endorsement.
- First school in NW Ohio to institute a successful block scheduling program.
- Highlighted twice in local newspaper for one of the most successful and aggressive School Improvement Programs in the state.
- Erie High School nominated for Ohio's Best Award.

PERSONAL CAREER ACHIEVEMENTS & HIGHLIGHTS

- Elected to serve as member of the Ohio State Committee for North Central Association of Colleges and Secondary Schools 1998–2001.
- Invited to share knowledge and expertise regarding the Outcomes Endorsement process and challenges with other school accreditation teams throughout the state.
- Frequently invited to make presentations and facilitate programs at school and education group functions in Ohio concerning school improvement efforts.
- Recipient of Lake Erie School District's "Golden Apple" award.
- Orchestrated development of district-wide Health Team & Safety Plan.
- Member of District Strategic Planning and Continuous Improvement Teams.

BURLINGTON HIGH SCHOOL – Deer Run, Ohio   1987–1992
Associate Principal / Director of Student Activities

BAYSIDE HIGH SCHOOL – Bayside, Ohio   1984–1987
Assistant Principal
Athletic Administrator / NHS Advisor / Senior Class Advisor / Yearbook Business Manager

Note: Prior experience as a Secondary Social Studies Instructor is available upon request.

EDUCATION / ADDITIONAL TRAINING

Bowling Green State University, Bowling Green, Ohio ~ Post-Graduate Work
Additional hours in Administration and Supervision / Ohio CEUs (1985–Present)

Bowling Green State University, Bowling Green, Ohio ~ Master of Education (1984)
Major: Administration and Supervision

Miami University, Oxford, Ohio ~ Bachelor of Arts (1982) ~ Major: History ~ Minor: Education

Participated in numerous educational training and leadership seminars.

LICENSES / CERTIFICATIONS

Ohio Certification in: High School Principal – through 2009
Comprehensive Social Studies (7–12) – Permanent

PROFESSIONAL MEMBERSHIPS

Ohio Association of Secondary School Administrators
North Central Association of Colleges & Secondary Schools
Phi Delta Kappa Education Honorary ~ Phi Alpha Theta History Honorary

SARAH A. BALLARD

Home: (615) 532-8064

1210 Burkland Road—Goodlettsville, Tennessee 37072

Email: SBallard@aol.com

PROFESSIONAL OVERVIEW

- More than 20 years of combined experience in the areas of **TEACHING, COUNSELING, STAFF AND PROGRAM DEVELOPMENT,** and **ADMINISTRATION.**

- Flexible and easy-going with the ability to quickly develop a good rapport and put students—of all ages—at ease.

- Strong ability to teach, motivate, and counsel children and adults—in a training, tutorial, or classroom environment—to excel in both personal and professional development.

- Well-versed and proficient in the design and development of instructional programs and curriculum to meet organizational goals and student needs.

- An accomplished change agent with an established track record in getting positive results working with students, parents, faculty, administrators, and community.

ACADEMIC BACKGROUND

Doctor of Philosophy—Program and Staff Development—1999
Middle Tennessee State University—Murfreesboro

Master of Arts Degree in Education—Emphasis: Guidance Counseling—1986
Tennessee State University—Nashville

Teacher Certification in Grades K–12—1981

Bachelor of Science Degree in Secondary Education—Emphasis: History—1981
Belmont University—Nashville, Tennessee

PROFESSIONAL EXPERIENCE

PRINCIPAL / TEACHER Grades 7–8—1995 to Present
The Hightower School—Nashville, Tennessee

Effectively manage daily operations of private elementary school with a population of 150 students in grades K–8. Hands-on involvement with faculty and staff development, curriculum development, ordering textbooks and materials, budget, and fundraising. As Head Teacher, taught 7th–8th grade combined class of 26–30 students. Subjects included social studies, science, 8th grade math, and Bible.

- Enrich the quality of education by identifying and nurturing the needs of individual students. Challenge their abilities and encourage them to set higher goals.

- As a member of the Building Committee, gained valuable experience in planning and designing state-of-the-art elementary school aimed at effectively combining the space needs of both students and teachers, and which ultimately served as a model school for other districts.

A distinctive headline font is used to add interest to the Times New Roman font used for the rest of the resume. This is a clear, well-organized, easy-to-absorb resume for an experienced administrator.

SARAH A. BALLARD   PAGE 2

PROFESSIONAL EXPERIENCE (CONTINUED)

ASSISTANT PROFESSOR OF EDUCATION—1986 to 1995
University of the Midwest—Dubuque, Iowa

Developed highly successful pilot program to train student teachers how to efficiently organize and present all subjects to grades 1–8 in a one-room school setting. Established a one-room lab school used in training and evaluation.

- Significantly raised the percentage of student teachers that stayed with the teaching district (from 78% to 95%).

- After receiving national media exposure, the lab school became a model one-room school for rural school districts nationwide.

TEACHER Grades 6–8—1981 to 1986
Belmont Junior Academy—Nashville, Tennessee

Taught 7th–8th grade social studies and English (1984–86). Taught 6th grade self-contained classroom (1982–84). Supervised homeroom for 6th grade and taught 6th–8th grade social studies (1981–82).

- Reached and motivated academically challenged students and turned them around by providing one-on-one attention.

PROFESSIONAL AFFILIATIONS

Association of Supervision and Curriculum Development—1990 to Present

Nashville Area Chamber of Commerce—1995 to Present

PERSONAL INTERESTS

Visiting historical sites … Genealogy and family history … Reading … Spectator sports

Sandi Palmer

1202 Coolidge Drive • Atherton, IA 50010 • (515) 297-3904 • sandi1436@aol.com

Objective

A position as Director of Education at Sylvan Learning Center that will fully utilize strong leadership abilities, innovative organizational skills, and sound instruction and learning techniques that motivate children to become independent, life-long learners.

Professional Profile

Personal Motto: "Classroom management is the key to successful teaching."

- Organized, take-charge education professional with strong follow-through ability and excellent management skills; able to plan and oversee projects from concept to successful conclusion.
- Motivated, high-energy educator with strong track record of fostering student creativity and responsibility while enhancing learning.
- Effectively prioritize a broad range of responsibilities in order to consistently meet deadlines.
- Develop excellent rapport with individuals at all levels—strong interpersonal skills.
- Provide individualized instruction based on student's need as the situation dictates.
- Actively supervise and mentor numerous block students and student teachers.

Experience

Lower Elementary Teacher
Atherton Community School District, Atherton, IA, 1974–present

Teach full academic curriculum at first, second, and third grade levels. Strong emphasis on reading, writing, and mathematics. Write curricula; assess and evaluate student performance; design report cards; and maintain excellent communication with students, parents, and staff.

Instruction
- Encourage students to make responsible choices by teaching consequences. Consistency of follow-through is key.
- Provide classroom training, performance evaluation, and motivation as a mentor to student teachers completing college requirements for an education degree.
- Develop and integrate classroom enrichment activities such as research projects in the library, Internet research, reading to younger children, and playing games related to regular curriculum.
- Motivate students through rewards system—earn play money or fines to be used in various ways. Earn opportunity to e-mail family or friends about successes.
- Integrate computer technology into the classroom; designed two unique web pages; established e-mail accounts for communication needs between students, parents, and teacher.

continued on page two

This resume uses a subtle watermark of a desk and apple to distinguish this administrator from other candidates. She made it through two intense interviews to become a finalist for the position described in the Objective.

Sandi Palmer

Experience *(continued)*

Analysis/Planning

- Appointed by administration for lengthy terms on reading and math curriculum teams. Developed, validated, and enhanced curriculums for both subjects.
- Served three-year term on Building Level Team. Represented staff in site-based management approach; evaluated and implemented new ideas presented by staff; planned staff development days and faculty meetings.
- Designed three diverse report cards that reflected school philosophy and needs of staff.

Education

Bachelor of Arts, University of Northern Iowa, Cedar Falls, IA (formerly State College of Iowa) Major: Education with emphasis on math.

Attend Continuing Education courses at Iowa State University, University of Northern Iowa, Drake University, and Heartland Area Education Agency.

Organizations

Atherton Community Education Association (ACEA), 1974–present
- Served two terms as president.
- Streamlined meeting procedures to effectively utilize time.
- Represented teachers on negotiations team; negotiated contract for certified staff.

P.E.O., Atherton, IA, 1989–present
- Current president of 50-member organization; served two previous terms as president.
- Increased attendance at meetings through positive one-on-one communications.
- Sponsored International Peace Scholar through fund-raisers.
- Donated to ACCESS and sponsored a team in the 8-Hour Run for Life (cancer).

RESUME 88: BY VIVIAN BELEN, NCRW, CPRW, JCTC

EMILY RAPPAPORT
111 River Drive ■ Park Ridge, NJ 07656 ■ (201) 695-2498 ■ erap@aol.com

EDUCATIONAL PUBLISHING/MATERIALS DEVELOPMENT

Highly qualified reading specialist offers accomplishments in publishing instructional reading materials.... Possess a strong background in classroom/remedial instruction.... Author of children's stories.

——*Areas of Expertise*——
Children's Literature—Curriculum Development—Staff Training
Print Production—Copyright Negotiations—Contracts

EDUCATION/PROFESSIONAL:

Montclair University, Upper Montclair, NJ—**MA DEGREE**/Certified Reading Specialist
William Paterson University, Wayne, NJ—**BA DEGREE**/Elementary Education
Education Association, New York, NY—Programs in Self Development & Communication
    Self Expression & Leadership Program   Communication: Access to Power I & II
    The Forum   Advanced Course in Communication
Beta Chi Chapter of Pi Lambda Theta, National Honor Professional Association in Education
State of New Jersey Certification: Reading Specialist/Reading Teacher (K–12)/Elementary Education

PUBLISHING EXPERIENCE:

NATIONAL STUDY SKILLS, INC., Paramus, NJ   2000–2004
A national supplemental learning program that emphasizes self-learning through repeated practice.

Coordinator/Materials Development & Instruction

Designed and developed instructional reading materials along with instructor's manual for use in more than 900 math and reading centers in North America.

- Recruited to set up new reading department at U.S. headquarters, servicing both advanced and remedial levels from preschool through high school.

- Produced three anthologies and four workbooks, including skills exercises and supporting literature—first-of-their-kind materials for this organization.

- Conducted extensive research to locate appropriate literature. Successfully negotiated contracts with publishers for rights to reproduce.

- Directed production of anthologies, coordinating with printers, illustrators and typesetters. Ensured that drawings conveyed a multicultural image and set a tone of egalitarianism.

- Authored original stories designed to accommodate Kumon instructional methodologies.

- Developed the corporation's recommended reading list for elementary school level.

- Spearheaded implementation of new reading materials by conducting training programs for regional managers and instructional staff. Presented an overview at national conference.

- Evaluated effectiveness of materials through on-site observations at several centers. Received excellent feedback from senior instructors.

Continued.....

Note how this individual's educational publishing qualifications—her primary area of expertise—are enhanced by extensive teaching experience, detailed on page 2.

EMILY RAPPAPORT   Page 2

(201) 695-2498

TEACHING EXPERIENCE:

LANGUAGE GROUP, Fort Lee, NJ   1991–2000
ESL Teacher (Part-Time)
- Assignments included accent reduction classes at Kean College as well as one-on-one training with international corporate clients.
- Made presentations to executive management of corporations to assess needs and develop English language training programs for their staff.

EAST ORANGE BOARD OF EDUCATION, East Orange, NJ   1998–1999
Developmental Reading Teacher
- Incorporated Bloom's Taxonomy of Higher Order Thinking (HOTS) into reading curriculum. Increased students' critical thinking skills.
- Initiated cooperative learning skills to enhance listening, verbal, thinking and writing skills. Facilitated improved group interaction.

PARAMUS BOARD OF EDUCATION, Paramus, NJ   1996–1998
Reading Teacher/Supplemental Reading Teacher
- Participated in pilot program to provide support to a classified student within a self-contained classroom. Trained classroom teachers in whole language approach to reading instruction.
- Implemented literature-based reading program for both remedial and developmental students. Included journal writing as means to assess that "what is said is clearly understood."

RIDGEWOOD BOARD OF EDUCATION, Ridgewood, NJ   1992–1995
Supplemental Teacher
- Spearheaded a special project based on creating books from inception—writing and illustration through binding. Led "Book Talks" program for student body and parents.

ST. ANTHONY'S SCHOOL, Fairview, NJ   1989–1992
Second Grade Teacher
- Taught self-contained class. Integrated many creative extended activities, enhancing reading instruction. Worked with local environmental center to create educational materials.

COMPUTER SKILLS:

Microsoft Windows, Word, and Excel—Internet Research

RELATED EXPERIENCE/ACCOMPLISHMENTS:

- Active member of *Search Committee* for President of William Paterson College. Worked closely with Department Chairpersons to screen resumes and interview candidates.
- Selected *Member of the Year* by Women's Club of Park Ridge. Instrumental in planning for the transition to new countywide library lending system.
- *PTA President* for local school. Raised record amount of money to outfit school classrooms with ceiling fans.

References available on request.

MIRA SAHMANI

2001 Pinehurst Avenue, Suite 22
Toronto, Ontario A2B 3C3
Home: 416-555-6677 ◆ Pager: 416-555-7788

Objective: **DAYCARE LICENSING ADMINISTRATOR**

QUALIFICATIONS

BACKGROUND:
ECE with 21 years of experience in child and daycare settings, including 12 years as an Executive Director responsible for the effective programming, operation, and compliance of community-based daycare facilities.

LEGISLATIVE KNOWLEDGE:
- Comprehensive knowledge and understanding of Day Nurseries Act, with the proven ability to interpret its standards and apply its guidelines to the successful operation of a daycare environment.
- Operational familiarity with Child & Family Services Act, in particular relating to Children's Aid responsibilities and guidelines.
- Comprehensive experience interpreting and applying standards set forth in appropriate Health & Fire regulations.
- Operational familiarity with Freedom of Information and Protection of Privacy Act, specifically as it relates to all criminal reference checking of daycare applicants and volunteers.

SPECIFIC STRENGTHS / SKILLS:
- Outstanding communication skills, with particular strength liaising with staff, parents, community members, Board of Directors, host school officials, professionals, and municipal and government officials.
- Shrewd financial management and budgeting skills, with experience managing all fees, accounting, pay equity, and Operating/Wage Enhancement grants.
- Ability to thrive in complex and challenging situations.
- Excellent organizational and analytical skills as demonstrated by exemplary daycare management record.

EMPLOYMENT EXPERIENCE

EXECUTIVE DIRECTOR   1994–Present
Glendale Centre for Kids   Toronto, Ontario
- Ensured compliance with all Ontario and Municipal laws and regulations concerning the operation, practice, and programming of the daycare.
- Created centre's Operational Philosophy and Mission Statement, and monitored compliance at all times.
- Developed centre's Policy & Procedures Manual to comply with and exceed all government guidelines.
- Chairperson for all monthly Ward 10 meetings, organizing agenda and speakers and ensuring effective sharing of information and ideas.
- Managed a staff of 10 childcare professionals, including Assistant Director, Early Childhood Educators, and Assistant Teachers—evaluated performance, hired new staff, and resolved staff issues as required.
- Ensured open lines of communication between centre and all concerned parties, including parents, staff, Board of Directors, and government officials.

An expansive Qualifications summary leads off this chronological resume for a child-care administrator seeking a position as a Daycare Licensing Administrator.

MIRA SAHMANI   Home: 416-555-6677   Pager: 416-555-7788   2

EXECUTIVE DIRECTOR   1992–1994
Clearwood Community Childcare   North York, Ontario
- Coordinated creation and implementation of all policies and procedures for operation of new daycare facility.
- Created highly respected daycare centre within culturally diverse community, demonstrating excellent communication and listening skills, compassion, and creativity.
- Negotiated with host school, PCTA, and school board to secure daycare interests and develop mutually beneficial relationship.
- Provided consultative advice and training to new Board of Directors regarding roles and responsibilities.
- Managed a staff of 8 childcare professionals, overseeing all hiring, performance evaluations, and staff development.
- Successfully balanced Director role with additional teaching responsibilities.

INFANT HEAD TEACHER   1991–1992
Lilliput Childcare   Toronto, Ontario
- Created and implemented play activities to develop infant sensory acuity and ensured all basic daily needs were met.
- Implemented innovative program to teach parenting skills to teenage parents in host school.
- Implemented cooperative opportunities for high school students to volunteer in daycare to support Home Economics curriculum.
- Provided consultative advice for young parents, coordinating suitable community resources as required.

ASSISTANT SUPERVISOR   1990–1991
Rodale Community Daycare   Oshawa, Ontario
- Balanced administrative and teaching responsibilities in 70-child for-profit daycare.
- Created comprehensive program for preschool–kindergarten children.
- Assisted in hiring, staff development, enrollment, policy-making, and marketing activities.

PRESCHOOL HEAD TEACHER   1989–1990
Von Trappe Daycare   North York, Ontario
- Created and implemented play and learning activities for toddler/preschool children.
- Modified program components as necessary to provide maximum benefit and enjoyment for children.

EDUCATION / PROFESSIONAL DEVELOPMENT

Practical Parenting Training Program   City of North York, 2003
True Colours   City of Toronto, 2003
Child Abuse Prevention Training Program   City of Toronto, 2001

Degree—Early Childhood Education   University of Toronto, 1988

Personal and professional references provided upon request.

CHAPTER 12

Resumes for Corporate Training and Development Professionals

- Corporate Training Managers
- Training and Development Professionals
- Corporate Trainers
- Training Consultants
- Executive Training and Development Professionals
- Technical Trainers/Training Managers
- Sales Trainers
- Performance Technologists
- Coaches/Mentors
- Software Trainers

Felicia Bowman

**Corporate Trainer
Available Immediately!**

Summary of Qualifications

1 Master's degree in Adult Education/Training with hands-on delivery and development

2 Experience in training and program development for major corporation

3 Delivered dozens of workshops for team building, technical training and other workplace topics

4 Conducted analysis of work teams and job & task components and presented findings

5 Excellent computer skills, including development of online training and tools

6 Member: ASTD (national and local), SHRM, and ISPI

555 Wilshire Road
Tampa, Florida 33624
(813) 555-0248
fbowman@hotmail.com

Educational History and Degrees

For Felicia Bowman

University of South Florida
Adult Education–Training–Human Resource Development, M.A.
Tampa, Florida, 1998

University of South Florida
Psychology, B.A.
Tampa, Florida, 1995

Key Strengths

Creativity—Ability to create unique solutions, analogies and illustrations for complex problems

Patience—Ability to work with all departments with all levels of employees

Knowledge—Ability to use extensive insights in Adult Learners' understanding and information processing

Structured—Ability to plan and prepare programs and workshops in a long term, time-based critical path schedule in order to meet targeted launch dates

Communication—Ability to express complex ideas and important points in a way that is understandable and simple for the majority of Adult Learners

Professional Experience

Training and Documentation Specialist, Lockheed Martin
Lakeland, Florida, 1999–Current

Team member of highly creative Training Group for corporate offices and 3 major business sectors of this $27 billion company.

✓ Completed 12 major job and task analysis projects to document technical work processes.

✓ Designed 4 training programs, each in multiple forms of media, including the Internet, CD-ROM, PowerPoint and NetMeeting.

✓ Used interactive team development processes to assess the functionality of teams in the Shared Services division.

✓ Delivered 3 specialized training modules for highly technical computer systems.

✓ Facilitate team-building exercises, communication enhancement workshops and ongoing meeting facilitation.

✓ Offer constructive and strategic input on organizational structural changes.

✓ Participate in business development projects and strategic planning.

Continued on Page 2

The vibrant, unusual format for this traditionally written resume really makes it stand out and demonstrates this job seeker's creativity.

Corporate Trainer—Felicia Bowman—page 2

Program Assistant, Counseling Center for Human Development, University of South Florida
Tampa, Florida, 1996–1999

Created policies, procedures and training for clients of USF's Counseling Center. Also provided administrative and computer troubleshooting support.

✓ Produced detailed publications and handbooks, including the Counseling Center's Handbook, internship materials and brochures.

✓ Designed and produced promotional materials and presentations for professional workshops to clients and university administration.

✓ Trained staff on Internet usage and software programs such as Microsoft Word, Excel, PowerPoint and Scheduler.

✓ Resolved client issues and provided customer service. Took incoming calls and provided referrals to other resources.

✓ Provided computer support for staff in the areas of software support and system troubleshooting.

✓ Conducted administrative support for the campus-wide Employee Assistance Program.

Program Assistant, University of South Florida, Veteran Services
Tampa, Florida, 1994–1995

Performed administrative and financial services in USF office that serviced

veterans in their search for continuing education and employment.

✓ Reported directly to the Veteran Services Program Coordinator and ran the office when she was not present.

✓ Supervised 3 employees and ensured that reports and forms were properly filled out.

✓ Provided training in office procedures and policies.

✓ Handled all travel and budgeting administration.

✓ Solicited assistance from other campus offices in providing opportunities for work placement openings.

✓ Counseled veterans on their education and work options, and helped them define goals.

✓ Coordinated VA Work-Study Program for USF.

Courses Completed During Master's Program

Adult Education in the United States	Program Management
The Adult Learner	Foundations of Research
Methods of Teaching Adults	Consulting Skills
Instructional Design	Group Processes
Trainers in Business and Industry	Personnel Policy

Sample Presentations & Projects Completed During Master's Program

Experiential Learning in Adults

Presentation Skills Workshop

Future Trends in Adult Learning

Book Review: The Adult Learner, A Neglected Species

Andragogy Versus Pedagogy: Adults Are Different Than Kids

Professional Associations

Member of top local and national training organizations

National Chapter of American Society for Training and Development (ASTD)

Suncoast Chapter of American Society for Training and Development (ASTD)

Society for Human Resource Management (SHRM)

International Society for Performance Improvement (ISPI)

2 . . . . . · · · · · · · · · · · · · · · ·

RESUME 91: BY LAURA A. DECARLO, CCM, CERW, JCTC, CCMC, CECC

Parker Martine

950 Douglas Avenue, Charlotte, NC 26547
(910) 634-5788 • ptine@spice.net

Corporate Trainer / Professor / Consultant
HUMAN RESOURCES and ORGANIZATIONAL DEVELOPMENT (OD)

Organizational Change Agent with 15 years of expertise in building and developing training solutions for corporate performance optimization. Emphasis on aligning human resource functions with corporate initiatives to deliver world-class standards of productivity, efficiency, and quality. Excel in developing and presenting subject-appropriate curriculum for corporate training and college instruction.
Key areas of experience:

• Training & Development	• HR System Design	• Curriculum Development
• Organizational Learning	• Capability Assessment	• Change Management
• HR System Design	• Gap Analysis	• Instructional Systems Design
• Needs Assessment	• Training Facilitation	• Intervention Strategies
• Workshop Presentation	• Diagnostic Instruments	• Focus Sessions
• Curriculum Design	• Group Dynamics	• Career Development

EDUCATION and CERTIFICATION

- MA, Human Resources Administration, University of North Carolina, Chapel Hill, NC
- BSe, Instructional Systems Design, University of Central Florida, Orlando, FL
- Instructional Design Certification, The 4MAT System, Chicago, IL

PRESENTATIONS and PUBLICATIONS

- *"ISD in the DoD"*—Presented at the National Conference, American Society for Training and Development (ASTD), Orlando, FL—2001
- *"An Analysis of Theogi's Group Methodology as Applied to the Workplace"*—Published in the *Journal of Human Resource Management*, Vol. I—2001

PROFESSIONAL EXPERIENCE

PROFESSOR / HR PROGRAM DIRECTOR   **1994 to Present**
DEPARTMENT OF BUSINESS, WAKE FOREST UNIVERSITY, Raleigh, NC
Directed satellite campus Human Resources Development program, teaching courses at both satellite and main campus.
- ***Program Management:*** Managed the human resource development curriculum and faculty with responsibility for selection and development of elective courses and faculty recruitment.
- ***Instruction & Curriculum Design:*** Developed and taught courses, including Human Resources Development: An Introduction ... Instructional Systems Design ... Utilizing the 4MAT System ... Organizational Development ... Human Relations in Organizations ... Group Dynamics I & II ... Career Development in the New Economy ... Organizational Design Systems I ... Trainer's Toolbox.

The extensive list of "key areas of experience" can serve as a keyword summary for this experienced corporate trainer and university educator.

Parker Martine

Resume Page Two

PROFESSIONAL EXPERIENCE continued

INSTRUCTIONAL DESIGNER   1991 to 1994

THE CORPORATE SOLUTION, Jonesboro, NC

Developed corporate training programs and organizational training solutions for numerous Fortune 500 companies.

- *Curriculum Development:* Utilized Instructional Systems Design (ISD) Model to design curriculum and adjust programs according to feedback from human resources personnel.
- *Course Validation:* Validated all components of instructional programs to determine compliance with desired competencies.

SENIOR CORPORATE TRAINER   1988 to 1991

TERRAN INSTITUTE OF JUSTICE, Beacon Hill, NC

Recruited to develop and manage corporate training program.

- *Program Management:* Coordinated professional development of staff and faculty. Performed training, coordination, and implementation functions. Organized and coordinated in-house and external training functions.
- *Diversity Programming:* Identified corporate requirements to integrate programming in EEO, multiculturalism in the workplace, and cultural communications.
- *Curriculum Integration:* Worked with external consulting firm to adapt existing training program into an in-house function, reducing training costs by more than 40% annually.
- *Instruction & Training:* Developed and taught programs for management training, personnel orientation, and thinking outside of the box.

REFERENCES

Personal and professional references available upon request.

RESUME 92: BY HELEN OLIFF, CPRW, CFRWC, ECI

CATE JAR

45 Hilgard Avenue, Los Angeles, CA 90095
310-616-2020 ▪ cj@netscape.net

TRAINING & DEVELOPMENT PROFESSIONAL
Productivity ~ Personnel Development ~ Progressive Learning Programs

Goal: Developing the maximum potential of personnel—a company's #1 resource.

SUMMARY OF QUALIFICATIONS:

Progressive Educator & Personnel Developer with 10+ years of experience in public and private training. Skilled in course development, lesson planning, and classroom delivery for diverse groups. Demonstrated proficiency in IT training, life skills development, and professional development programs. Detail-oriented organizer and planner with strong communication and problem-solving skills. Motivated by full transfer of knowledge and development of maximum potential in the workplace.

AREAS OF EXPERTISE:

- Employee Training Programs
- Technical & Life Skills Training
- Training Needs Assessments
- Program Planning & Evaluation

- Adaptable Training Styles
- Curricula Development & Modification
- Communicating for Understanding
- Workforce Resistance to Learning

KEY ACCOMPLISHMENTS:

Corporate Training

- Modified a **classroom-style computer course** and delivered **corporate training** for groups of 20 to 25 employees. Included Microsoft Office (MS Word, Excel, PowerPoint, and Access), Windows, and Internet Explorer. (Computer Learning Center)
- **Trained personnel** in public schools on Microsoft Office suite. **Revamped the curricula** to ensure business examples relevant to an academic audience. Included a grade book example in Excel, a database of class novels in Access, a lesson plan outline in Word, and a PowerPoint presentation for interactive classroom exercises. (Tech Decisions)
- Reputation for **putting adults at ease with technology.** (CLC, TechDecisions, InfoSys, and New Tech)

Program Development

- Surveyed and assessed **training needs** among staff/students to guide an IT training plan. (Fairfax)
- Developed an **end-to-end computer training and technology integration program** for educators. Training emphasized computer usage for business and teaching. (Fairfax)
- Applied a **service-in-action approach** to instill **progressive learning** about community service. Planned a student-led community-service project for the children's ward at Fair Oaks Hospital. (Fairfax)
- Created an effective child **development workbook** for family planning. Helped students compute and comprehend the material cost of childbirth and fostered useful developmental awareness. (Fairfax)

Skills Assessment & Development

- Administered a **personal development program** for employment and college preparedness. Encompassed self-knowledge, self-care, goals, strong interests, and job search. Invited guest speakers from various disciplines in private industry.
- Developed **life skills curricula** in budgeting, banking, finding housing, reading a lease, and furnishing an apartment. Used didactic and facilitated instruction and individual and group projects.

Accomplishments are presented up front, divided into three distinct and relevant areas. This was important to help this job seeker avoid getting "pigeonholed" into only technical training.

CATE JAR   PAGE 2

RELEVANT POSITIONS HELD:

LOS ANGELES UNIFIED PUBLIC SCHOOLS (Los Angeles, CA)
Technology Integration & Training Specialist, 1998 to Present
Provide all computer training and integration of technology into school curricula for students and staff.

- Assist with the development of the school's long-range technology goals and plans.
- Maintain 3 computer labs—including installations and upgrades—for faculty, students, and staff.
- Provide Level One troubleshooting and computer support to student end users.

Manager, Life Planning & Development Program, 1998 to Present
Currently oversee an early childhood development program with 14 students and 23 student teachers.

- Evaluate program success via parent and community feedback and student-teacher self-assessments.
- Supervise a mix of didactic lessons, facilitated discussions, group projects, and self-study methods.
- Select and ensure relevant program content for human development, family life cycle, parenting styles, teen pregnancy, and family planning.

COMPUTER LEARNING CENTER (Oakland, CA)
IT Trainer & Program Planner, 1995 to 1998
Responsible for training corporate customers on all aspects of Microsoft Office Suite.

- Developed course objectives for Excel, Word, PowerPoint, and English language, based on student goals, selected textbook, and faculty suggestions. Trained 25 adults—ages 18 to 40+.
- Developed teaching aides for Excel, Word, and PowerPoint classes, to help clarify difficult concepts.
- Earned outstanding evaluation for MS Office training program developed/delivered for Chantilly Golf Club.

TECHDECISIONS (Oakland, CA)
Corporate Technology Trainer, 1992 to 1995
Sales Support & Presentation Specialist, 1990 to 1992
Responsible for creating courseware, help-desk, and presentation materials for corporate clients.

- Helped develop courseware to integrate technology into secondary/middle school curricula for the North Carolina public school system.
- Provided online help-desk support for research, textile, government, and educational customers.
- Developed presentation materials and reports to support a federal sales and marketing team.
- Developed/implemented a library program for managing and tracking software licensing agreements.

OTHER WORK EXPERIENCE:

INFOSYS SERVICES (San Francisco, CA)—Office Administrator, 1987 to 1989
NEW TECH CORPORATION (Sacramento, CA)—Office Manager, 1985 to 1986

EDUCATION & PROFESSIONAL TRAINING:

B.S. Education—California State University (Sacramento, CA)

Current Teaching Certifications:
- **English**—University of California (Los Angeles, CA)
- **Technology**—Cal State San Marcos, Extended Studies (San Marcos, CA)

Computer Skills:
- **Office Systems**—MS Office 2000 (Word, Excel, PowerPoint, and Publisher), Adobe Acrobat, Internet browsing (Explorer and Netscape), e-mail (Outlook and First Class), operating systems (Windows NT/2000/98/95 and Mac OS 8.1/8.0)
- **Specialty Systems**—Blackboard, Inspiration, Access 2000 DBMS, and ACIS Inventory System

RESUME 93: BY JANET L. BECKSTROM, CPRW

Roberta T. Juarez

3482 Homestead Court ◆ Rochester, MI 48309 ◆ 248-555-6308

Profile

◆ Possess many traits of an effective communicator:
- Dynamic presence   - Humor
- Engaging demeanor   - Instinct
- Outgoing personality   - Proven platform skills

◆ Technical areas of expertise:
- Coordination of benefits   - Litigation
- Eligibility investigation   - Tort law
- Subrogation   - No-Fault insurance
- Fraud   - Workers Compensation
- Arbitration   - Benefit provision language

◆ Entrepreneurial spirit—identified niche and created company to fill it; more than 15 years of experience as business owner with responsibility for all aspects of operations.

◆ A visionary who sees the big picture. Not afraid to take risks.

Highlights of Experience

Training/Public Presentation

◆ Developed corporate training program for newly created department and off-site support personnel.

◆ Presented more than 125 training and informational sessions to all levels of employees, from management to caregivers; adapted presentation style based on setting and audience's level of expertise.

◆ Created customized program as featured speaker at National Third Party Liability Group seminar (400+ audience over 3 days). Developed supporting literature for inclusion in educational packets; utilized appropriate speaker tools to enhance presentation.

◆ Addressed Eastern Michigan University's Adult Learning Seminar/ Extended Degree program as a successful graduate of the program.

◆ Provided testimony in legal hearings and court cases.

Program Administration

◆ Developed corporate understanding of previously neglected area of Coordination of Benefits (COB) and cost avoidance; during one year alone saved or recouped $2.8 million for client organization.

◆ Drafted policy and procedural documents on wide range of topics.

◆ Developed first-ever COB procedure manual utilized by employees in corporate and satellite locations.

◆ Collaborated with client corporation to expand and empower internal department, lessening need for contractor. Continued to provide consultative support on as-needed basis.

Professional Experience

JUAREZ RESEARCH • Rochester, MI   1990–Present
Under exclusive contract with Health Care Network of SE Michigan
Founder/President

HEALTH CARE NETWORK OF SE MICHIGAN • Detroit, MI   1984–1990
Contract Enrollment Entry Specialist
Marketing Representative
Medicaid Sales Representative

Education

SAGINAW VALLEY STATE UNIVERSITY • Saginaw, MI
Bachelor of Science in Business Administration   2000

MOTT COMMUNITY COLLEGE • Flint, MI
Associate of Business   1996

"Roberta was extremely knowledgeable . . ."
—Medical Records Technician

"Great info . . . you explain complex issues very well!"
—Case Manager

"Ms. Juarez presented the information in several different formats, using language that could be understood by everyone, and in a way that we could all apply to our own lives."
—Medical Records Manager

"Nice, because [it was] very informal and to the point—questions could be asked spontaneously."
—Claims Manager

"Thank you! Your seminar gave me a whole new perspective on how and why . . ."
—Surgical Staff

"Examples given of different scenarios broadened understanding."
—Finance Department Manager

"Roberta enlightened me to issues I never knew about!"
—Support Staff Coordinator

A functional format allows the grouping of training and program administration experience for greatest impact. Note the seven short, powerful testimonials.

MARISOL RODRIGUEZ

24 Collingsworth Drive
Rochester, NY 14625

585-586-7718
marisolz@frontiernet.net

EDUCATION & TRAINING COORDINATOR

Program Development & Implementation / Needs Assessment / Employee Development

Talented and motivated Training & Development professional with 15+ years of experience responding to the employee training and development needs of a manufacturing facility employing more than 3,000 people. Superb project management and administrative capabilities combined with exceptional communication and interpersonal skills. Offering knowledge and expertise in these key areas:

- ➢ **Assessing both technical and soft-skills training needs.**
- ➢ **Managing development and implementation of new programs.**
- ➢ **Counseling individuals on available academic and vocational opportunities.**
- ➢ **Making business cases to senior management to justify new training initiatives.**
- ➢ **Dealing collaboratively with a unionized workforce to achieve common goals and objectives.**
- ➢ **Recruiting, training, and supervising training staff to meet ongoing needs.**

RELEVANT EXPERIENCE

GENESEE VALLEY MANUFACTURING CONSORTIUM; Rochester, NY
A leading manufacturer and supplier of electromechanical assemblies and devices to the aerospace industry. Over the past 10 years, the firm has transitioned from a wholly owned subsidiary of GE to an independent supplier owned by 2 different multinational firms.

Human Resources Development / Training Coordinator   **1988–2004**

Pioneered in-house training department to serve the needs of a 3,600-employee workforce. Defined department's vision and mission, developed and administered $3.8 million annual operating budget, and recruited key team members to build an effective training staff.

- Conferred with senior managers and line supervisors to assess needs and design/implement strategies that achieved employee development goals.
- Instituted selection criteria that ensured training staff possessed appropriate technical knowledge and communication skills to effectively address ongoing training needs.
- Managed relationships with external training vendors, including evaluating course offerings, facilitating employee registration, negotiating fees, and authorizing disbursements.
- Developed and coordinated schedules for internal and external training programs, managed all logistics for on-site and off-site training, and ensured employee attendance.
- Counseled both hourly and exempt employees on educational opportunities and tuition assistance availability for a variety of academic and vocational programs.
- Facilitated various technical and soft-skills training classes for diverse groups of employees.
- Managed daily operations, fulfilling a broad range of administrative and managerial duties.

Key Accomplishments:

Managed transition of training department during ownership change. Maintained department's high levels of effectiveness and value-added activities, which engendered "buy-in" from GE corporate management. Department was recognized as a Best Practices model for GE in the area of employee development and training.

Championed the development and implementation of Computer Learning Lab that afforded employees at all levels the opportunity to advance their skills in a variety of areas. Made business case to senior management to secure funding, conferred with vendors and consultants on the design and construction of the facility, and managed program implementation and launch. This 15-station computer lab allowed employees to enhance their basic skills, learn common PC applications, and attain job-specific certifications in a self-paced, interactive environment.

A storytelling format is used for the Key Accomplishments section, providing rich detail for these most significant activities.

RESUME 94, CONTINUED

Marisol Rodriguez   Résumé – Page Two

ADDITIONAL PROFESSIONAL EXPERIENCE

Quality Analyst
Coordinated and implemented machine and process capability studies; troubleshot quality-related problems; and made recommendations for process improvements. Played a key role in introducing Statistical Process Control (SPC) methodologies to manufacturing facility, including conducting workshops to educate plant personnel.

Claims Examiner — Department of Labor
Reviewed information provided by claimants and employers to determine eligibility for benefits under provisions of NYS Unemployment Insurance guidelines. Interviewed claimants and collected data related to employers' challenges to eligibility.

Teacher, Reading / Science
Taught Remedial Reading at the elementary level, as well as secondary science in public school settings.

EDUCATION

Bachelor of Science, Anthropology / Sociology (Double Major)
State University of New York College at Geneseo; Geneseo, NY
Magna Cum Laude Graduate / Dean's List — Seven Semesters / Completed Degree in 3 Years

PROFESSIONAL DEVELOPMENT

CompTIA A+ DOS/Windows Service Technician	2000
CompTIA A+ Core Service Technician	2000

National Aeronautics and Space Administration (NASA) Professional Trainer
Goddard Space Flight Center, Greenbelt, MD
Comprehensive program encompassing 168 hours of training in these key areas:

- Needs Analysis
- Dealing with Challenging Learners
- Professional Trainer
- Interactive Teaching
- Designing & Conducting Skills Labs

Advanced Training in Microsoft Office Applications (Word, Excel, Access, PowerPoint)

References Provided on Request

MARTHA A. FRANKLIN

14452 Springfield Lane · Springfield, OH 45502
Cell: (937) 321-1612 · Email: marthafranklin@email.net

AWARD-WINNING SENIOR SALES TRAINER AND DEVELOPMENT MANAGER
who employs instructor-led classes, shadow Internet/web sessions, and team training methods to build skills in internal and external clients.

Maximize sales teams' productivity by using learning management systems that involve group training, projects, and e-learning platforms to offer a high return on investment (ROI). Oversee the entire training process, from the introduction of select programs and curriculum development to providing field training and seminar management. History of improving the company's bottom line by offering online learning alternatives coupled with focused and effective field sales training that secured higher closure rates and reduced employee turnover.

Local, National, and International Clients

TRAINING SKILLS OVERVIEW

· High-impact Presentations	· Business Development Programs	· SPIN Selling
· Learning Systems	· Consultative Sales Techniques	· Role-specific Training
· Program Introduction	· Curriculum Development	· Internal/External Training
· Seminar Management	· Training Needs Assessment	· Sales Team Retention

PROFESSIONAL CAREER

Sales Training and Development Manager · December 2001–Present
JBL, Inc., Springfield, OH

- Facilitate sales and leasing training on a one-on-one or group basis that encompasses career development and performance evaluation of Northeast, Mid-Atlantic, and Midwest trainers and instructional designers.

- Assisted in lowering overall turnover to 34% (below industry average) after introducing a management essentials program.

- Introduced innovative e-learning programs for community purchases and a prospect-management system for leasing consultants.

- Received the Excellence Award in 2003 for the design of a sales training curriculum that contributed to raising industry benchmark scores by 40%.

- Co-developed a learning management system for JBL University in 2003.

- Increased lease closings approximately 75% after implementing a 3-day leasing consultant development program.

- Devise and implement sales training focused around customer service, business development, and client-focused topics.

- Manage sales training initiatives, including an application database program, a customer-service program focused on resident retention, and a leasing consultant development program.

An attractive, unusual format and ample white space make this resume very readable.

RESUME 95, CONTINUED

Franklin, M.   Page Two

Training and Development Project Manager · June 1999–December 2001
Hanson Technologies, Inc. (Merged with Brownstein, Inc.), Springfield, OH

- Designed, introduced, and presented training to internal consultants and external clients in the U.S. and Europe after reviewing core and functional competencies.

- Trained on core consulting, presenting to influence, project management, and new employee (team development, diversity, team building) orientation.

- Reviewed and selected vendors and managed the partnership with an online university.

- Enhanced each sales team by offering focused training sessions on presentation skills, account management, and proposal writing that substantially grew the client base after each workshop.

- Coached, mentored, and networked with each project team.

- Integrated role-specific training with project-linking competencies.

- Led the integration team with focus group facilitation, data gathering, and broadcasting.

Program Manager, Training and Career Services · May 1995–June 1999
Sales and Recruitment Representative · January 1992–May 1995
Sylvan Learning Centers, Inc., Springfield, OH

- Managed a staff of 5 training associates and career counselors.

- Provided post training, counseling, and career analysis to ensure a high number of student placements.

- Increased placement by 50% after introducing an entire career transition curriculum (e.g., resume writing, job searching, networking with high-tech employers, and interviewing).

- Recruited students by speaking and presenting at area schools and participating in job/career fairs.

EDUCATION & SOFTWARE

Wittenberg University   Wright State University
Master of Arts, Teaching · 1995   **Bachelor of Arts, English** · 1990
Cum Laude, GPA: 3.72

MS Products: PowerPoint, Project

RAMONA GOMEZ-ROSARIO

7000 Prairie View Lane, Laredo, Texas 89534
(956) 256-0979 ▶ E-mail: mgr@msn.com

EXECUTIVE TRAINING AND DEVELOPMENT

PROFILE ▶ **Career interest in International Business Services** using fluency in Spanish and French language at near-native speaking level (translate, read, and interpret) and more than 10 years of experience as a trilingual educator. Seeking opportunities in

~~ Training senior staff in cultural protocols, cultural nuances, and social / business etiquette

~~ Facilitating an executive language-immersion program for overseas assignments

~~ Conducting bilingual technology application training courses

~~ Developing bilingual training manuals for Standard Operating Procedures

~~ Serving as translator / interpreter during strategic negotiations

▶ **Comfortable relating to people of diverse cultures and ages.** U.S. citizen who has traveled extensively throughout Europe, Mexico, South America, and Canada. Willing to relocate and travel (internationally or domestically). Professional demeanor.

▶ **Technology:** Trilingual keyboarding fluency in word processing, database development, spreadsheet applications, and PowerPoint presentations. Proficient in delivery of online "webinars."

EDUCATION ▶ **Master of Arts—Spanish Language and Literature,** 1994
Bachelor of Arts—Spanish (Minor: Education), 1992
Texas State University

HONORS: Sigma Delta Pi Spanish Honorary Society, GPA: 4.0

▶ **International Study,** 1991–1992
Instituto Internacional, Madrid, Spain

Study area: Spanish history, language, culture, literature

Classes taught in Spanish by professors from the Universidad Complutense and Universidad Autonoma of Madrid.

Completed entire coursework for major in Spanish, while living in Spain.

▶ **Teaching Licenses:** States of Texas and Florida

EMPLOYMENT HISTORY

▶ **SPANISH / FRENCH PROFESSOR**
Rio Vista University, Laredo, Texas (1999–present)

▶ **SPANISH INSTRUCTOR:** CLASS TAUGHT ENTIRELY IN SPANISH
University of Miami, Miami, Florida (1994–1999)

This resume was created to help a trilingual language professor transition from academia to the international business world in a training and development capacity for executives.

RESUME 96, CONTINUED

RAMONA GOMEZ-ROSARIO   PAGE TWO

LEADERSHIP ACHIEVEMENTS

▶ AS SOUTHERN ASSOCIATION OF COLLEGES COMMITTEE MEMBER: Proposed new methods to improve business processes related to academic instruction. Identified trends that could affect enrollment ratios.

▶ AS TECHNOLOGY COMMITTEE MEMBER: Assessed classroom needs for technology equipment (computers, scanners, peripherals) benchmarking against $90,000 annual budget.

▶ AS TEXTBOOK COMMITTEE CHAIR: Reviewed and evaluated scope, sequence, and content of topic-specific textbooks to determine instructional viability. Justified the cost / benefit of adjunct materials (CD-ROM, audio visual, and others).

▶ AS SPANISH AND FRENCH LANGUAGE INSTRUCTOR: Created student-centered learning environment through use of innovative techniques including positive reinforcement and performance incentives, as well as curriculum design and implementation.

AFFILIATIONS (ACTIVE)

▶ American Council of Teachers of Foreign Languages
▶ National Educators Association
▶ Texas Educators Association
▶ Laredo Educators Association
▶ American Association of Teachers of Spanish and Portuguese

FAVORITE QUOTE APPLICABLE TO BUSINESS COMMUNICATIONS

"Usted puede tener las ideas brillantes, pero si usted no los puede obtener a traves de, sus ideas no lo obtendrian dondequiera." (Spanish)

"Vous pouvez avoir des idees brilliants, mais si vous ne pouvez pas les recevoir a travers, vos idees ne vous recevront nullepart." (French)

"You can have brilliant ideas, but if you can't get them across, your ideas won't get you anywhere." (English)

— Lee Iacocca

RESUME 97: BY DIANE BURNS, CPRW, CCMC, CCM, CEIP, JCTC

Allen S. Louis

207 Mark Landing Court
Baltimore, MD 20175

410.555.6217
asl@aol.com

Professional Trainer

Polished school teacher and adult trainer. Comfortable and competent public speaker.
Promote growth, success, and a desire to meet established objectives
from students/participants.

Ambitious, results-oriented, and responsive to new ideas and challenges.
Superior oral and written communication skills.

Administrative Experience

Acting Administrative Intern, Oakland Mills Middle School   2003 to 2004

- Oversaw/supervised the entire administrative and teaching staff (135 personnel), assuming the duties of principal or assistant principal in their absence. Counseled staff as required. Responded to emergencies and immediate situations. Composed written correspondence and other materials.
- Participated in the planning, development, implementation, and evaluation of instructional programs. Managed administrative needs. Enforced policies.

Teaching Experience

Sixth Grade Social Studies, Oakland Mills Middle School, MD   2003 to Present
Sixth Grade Social Studies, Thunder Middle School, MD   2001 to 2003
Fourth Grade Teacher, Clark's Elementary School, MD   2000 to 2001
Fourth Grade Teacher, Mine's Elementary School, MD   1999 to 2000

- Formulate appropriate performance objectives, select and organize classroom content, design diversified instructional strategies, and evaluate objectives. Properly organize and manage the classroom environment. Teach, guide, test, and evaluate student performance. Present information to students using creative teaching methods. Interact with students, parents, teachers, and staff.

Presentations

- Presenter: Teacher's Association of Baltimore County, Teacher Portfolio Workshop, 2003
- Presenter: SQ3R (Reading Strategies) Inservice, 2002
- Delegate to the Maryland State Teacher's Association Convention
- Delegate to the National Education Association Convention

In this resume, teaching and presenting experience are highlighted. It's not until you reach page 2 that you realize this individual is in the military. And even in that role, human resource experiences (relevant to his training goal) are emphasized.

Education & Certifications

Arizona State University
Master of Science in Teaching, 1994 (GPA: 4.0)
Major: Elementary Education with a specialization in Social Studies

University of Maryland
Bachelor of Arts in Political Science, 1995

Maryland Teaching Certificate, Advanced Professional 1–6 & Middle School, 1999
Arizona Teaching Certificate, K–6, 1999

**Completed 12 semester hours towards certification as Administrator I
Arizona State University and University of Maryland, 1996 to present

Inservice / Staff Development

- Computer Technology: ClarisWorks
- Computer Technology: Hyperstudio, ClarisWorks, PowerPoint, and Internet
- Initiative and Confidence Course Certification
- *Baltimore Sun,* Newspaper in Education (NIE) Workshops
- Strategic Reading Instruction
- Previewing the Principalship
- Funding for Environmental Service Projects: Grant Writing

Military Experience

United States Navy Reserves, Commander (Administrative Manager)
SECRET Clearance   1993 to Present
Completed Signal Officer Basic Course (Academic Average: 90%)
Commended for above-average performance as a group leader, demonstrating decisiveness and ability to delegate.

- Plan, develop, and direct personnel systems to support the implementation of programs, i.e., personnel actions, assignments, awards, classifications, decorations, reenlistments, strength accounting/staffing, records maintenance, and pay management.
- Supervise a staff of 20 in the Personnel Actions Center supporting administrative actions for 200 personnel.
- Assisted a primary instructor in a specialized presentation. Formulated and developed communications-electronics class formats and curriculum.

Allen S. Louis, Page 2

BARBARA FLEMING

400 Sherwood Cr., Toronto, ON, K2R 2Z3
H: (613) 229-6390 | Email: barbaraf@hotmail.ca

E-LEARNING DESIGN SPECIALIST

Start Up, Turnaround, High Growth & Government Organizations

Proven expert in the design and implementation of cost-effective staff training, e-learning, customer service, sales management, and marketing solutions. Recognized for innovative leadership and counsel in transitioning under-performing departments into top producers. Decisive, energetic, and focused. Talented team leader, team player, and project manager.

▶ Training & Development Leadership	▶ Quality & Performance Improvement
▶ Organization Design & Development	▶ Team Building
▶ Communication	▶ Seminar Planning
▶ Presentations & Public Speaking	▶ Individual & Group Coaching

Specializing in Online Interactive Strategies

PROFESSIONAL EXPERIENCE

CANADA CUSTOMS & REVENUE AGENCY
Training and Learning Directorate, Toronto, ON   2003–present

▶ **Learning Design Specialist**

- Lead project teams, including technical subject matter experts in tax and finances.
- Design and develop programs for more than 50,000 employees needing new skills.
- Analyze and design learning/training activities/programs by following a structured approach. No "off-the-shelf" training products. Customize designs to particular and unique specifications as demands change frequently.
- Conduct client needs assessments and advise clients about learning solutions.

GLOBAL BANK, Vancouver, BC   2001–2003

▶ **Trainer**

- Designed and wrote training materials for Operations staff and structured training and support Increased productivity 100% and reduced overtime by 15%.
- Facilitated 3-day off-site team building and goal setting for HR department, resulting in 80% goal completion in 3 months.
- Liaised with Credit and Customer Service departments.
- Managed development and presentation of material for employee orientation.

BLUE JAY INVESTMENT SERVICE, Toronto, ON   2000–2001

▶ **Marketing / Sales Assistant**

- Expanded market presence online, growing by 70% in one year.
- Delivered marketing package for prospective clients.
- Pioneered and managed monthly client newsletter.

With a wealth of experience in the emerging field of online learning, this job seeker emphasizes her expertise with a bold headline and strong profile.

RESUME 98, CONTINUED

BARBARA FLEMING
Page 2

NORTHERN FUND VENTURES INC., Toronto, ON   1996–2000

▶ **Regional Marketing Manager** *(1999–2000)*

- Spearheaded implementation of regional grid strategy leading to an explosion in individual penetration rate from 11% to 98%.

- Reduced error rate from 15% to 5% through initiation, design, and implementation of tracking system and error opportunity reducing procedures.

- Formulated national seminar on customized, cost-effective marketing support for financial advisors. Increased sales 175%, best in company.

- Solved marketing voids by creating training matrix, and delivered off-site training retreat under budget, exceeding all success measures.

- Managed marketing team of 6 and marketing material distribution.

▶ **Senior Marketing Representative** *(1997–1999)*

- Increased sales by 35% in 2 geographical areas.

- Trained staff and led teams in production of training and marketing materials.

▶ **Investor / Dealer Service Representative** *(1996–1997)*

- Provided service to dealers, brokers, advisors, clients, and suppliers.

TECHNICAL QUALIFICATIONS

Presentation/Graphics:	Microsoft PowerPoint
Basics/Database:	Windows 95/98/NT / Microsoft Access
Software:	Microsoft Office (Word, Excel) / MS Project / MS Mail

EDUCATION & TRAINING

MS Train the Trainer—General Training Canada Corp., Ottawa, ON	1995
CPH, CSC—Canadian Securities Institute—Ottawa, ON	1995
Bachelor of Arts *(History/English)*—Concordia University, Montreal, QC	1993

Janene Connolly

4208 Nottingham
Livonia, Michigan 48135
(555) 217-5313
jancon217@aol.com

Performance Technologist with nine years of experience in training and instructional design. Expert in facilitating adult groups through complex problem-solving to action and improvement. Implemented programs for total financial conversions at several banking institutions. Worked with organizations to create industry-leading training processes to meet the dynamic needs of the organization and, as new technology emerges, to strengthen the overall performance of employees to meet competitive market demands. Core competencies:

- Organization Needs Assessment
- HR Policies & Procedures
- Technology Conversions
- Seminar/Workshop Design
- Executive Training & Leadership
- Customer Service Training

EDUCATION

Master's Degree, *Adult Instruction & Performance Technology*, UNIVERSITY OF MICHIGAN–DEARBORN, Dearborn, MI — Expected graduation: December 2005
Bachelor of Arts, *Art*, UNIVERSITY OF DETROIT MERCY, Detroit, MI — graduated Magna cum Laude
Certified — Business as Unusual Trainer
Certified — Business Sales Development Trainer

PERFORMANCE TECHNOLOGY PROJECTS

- Designed a sales training program for Mail Boxes Etc. sales staff.
- Designed and developed a job aid and a focus group process for the Livonia Ford Transmission Plant to facilitate an employee move process.
- Wrote a paper published on the University of Michigan web site: *Making the Transition from Classroom Training to Distance Learning.*

PROFESSIONAL HISTORY

DEARBORN FEDERAL CREDIT UNION, Dearborn, MI
A full-financial institution
INSTRUCTOR 2003–Present

Facilitate training, employee development, orientation, and technology conversion classes for a 450-employee financial institution. Develop "on-the-job" training techniques and deliver instruction for various departments, to include tellers, member services, call center, loans, and collections. Noted for resourcefulness, ability to handle diverse situations with ease, and talent for explaining material in an interesting and clear manner.

- Design and develop training programs to meet company service standards.
- Conduct training needs assessments to determine employee performance gaps.
- Facilitate soft skills and technical instruction for all levels of employees.
- Create training manuals to enhance the employee learning process.
- Design effective job aids to enhance employee on-the-job performance.
- Develop evaluation processes to judge performance results and to adjust future training sessions.
- Mentor training staff in adult learning techniques and instructional design concepts.

A strong summary and a separate section for important projects are used to enhance the impact of this chronological resume.

Janene Connolly

PAGE TWO

FIRST OF AMERICA BANK, Royal Oak, MI   1989 – 2003
Financial Institution
LEARNING SPECIALIST (1999–2003)

Provided stand-up training and verbal and written presentations for retail branch software conversions, new hire training, sales skills, supervisory, and procedural training. Worked with corporate department heads to evaluate training needs, and presented classes to assure all employees performed their jobs effectively.

- Applied adult learning concepts as facilitator of employee training programs.
- Exercised effective communication skills in working with all levels of employees.
- Acted as facilitator manager for all Michigan and Illinois platform trainers during the 2002 First of America/National City Bank conversion.
- Assisted instructional designers in the development of conversion training agendas, manuals, and job aids for all branch employees in Michigan and Illinois.
- Conducted stand-up training and train-the-trainer sessions for three major software conversions. Training encompassed employees in four states.

TRAINER / RETAIL BRANCH SUPPORT (1996–1999)

Trained employees in various training modules to include telephone help desk support, error resolution, written communications, and software testing.

- Traveled to Florida for three weeks, as the only new accounts facilitator, to provide training for the East Coast Florida Branch Conversion.
- Developed and distributed training manuals and job aids to be used at Michigan training sites for all Michigan branch employees.
- Trained more than 200 branch "new accounts" staff on multiple on-line applications within a one-month time frame.

CUSTOMER SERVICE / BANKING (1989–1996)

Opened new customer accounts, cross-sold various financial products, and provided customer service.

- Sold bank products and provided high-quality service to bank customers.
- Performed manager / supervisor functions in the absence of the branch and assistant managers.
- One of the first employees to initiate micro-marketing (phone sales, mailings) techniques that resulted in personal sales increases of 150%.
- Played a vital role toward the branch consistently meeting, or exceeding, loan goals for specified time periods.

PROFESSIONAL AFFILIATIONS

American Society for Training and Development
International Society for Performance Improvement
Pi Lambda Theta, International Honor Society in Education

COMPUTER SKILLS

MS Word • MS Excel • MS Project • MS PowerPoint • Lotus Notes

CARLOS MENDEZ

15243 South Drive ◆ Olathe, Kansas 66066
913-555-1212 ◆ cmendez@email.com

TECHNOLOGY PROFILE
Trainer ◆ Leader ◆ Coach ◆ Mentor

Technical Trainer and Team Leader with 18-year career delivering world-class customer support training programs in networked multi-function printer market. Change agent advancing technology in the workplace. Proven negotiation skills contributing to successful goal- and task-oriented problem-solving. Strong work ethic demonstrated through commitment to company growth and productivity.

Certification: Microsoft Certified System Engineer (MCSE), 1998

Operating Systems: Windows 2000, Windows NT 4.0, Windows 95/98, Novell NetWare 3.12/4.x

Software: Microsoft Office Suite

PROFESSIONAL EXPERIENCE

UNIVERSAL COPIER CORPORATION, Kansas City, Missouri   1986 to Present
Global company offering customized solutions for simplifying document life cycles

Senior Technical Trainer, 6/01 to Present

Hire and train permanent customer support analysts sourced from pool of sub-contractors. Monitor on-phone performance of support analysts, providing ongoing feedback to management and analysts. Develop and present training programs on products and network connectivity based upon personal research and testing. Edit user documentation that is incorporated into training curriculum. Organize, facilitate, and moderate bimonthly national conference calls for field analysts. Conduct periodic workshops to update all telephone analysts on software changes. Present focused training classes to non-technical managers on new technology and product advancements.

❖ Initiated and led start-up of focal training team to centralize generic training and eliminate redundancies in customer support center, thus improving productivity and reducing average class cost by $5000.

❖ Earned multiple annual achievement awards, including one in 1999 for moderating live talk show that provided critical solutions for hundreds of field analysts.

❖ Created training strategy that increased service level of support center from 15% to 85% within four months.

❖ Supervised launch of easy-access problem-solving Web site for offering valuable resources to all field personnel.

❖ Designed step-by-step job aids for telephone analysts that reduced research and telephone time.

❖ Increased customer satisfaction by facilitating communication between engineering department and customer support communities.

Continues on page 2

As with most technology resumes, this resume includes specific mention of technology expertise. Bullet-point accomplishment statements are clearly distinguishable from the summary of position activities.

RESUME 100, CONTINUED

Page 2, Resume of Carlos Mendez   913-555-1212

Technical Trainer, 3/95 to 6/01

Devised and presented stand-alone, multi-function desktop training for customer support analysts. Assisted with selection, testing, and hiring of new staff. Monitored telephone performance of analysts. Facilitated workgroup startup and meetings. Coached team of 15 in absence of manager.

❖ Developed and delivered state-of-the-art training to support centers in New York and London that achieved worldwide company recognition and generated $11,000 in revenue. Earned annual company achievement award in 1999.

❖ Designed first training and support Web site for support center, receiving company-wide recognition when showcased at annual Teamwork Day in Las Vegas, Nevada, in 1993.

❖ Led team effort to create the SOS (Help) Office that served as an escalation point for customer support analysts.

❖ Created company-wide troubleshooting guide for multi-function copier products.

❖ Earned President's Award for demonstrating new LAN/FAX product at NetWorld show in Washington, DC, in 1995.

Additional Relative Experience:

Facsimile Customer Support Analyst, 1/93 to 3/95
Data Communications Analyst, 4/91 to 1/93
Personal Computer Support Representative, 6/90 to 4/91
Customer Support Representative/Word Processor, 11/88 to 6/90
Senior Administrative Aide, 6/87 to 11/88
Administrative Assistant, 1/86 to 6/87

CITY OF OLATHE, KANSAS   1982 to 1986

Mediator/Intake Specialist
Resolved disputes for walk-ins and referrals from the Olathe Police Department.

EDUCATION

Networking Technologies Certificate, Sunflower College, Avery, Kansas, 2001

AAS Degree in Mid-Management, State Community College, Stanley, Kansas, 1994

Company-Sponsored Professional Development

- Management Development, 2004
- Leadership through Quality, 2003
- Train the Trainer, 1996
- Preparing for Leadership, 2003
- Network Printing Core, 2004
- Sales Training, 1994

CHRISTOPHER SAMPSON

1019 Swan Road
Detroit, Michigan 48823

547-503-4521
E-mail: csampson_101@hotmail.com

OBJECTIVE

To obtain a position as a Curriculum Software Trainer

HIGHLIGHTS OF QUALIFICATIONS

✓ More than 14 years of progressive experience as a Consultant, Trainer, Project Manager, and System Analyst.
✓ Extensive experience writing curriculum, training manuals, and training scripts and recommending design changes for multimedia applications.
✓ Highly effective liaison between widely diverse levels of staff and users to problem-solve technical and functional issues.
✓ Adept at tailoring training presentations to meet the consumers' needs.
✓ Critical evaluation and resolution of training issues from prototype testing to full production to increase software marketability for all levels of users on a national basis.
✓ Ability to work with diverse customers and maintain a high level of customer service.

EXPERIENCE

T. ROWE PRICE, Detroit, Michigan   2001 to Present

Senior Programmer/Analyst
Led team and managed project to certify that all facets of computer interfacing between client companies and T. Rowe Price's Retirement Plan Service and Information Technology Department were fully compliant with Sarbanes-Oxley regulations.
✓ Completed project ahead of time by serving as a liaison and selling the importance of the project and obtaining the cooperation of departments.
✓ Facilitated design meetings between consultants, business analysts, and technicians.
✓ Determined priority and format for testing 6 Retirement Plan Systems and 75 programs.

UNITED GUARANTY INSURANCE COMPANY, INC., Detroit, Michigan   1999 to 2001

Consultant
Coded and tested programs for Information Warehouse System to enhance systems for acquired companies.
Developed design specification and project estimates for completion of enhancement.

ANALYSTS INTERNATIONAL CORPORATION (AIC), Macon, GA   1997 to 1999

Trainer/Business Analyst (SYSTEMATIC TELECOMMUNICATIONS SERVICE, INC.) 1998–1999
Created training database with 200+ files for training exercises.
✓ Wrote and tested training scripts on multiple databases.
✓ Developed curriculum and generated graphics for training materials.
✓ Recommended design changes on a multimedia application of a nationally utilized billing and sales software package.
✓ Developed curriculum and conducted Train-the-Trainer classes on a Cellular Billing and Sales software package used within a client/server environment.

The Highlights of Qualifications section combines strong qualifications that "sell" this technical individual for the pure training positions he's seeking.

RESUME *101*, CONTINUED

CHRISTOPHER SAMPSON　　　　　　　　　　　　　　　　　　　　　Page Two

EXPERIENCE (Continued)

Consultant (ALANTIC GAS AND LIGHT) 1997
Programmed and tested complex developmental programs for appliance warranty project. Modified loan program, audit program, and financial accounting control software.

FLORIDA GAS & LIGHT COMPANY, Miami, Florida　　　　　　　　　　　　1991 to 1997

Systems/Data Analyst 1995–1997
Re-engineered a Customer Information System of 1.8 million customers into a "real-time" payment and billing system for 35 work groups in one implementation.
- ✓ Led team of 10 analysts and resolved the technical and functional problems to increase user confidence.
- ✓ Interviewed users and wrote more than 20 functional requirement documents.
- ✓ Wrote design specifications for more than 50 enhancements.
- ✓ Served as a highly visible liaison between all levels of users and programmers to problem-solve 100+ technical and functional issues both pre- and post-implementation of system.
- ✓ Created and marketed prototypes to all levels of users through User Acceptance Testing.
- ✓ Consulted with Cleveland Gas and Light on the design, implementation, and administration of system.

Training/Planning Analyst 1991–1995
Analyzed, updated, and designed computer-based training in conjunction with computer programmers.
- ✓ Wrote 50+ User Procedures, Participant and Instructor Guides, and Online Help Procedures (materials used nationally by numerous utility companies).
- ✓ Conducted presentations, demonstrations, and in-depth training classes for diverse audiences from senior managers to clerical staff.
- ✓ Customized training programs to meet the needs of the customers.

EDUCATION

MBA, Computer Information Systems 1991
MICHIGAN STATE UNIVERSITY, East Lansing, Michigan, *cum laude*

BS in Business Administration, Computer Information Systems 1989
MARYGROVE COLLEGE, Detroit, Michigan, *cum laude*

References Available Upon Request

RESUME 102: BY LISA LEVERRIER STEIN, MA, MS, CPRW, JCTC

Tim Wilson

6413 Chesapeake Lane
Atlanta, GA 30092

Home Phone   (404) 444-1234
E-mail   twilson25@aol.com

Corporate Training Manager

*Expertise in the Design, Development, Delivery, and Administration
of National Corporate Training Programs*

- Organizational Needs Assessment
- Performance & Productivity Improvement
- Staff Training & Team Leadership
- Vendor Selection & Management
- Training Reporting & Tracking

- Training Program Design & Instruction
- Training Coordination & Scheduling
- Training Budgets & Cost Reduction
- Instructor Certification Implementation
- Meeting Planning & Logistics

Equally extensive experience in Project Management and Call Center Operations Management. Supervisory responsibilities for teams of up to 30 professionals and support staff. PC and Mac proficient in Microsoft Word, Excel, and PowerPoint; WordPerfect; WordPro; and PageMaker.

Professional Experience

VISA International — Atlanta, GA   2001 to present
National Training Implementation Manager

Recruited to lead training implementation across 9 regional credit card centers for large retail and credit card company. Manage issues between curriculum development division and training delivery function. Supervise and coach group of 5 national trainers. Select and manage vendor relationships and contracts. Responsible for all logistics for large-scale training programs including space allocation, materials, room set-up, catering, and meeting planning.

Training Programs

- Orchestrated design, development, and delivery of new training program for front-line managers. Planned all logistics for delivery of 48 hours of classroom training in 9 credit card centers within 12 months.
- Coordinated and implemented offerings of instructor certification program in 9 credit card centers nationwide.

Organizational Improvements

- Designed and implemented course evaluation forms for all areas of training, resulting in measurements on course and trainer effectiveness.
- Developed administrative checklists for existing courseware to track materials, course registration, and attendance.

MasterCard International — Jacksonville, FL   1994 to 2001
Instructor / Course Developer / Registrar Manager (1997 to 2001)

Recruited to maintain and deliver series of management development courses for large credit card company with more than $13 billion in annual receivables. Supervised team of managers and associates. Managed all vendor relationships and contracts and the entire registrar function.

Training Programs

- Delivered courses including *Passport to Excellence, The Business of UCS, Time Management, Performance Management, Managing Conflict,* and *Policy Deployment* to audiences in three operation center locations.

Note how the bullet points in the Professional Experience section are broken down into "Training Programs" and "Organizational Improvements," making the accomplishments in these two important areas easy to absorb in a quick read of the resume.

Tim Wilson

Organizational Improvements

- Reduced backlog of associates needing required orientation course by 78% in 12 months.
- Planned all course offerings and assisted in design and production of annual course catalogue.
- Scheduled all aspects of Universal Leadership Program for three operation centers.
- Reduced company expenses by $50,000 annually by redesigning course registration and cost allocation procedures.
- Analyzed registrar software needs and recommended improvements.

Recognition and Rewards

- Team Award, 1999
- Human Resource Spirit Award, 1998
- Team Leader Award, 1997

Team Manager — Call Center Operations (1994 to 1997)

Recruited to manage group of 30 customer service call center associates in bankcard processing environment. Managed call flow between two national call centers to meet and exceed customer service quality indicators. Hired, trained, and coached associates. Managed all aspects of call escalation to handle customer inquiries and concerns.

- Created functional team for weekend shift to enhance management of call volume and meet staffing requirements. Result was improved customer service and reduced need for hiring additional headcount.
- Suggested improved electronic communication vehicle which positively affected daily task management of more than 2,000 associates.
- Spearheaded logistics for high-profile community project, including staffing, scheduling, and ticket sales and production.
- Selected to deliver training for credit card application system for 700+ associates within 2 weeks.

Previous Professional Experience

Vice President / CFO — Launched entrepreneurial venture offering high-end sportfishing charter excursions to an exclusive clientele. Independently managed all financial planning, general accounting, banking, sales, customer service, advertising, and public relations functions.

Sales Executive — Top-producing sales associate of both residential and commercial properties throughout the Jacksonville, Florida, metro market. Managed the entire sales cycle, including market analysis to determine fair market pricing, property presentations, price/contract negotiations, mortgage consultations, and final property settlement/owner transfer.

Customer/Account Manager/Accountant — Several progressively responsible accounting and office management positions in the telecommunications and national retail chain industries. Demonstrated excellent communication, organizational, analytical, and project management skills.

Education / Professional Development

Certificate in Training & Human Resource Development, 2003 — University of GA, Athens, GA
Coursework in Instructional Systems Design, Adult Learning, Consulting, and Testing & Evaluation

University of Virginia / Tidewater Community College / Florida Community College, 2002
Coursework in Business Management

Myers-Briggs Type Indicator (MBTI) Certified, 2000 — Type Resources, Inc.
American Society for Training & Development (ASTD), National Member, 1994 to Present

RESUME 103: BY LOUISE GARVER, JCTC, MCDP, CEIP, CMP

RAYMOND P. GARNER

CORPORATE TRAINING EXECUTIVE

2219 Forest Park Lane
Chicago, IL 60653

garner@comcast.net
(773) 373-0882

CAREER OVERVIEW

Dynamic management career leading the design and execution of innovative training, management development, and organization development programs for a global Fortune 500 corporation. Achieved recognition for successful collaboration with the senior management team to plan and implement strategies that improved customer focus, productivity, profitability, and employee satisfaction.

Core Competencies

**Change Management • Management/Employee Development • Performance Management Systems
Succession Planning • Continuous Process Improvement • Team Building**

AWARDS & HONORS

- Member of the Advisory Board for U.S. Training Industry Survey on "Report to the President of the United States of America."
- Featured as one of the "most innovative professionals in the field of corporate training and organizational development" in the September 2003 issue of *Human Resources Executive*.
- Honored with the Training Director Forum's Annual Award for successful change management implementation in 2003.
- Frequent presenter on organizational development and change management topics at the Association for Training & Development International Conference.
- Honored with 5 Danver Corporation Quality Awards for leadership and results in change management and management/employee development initiatives.

EXPERIENCE

DANVER CORPORATION – Chicago, IL – 1983 to Present

Vice President of Organizational & Management Development	**1996 to Present**
Director of Corporate Training & Organizational Development	**1990 to 1996**
Manager of Division Training & Development	**1986 to 1990**

Member of the senior leadership team. Provide strategic management direction to the organizational development and training functions at $160 billion multinational corporation employing 30,000. Spearhead the design and implementation of organizational, management, and employee development programs throughout corporate and worldwide business units. Direct team of senior training consultants and directors plus an annual multimillion-dollar budget. **Achievements:**

Organization Development

- Transitioned corporation into learning and development environment, fostering teamwork and high employee involvement resulting in measurable improvements in performance and morale.
- Created a nationally acclaimed performance management and succession planning system implemented company-wide; featured in Tom Peters' newsletter *On Achieving Excellence.*
- Designed and implemented culture change training program division-wide to support 30% product-line growth.
- Recommended external consultants to facilitate improvement in product-line performance through automated systems that streamlined workflow while reducing costs by $14 million.

To distinguish himself from other candidates, this job seeker placed prestigious honors, awards, and media recognition on page 1, just above his employment. Subheadings were used within the position descriptions to call attention to his achievements in different areas.

RESUME *103*, CONTINUED

RAYMOND P. GARNER   PAGE 2

DANVER CORPORATION continued…

Management Development

- Innovated internal enterprise marketing Management/Leadership Training and Consulting Services for external customers, saving $1.5 million in year one of implementation.
- Developed and facilitated Leadership and Teamwork seminars/retreats for CEO and senior management teams. Results strengthened coordination between market segments, reduced product development cycle time, improved profitability, and increased customer satisfaction.
- Created company's first core Management/Leadership Development curriculum organized into 3 skill levels (foundation, operational, and strategic); expanded program to include all employees.

Employee Development

- Planned and created employee development planning process introduced company-wide that resulted in measurable performance improvements in 10 key functional areas.
- Consulted with incoming senior management and facilitated effective transition of new staff within a key business unit in record time.

Manager of Training and Organizational Development   **1983 to 1986**

Brought on board to create all training and organizational development programs for a business unit with 500 employees. Assessed organizational needs and developed programs for all employees. Managed $650,000 annual budget.
- Conducted customized training in effective negotiation skills, resulting in renewal of a major 10-year contract that surpassed the company's established return-on-equity objectives.

LANDMARK CORPORATION – New York, NY – 1981 to 1983

Senior Training Coordinator

Designed/implemented training programs for managers and professionals on performance management and coaching, leadership, conflict management, communications, and negotiations. Conducted train-the-trainer programs for line managers.

- Centralized training function to include 5 plant locations and reduced outsourcing costs by $250,000.
- Led Policy Development Committee in establishing procedures implemented organization-wide.

EDUCATION

Ed.D. in Organizational Development
Yale University, New Haven, CT

M.Ed. in Counseling and B.A. in Psychology
Columbia University, New York, NY

Certified Trainer: Zenger Miller Supervisory Training

American Association for Training and Development
Membership Chair ~ Programs Committee Chair

PART III

Cover Letters for Teachers and Educators

CHAPTER **13**

Writing a Winning Cover Letter

Now that your resume is written, you may think that you're all set to launch your job search. If it were only that easy! Just as critical to the effectiveness and success of your job search campaign is your cover letter. To begin our discussion of this vital element in your search, let's start with a concise definition:

> **Cover Letter:** A document that accompanies your resume and is used to highlight your specific skills, qualifications, competencies, achievements, and more that ***relate directly to the position for which you are applying.***

That's right...the best cover letters are letters that are targeted to specific positions (for example, a teaching position with a local high school, an administrative management position with a local community college, or a corporate training position with an international company). Targeted letters allow you to selectively include information about your past work experience, training and education, affiliations, professional activities, and more that directly support your candidacy for a particular position. In essence, you're taking everything about your career, laying it out on the table (so to speak), and then selecting only that information which is most important to your current job objective.

Here's an example of a wonderfully written cover letter that is targeted to this candidate's specific objective—a position in training and development. You can see the resume that accompanied this letter on page 228.

CATE JAR

45 Hilgard Avenue, Los Angeles, CA 90095
310-616-2020 • cj@netscape.net

TRAINING & DEVELOPMENT PROFESSIONAL
Productivity ~ Personnel Development ~ Progressive Learning Programs

Goal: Developing the maximum potential of personnel—a company's #1 resource.

June 15, 2005

Rochelle Kingsley
Executive Director
Meriden Business & Learning Center
500 South Broad Street
Meriden, CT 06450

Dear Ms. Kingsley:

I am writing because you expressed an interest in a Training & Development Professional who fits with your company. I believe that I am such a candidate! I am a progressive educator and personnel developer with 10 years of experience in productivity training and progressive learning programs—and you can put me to work day one for your company and your customers!

Here are some of my career highlights to date:

- **Training / Professional Development.** As a Corporate Trainer and IT Program Planner at Computer Learning Center, Technology Decisions, and other IS companies, I earned a reputation for putting adults at ease with technology.

- **Program Development.** As a Technology Integration and Training Specialist at Los Angeles Unified Public Schools, I surveyed and assessed training needs among staff/students to guide an IT training plan.

- **Skills Assessment & Development.** As the Manager of a life planning and development program, I developed and administered a personal development program for employment and college preparedness. It included self-care, career interests, goal setting, and job search.

I am looking forward to learning more about the needs and goals of your organization and how the right Training & Development Professional can help. You can reach me at 310-616-2020. I look forward to hearing from you soon and the opportunity for an interview. I will follow up in two weeks to determine a mutually agreeable time for a personal meeting.

Sincerely,

Cate Jar

Enclosure: Resume

A targeted cover letter (submitted by Helen Oliff, CPRW, CEIP, IJCTC, CFWRC).

All too often, job search candidates write what we refer to as general cover letters—letters that can be used to apply for any position with any type of organization. In essence, these letters simply summarize information that is already included on your resume and tend to be not nearly as effective as targeted cover letters. Because you do not have a specific position in mind when you write a general letter, you are not able to highlight information that would be most essential in a particular situation. As such, we strongly urge that you stay away from general letters and devote the time that is necessary to develop targeted cover letters that will sell you into your next position.

Another a real advantage to targeted cover letters is that the recipient will notice that you have taken the time to write an individual letter to him or her; and, of course, that leaves a great impression. When you are able to integrate specific information into your letter about the school, college, or company to which you are applying, it clearly demonstrates your interest in the position and the organization, before you've ever had the opportunity to speak with anyone there. Just think how impressed a prospective employer will be when he or she realizes that you've spent the time and energy necessary to research and "get to know" their school or company. This, in and of itself, will give you a distinct advantage over the competition.

Six Steps to Writing Better Cover Letters

To help guide you in writing and designing your own winning cover letters, we've created a step-by-step process and structure that will allow you to quickly and easily write letters that will get you and your resume noticed, not passed over:

1. Identify Your Key Selling Points
2. Pre-Plan
3. Write the Opening Paragraph
4. Write the Body
5. Write the Closing
6. Polish, Proofread, and Finalize

Now, we're going to explore each of these steps in detail to provide you with an action plan to write your letters with ease and confidence. Our most detailed discussion will be of Step 1: Identify Your Key Selling Points, which is the entire foundation for your cover letter.

STEP 1: IDENTIFY YOUR KEY SELLING POINTS

What qualifications, experiences, achievements, and skills do you bring to a school or company? It's time to evaluate and quantify what it is that makes you unique, valuable, and interesting to potential employers.

Know Your Objective

The best place to start is by clearly identifying *who* you are and what your job objective is. Are you an elementary, middle, or high school teacher? A principal or school administrator? A multimedia learning specialist or instructional programmer? A corporate training and development professional? It is critical that you be able to clearly and accurately define who you are in an instant. Remember, an instant is all that you have to capture your reader's attention, encouraging him not only to read your cover letter in full, but to read your resume and contact you for a personal interview.

Summarize Your Experience

Just as important, you must be able to clearly identify why an organization would be interested in interviewing and possibly hiring you. Is it because of the schools, universities, or companies you've worked for? The industries in which you've been employed? The positions you held? The promotions you earned? Your accomplishments? Your specific skills and qualifications? Your licenses and educational credentials? Your technical expertise? Your leadership skills? Your foreign-language skills and international experience? Why would someone be interested in you?

Sell Your Achievements

Your achievements are what set you apart from others with a similar background. They answer the reader's all-important question, "What can you do for me?" because they tell precisely what you have done for someone else. Cover letters and resumes without achievements are simply dry compilations of position titles and responsibilities. They don't sell your unique attributes, and they don't compel readers to pick up the phone and invite you in for an interview.

In thinking about your achievements, ask yourself how you've benefited the organizations where you've worked. In general terms, you can help an organization by

- **Making money** (revenues, profits, earnings, ROI/ROA/ROE increases, new customers)

- **Saving money** (cost reductions, streamlining, automating)

- **Creating new things** (courses, programs, techniques, methodologies, systems, processes, and more)

- **Improving existing things** (reengineering, redesigning, developing new processes, consolidating)

- **Improving student, teacher, or organizational performance** (productivity, efficiency, quality, delivery, and customer service)

- **Winning honors, awards, and commendations**

In writing your achievements, think about the two key pieces of information you want to convey about each of your successes: what you did and how it benefited the organization. It is the combination of both of these components that will make your achievements—and, in turn, you—shine.

Who you are, what you have achieved, and why an organization would want to hire you are critical questions you must ask yourself before you ever begin to write a cover letter. The answers to those questions will directly impact what you write in your cover letter and how you present that information. You must determine what you have to offer that relates to that organization's specific needs, what will be of interest to them, and what will entice them to read your resume and offer you the opportunity for an interview. That information then becomes the foundation for every cover letter that you write.

STEP 2: PRE-PLAN

Before you begin writing a single word of your cover letter, you must determine the appropriate strategy for that particular letter. You're not ready to write until you can clearly answer the following questions:

- **Why am I writing this letter?** Am I writing in response to a print or online advertisement, sending a cold-call letter to universities or companies, contacting someone in my network, writing to an organization at the recommendation of someone else, or writing a follow-up letter to a company to which I already sent a resume? The answer to this question will significantly impact the content of your cover letter—the introduction in particular.

- **Have I researched the organization (for example, the school, university, or company) or the position?** There will be instances where you know, or can find, information about an organization you are writing to, the services and programs it offers, the positions that are open, the types of candidates it hires, the hiring requirements, and so much more. Do your research! The more you know about a particular school or company and the position, the more on-target you can write your letters, relating your experience to their identified needs. If you know the school has a large number of special-needs students, be sure to stress your experience designing special-needs curricula. If you know the university is in need of strong programming and instructional leadership, be sure to focus your letter on the innovative programs you have created and their success. Your goal is to find common ground between you and the company and then leverage that to your advantage.

- **Do I have a contact name?** Have I double-checked the correct spelling of the name and the person's job title? Do I have the full mailing address or e-mail address? The fact is that if you write to the Human Resources department of a company, a university, or a school system, you'll never quite know where your letter and resume have landed. However, if you write to a particular individual in a particular department with particular contact information, you not only know who has your resume and cover letter, you also know who to follow up with. This is critical for job search success in today's competitive market!

STEP 3: WRITE THE OPENING PARAGRAPH

The opening paragraph of your cover letter is your hook—your "sales pitch"—that tells your reader who you are and why you are of value to that specific organization. It should be written to entice the recipient to read your letter in its entirety and then take the time to closely review your resume. And, because it is so critical, the opening paragraph is often the section that will take you the longest to write.

TIP: If you're having trouble writing the opening paragraph of your cover letter, leave it for the time being and move on to the body of the letter. Once you've written the rest, the opening paragraph will usually flow much more smoothly and quickly.

There are three specific questions you must address in the opening paragraph of your cover letter:

1. Who are you?

2. Why are you writing?

3. What message are you communicating?

Your answers to these questions, combined with the specific reason you are writing (for example, in response to an advertisement, on recommendation from a network contact, or because of an Internet job lead), will almost always dictate the type of opening you select. Review the introductory paragraphs for the sample cover letters in chapter 14 to help you get started developing your own introduction.

STEP 4: WRITE THE BODY

Now you're ready to tackle the real task at hand: writing the body of your cover letter—the substance, key qualifications, accomplishments, successes, and whatever other information you choose to highlight that will entice the reader to closely review your resume and offer you the opportunity for a personal interview.

In order to sell yourself (or any product) as "the answer," you must highlight the attractive *features* and *benefits* of that product. Put yourself in the shoes of the buyer and ask yourself

• What will catch my attention?

• What's interesting about this candidate?

• What's innovative or unique about this candidate?

• Why is this candidate different from (or better than) other competitive candidates?

• Do I understand the value I'll get from this candidate?

• Do I need this candidate?

• Do I want this candidate?

Whether or not you're conscious of it, every time you buy something, you ask yourself these questions and others. It's the typical process that everyone proceeds through when they're deciding whether to make a purchase. It is imperative that you remember this as you begin to write your cover letters. Understand that you must clearly communicate the answers to these questions in order to get people to want to "buy" *you.*

TIP: Your cover letter *should not* be written as "Here I am, give me a job," but *should be* written as, "Here I am; this is why I am so valuable; give me a chance to solve your problems." Focusing on the value and benefits you have to offer is a good way to capture the reader's attention. Remember, the employer's most compelling question is "What can you do for me?" not "What do you want?"

Your challenge, then, is to convey your value in a short and concise document—your cover letter. Unfortunately, there are no rules to guide you in determining what to include in each specific cover letter that you write. It is entirely a judgment call based on the specific situation at hand—the position, the organization, and the required qualifications and experience. What you include in your letter is not necessarily based on what you consider to be your most significant responsibilities and achievements from throughout your career, but rather what is *most relevant to the hiring company and its needs*.

Achievements, accomplishments, contributions, and successes are the cornerstone of any effective cover letter. It goes without saying that you want to demonstrate that you have the right skills, qualifications, and experience for a particular job. However, you do not want your letter to be a "job description"—a mere listing of job responsibilities. First of all, you've addressed a great deal of that information in the resume that you'll be sending along with your cover letter. You do *not* want your letter to simply reiterate what's in your resume. The challenge is to write a cover letter that complements the resume and brings the most notable information to the forefront.

Depending on the format of your letter, you can convey this information in a paragraph format, a bullet-point format, or a combination of both. Use whichever you feel is most appropriate to convey the particular information. If you decide to use full paragraphs, make sure that they are fairly short to promote readability. Edit and tighten your copy so that every word and phrase conveys information that relates to the employer's needs and your most relevant qualifications.

STEP 5: WRITE THE CLOSING

Now that you've written your introductory paragraph and the body of your cover letter, all you have left to do is the closing paragraph. Simple enough; in fact, this is generally the easiest section of your letter to write. To get started, ask yourself these two simple questions:

- What style of closing paragraph do I want to use?

- Is there any specific personal or salary information I want to include that was requested in the advertisement to which I am responding?

When it comes to choosing style, closing paragraphs are easy. There are basically only two styles—Passive and Assertive—and the distinction between the two styles is evident:

- **Passive:** A passive letter ends with a statement such as *"I look forward to hearing from you."* With this sentence, you are taking a passive approach, waiting for the hiring company or recruiter to contact you. This is *not* our recommended strategy.

- **Assertive:** An assertive letter ends with a statement such as *"I look forward to interviewing with you and will follow up next week to schedule a convenient appointment."* In this sentence, you are asserting yourself, telling the recipient that you will follow up and asking for the interview!

We strongly recommend that you end your cover letters with an assertive closing paragraph. Remember, the only real objective of your cover letter is to get an interview, so *ask for it!* Furthermore, we also advise that you outline an agenda that communicates you will be expecting their call and, if you don't hear from them, you will follow up. This puts you in the driver's seat and in control of your job search. It also demonstrates to a prospective employer that once you've initiated something, you follow it through to completion. This is a valuable trait for any professional.

Inevitably, there will be instances in your job search when you will not be able to follow up:

- If you are responding to a blind advertisement with a P.O. box, you won't know who to call.

- If you are responding to an advertisement that states "No Phone Calls," don't call.

- If you are sending out 1,000 letters to recruiters across the nation, don't waste your time calling them. If they're interested or have an opportunity for which you are suited, they'll call you.

- If you know that you'll never get the individual you want to speak with on the phone, don't waste your time or money.

The closing paragraph of your cover letter is also the preferred placement for any personal or salary information you will include. There are generally only two times you will want to include this type of information:

- **When it has been asked for in an advertisement.** Common requests include such things as salary history (what you have made in the past and are currently earning if you are employed), salary requirements (what your current salary objectives are), citizenship status, or geographic preference.

- **When you are writing "cold-call" letters to recruiters.** When contacting recruiters, we recommend that you at least minimally address your salary requirements (a range is fine) and any geographic preferences in the closing paragraph of your cover letter.

STEP 6: POLISH, PROOFREAD, AND FINALIZE

The process we recommend for writing your cover letters suggests that you first craft the opening, then the middle, and then the closing of each letter. Although the step-by-step process makes the task fairly quick and easy, you will probably find that your letters need final polishing, wordsmithing, and tweaking to ensure that each section "flows" into the next and that you have a cohesive-sounding whole.

Take the time to proofread your letter thoroughly and carefully. Read it for sense and flow; then read it again to check for spelling errors, punctuation mistakes, and grammatical inconsistencies. We cannot emphasize this point enough. The people who receive your cover letter and resume *do* judge your professionalism based on the quality and accuracy of these documents. In fact, in a survey of hiring authorities we conducted for a prior book, *90 percent of respondents* mentioned quality and appearance factors (such as typos, misspellings, smudged print, and low-quality paper) as reasons for *immediately discarding a resume*. Don't take a chance that your carefully written letter and resume will end up in the circular file before your qualifications are even considered.

Here are a few things to look out for during the polishing phase:

- **Spelling:** Use your computer's spell-checker, but don't rely on it totally. The spell-checker won't flag an "it's" that should be "its" or a "there" that should be "their." Make triple-certain you've correctly spelled all names: people, organizations, software programs, and so on.

- **Grammar and punctuation:** If you're not confident about your grammar and punctuation skills, purchase an all-purpose reference guide and use it as often as you need to. Don't let your cover letter be discarded because of basic grammar and punctuation errors.

- **Interesting language:** As much as possible, avoid cliches and outdated language (such as "Enclosed please find my resume"). It's difficult to find new ways to express familiar sentiments (such as "I would appreciate the opportunity for an interview"), and it's certainly not necessary to come up with unique language for every phrase. But make sure that your cover letter doesn't sound like a cookie-cutter, one-size-fits-all letter that could have been written by any job seeker.

Authors' Best Tips for Writing Winning Cover Letters

Here's our most important cover-letter advice, gleaned from our experience writing thousands of cover letters over the years.

DON'T REINVENT THE WHEEL

A great amount of our discussion has focused on the fact that your cover letters should be written individually based on the specific situation. And that is quite true. The more focused your letters, the greater the impact and the more likely you are to get a response and opportunity to interview. However, you *do not* have to reinvent the wheel with each and every cover letter you write. If you're a teacher writing in response to advertisements for other teaching positions, you can very often use the same letter with just a few minor editorial changes to match each opportunity. Remember to use your word-processing program's "copy and paste" function. It's a great, labor-saving tool!

SELL IT TO ME; DON'T TELL IT TO ME

Just like resume writing, cover letter writing is sales—pure and simple. You have a commodity to sell—yourself—and your challenge is to write a marketing communication that is powerful and pushes the reader to action. (You want him to call you for an interview!) Therefore, it is essential that when writing your letters you "sell" your achievements and don't just "tell" your responsibilities.

Here's a quick example. If you are an instructional specialist, you could "tell" your reader that you've developed more than 10 new instructional programs. Great! Or, you could "sell" the fact that you've led project teams in the design, development, and delivery of more than 10 new instructional programs over the past two years, eight of which are now fully disseminated throughout the entire Cincinnati Public School System. Which letter would capture your interest?

GET OVER WRITER'S BLOCK

Very often, the most difficult part of writing a cover letter is getting started. You can sit and look at that blank piece of paper or computer screen for hours, frustrated and wondering whether the whole world has such a hard time writing cover letters. If writing is part of your daily work responsibilities, the process might not be too arduous. However, if you do not have to write on a regular basis, cover letters can be an especially formidable task. That's why it is so important to follow the step-by-step process we have created. It is guaranteed to make cover letter writing faster, easier, and much less painful!

If you're still having trouble, consider this simple thought: **You do not have to start at the beginning.** Even after writing thousands and thousands of cover letters, we'll sit stumped, unable to come up with just the "right" opening paragraph. Instead of wasting time and brain power, and getting frustrated, we'll just leave it alone and move on to another section in the letter that we feel more confident writing. You'll find that once you get going, new ideas will pop into your head and the more difficult sections will come much more easily and confidently.

ANSWER THE EMPLOYER'S MOST IMPORTANT QUESTION: "WHAT CAN YOU DO FOR ME?"

A powerful cover letter can help you get what you want: a new, perhaps more advanced, and more satisfying position. It is certainly important that you understand what you want to do, the kind of organization you'd like to work for, and the environment in which you'll be most productive. Yet you must remember that employers aren't really interested in you. They're interested in *what you can do for them.* If you do not keep this thought in the forefront of your mind when writing your cover letters, you're likely to produce a self-centered-sounding "here I am" letter that probably won't do much to advance your job search.

When writing your cover letters, consider the employer's needs and make sure that you communicate that you can add value, solve problems, and deliver benefits for that employer. You can do this through a strong focus on accomplishments ("Ah, she did that for Acme Schools; she can do the same for me.") and through careful attention to the wording and tone of your letter so that you appear to be more interested in contributing to the organization than satisfying your own personal needs.

Then, be sure to review the Cover Letter Checklist on the next page to be sure that your letters meet all of our requirements for style, appropriateness, quality of text, quality of presentation, and effectiveness. Follow our rules and we guarantee that your letters will open doors, generate interviews, and help you land your next great professional opportunity.

Cover Letter Checklist

Before mailing, faxing, or e-mailing each cover letter you prepare, complete the following checklist to be sure that you have met all the rules for cover letter writing. If you cannot answer "yes" to *all* of the questions, go back and edit your letter as necessary before mailing it. The only questions for which a "no" answer is acceptable are questions #5 and #6, which relate specifically to the organization to which you are writing. As we have stated previously, there will be instances when you can find this information, but there will also be instances (for example, when writing to a P.O. box) when you cannot.

		YES	NO
1.	Do I convey an immediate understanding of who I am in the first two sentences of my cover letter?	❏	❏
2.	Is my cover letter format unique, and does my letter stand out?	❏	❏
3.	Have I highlighted my most relevant qualifications?	❏	❏
4.	Have I highlighted my most relevant achievements?	❏	❏
5.	Have I included information I know about the company or the specific position for which I am applying?	❏	❏
6.	Have I highlighted why I want to work for this company or school?	❏	❏
7.	Is my letter neat, clean, and well-presented without being over-designed?	❏	❏
8.	Is my letter error-free?	❏	❏
9.	Is my cover letter short and succinct, preferably no longer than one page?	❏	❏
10.	Do I ask for an interview in the letter?	❏	❏

CHAPTER 14

Sample Cover Letters

What follows are seven more sample cover letters for your review. Look at them closely. Select opening paragraphs, closing paragraphs, formats, and styles that you like, and then model your own cover letters accordingly. You'll find that by using these sample letters for hints, your letter-writing process will be much easier and faster. To see even more samples and get more help with writing your cover letters, see our book *Cover Letter Magic* (JIST Publishing).

Jennifer Tolles

75 Bolivar Terrace, Reading, MA 01867
jennifertee@aol.com ▶ 781-592-3409

April 30, 2005

Dr. Mark B. Cronin, Superintendent
Belmont Public Schools
644 Pleasant Street
Belmont, MA 02478

Dear Dr. Cronin:

Your school district's reputation for *excellence in education*—described so vividly in the recent *New England Journal of Elementary Education*—has prompted me to forward my resume for consideration for fall teaching positions. In addition to strong professional qualifications, you will find that I also have the intangible personal qualities that fit your culture and enable me to truly make a difference to the children I teach.

Please consider my qualifications:

▶ Recent bachelor's degree and Massachusetts teaching certification, grades 1–8.

▶ Year-long teaching experience as an LD Tutor for elementary and high school students—experience adapting classroom materials for individual students, delivering individual and group lessons, working collaboratively with classroom teachers, and promoting a positive learning environment for my students.

▶ Diverse field-teaching experiences (grades 1, 4, 6); successful experience planning and delivering integrated lessons that sparked students' interest, creativity, and desire to learn.

▶ Keen respect for each individual child and appreciation for the differences among us.

▶ A highly effective classroom-management style that creates an environment in which all children can learn.

I will call you within a few days to see when it might be convenient to meet. Thank you for your consideration.

Sincerely,

Jennifer Tolles

enclosure

This letter starts out by quoting a recent article about the school district to which the candidate is applying. Then she relates her experience and personal qualities directly to what she knows about the needs and the culture of that district (submitted by Louise Kursmark).

Casey T. Mulcahey

1984 N. Elms Road
Flushing, MI 48433
810-555-0234
caseymulcahey@verizon.net

May 19, 2005

Mr. Robert Jones, Superintendent
Flushing Community Schools
522 N. McKinley Road
Flushing, MI 48433

Dear Mr. Jones:

I understand the Flushing Community School district will have an opening for a secondary math teacher for the 2005–2006 school year. As you may know, I have been student teaching with Mr. Peterson in his math classes and with Mr. Menenga in a senior government class. I will soon be graduating from UM—Flint and am eager to begin my career. I hope you will take a few minutes to review my credentials in consideration for the open math position.

One of the first things you will notice about me is that I am not a traditional college graduate. In fact, it has been a long road to get to this point. But the trip, with all its detours, has been worth the effort. I love math, and more importantly, I enjoy teaching high schoolers. Because I was a troubled student, I can relate to the frustrations many students experience. I understand what it's like to study and struggle to get good grades. This gives me credibility with my students.

I have received good evaluations from both Mr. Peterson and Mr. Menenga. I believe they would tell you what I lack in classroom experience I more than make up for with enthusiasm and motivation. I hope you will give me a chance to share that enthusiasm with you in an interview. I will contact you to arrange a time. Thank you for your consideration.

Sincerely,

Casey T. Mulcahey

Enclosure

This new teacher tells a compelling story about his unusual journey to the profession—information that is important because it led to his dedication to teaching. Referral names are "dropped" effectively (submitted by Janet Beckstrom).

Jerome L. Crown

7529 Heritage Way, Loveland, OH 45140   jlcrown@zoomtown.com • 513-984-3090

May 15, 2005

Dr. Keith Kelly, Principal
Tristate Alternative Schools
9325 Cooper Road
Cincinnati, OH 45242

Dear Dr. Kelly:

I'd like to be your next science teacher.

As a recent college graduate with extensive coursework in the sciences, coupled with solid work experiences in high-volume/high-intensity environments dealing with the public, I think I have quite a bit to offer.

As I consider teaching the sciences in public education, and as I further consider what qualifications I might bring to the assignment, the following four points will be of interest to you:

- **I have extensive coursework in the sciences**—biology, chemistry, physics, and mathematics. I present a wide range of teaching capabilities to a needy principal.

- **I will be strong in front of the classroom.** I am a natural persuader and influencer, and am people-centered and highly verbal. My sales experiences were very successful and included training my peers, and my time with Juan & Pedro's developed my interpersonal and communication abilities.

- **I'm a whiz at documentation and paperwork.** With Juan & Pedro's, I managed the seating allocations for up to 1,000 guests a night. And with G.H. Troutman, I tracked and managed a 5,000-unit inventory rolling over nearly every month. I am organized and efficient.

- **I'm the right personality type.** I am an Influencer (DISC), and that means I love the give-and-take of discussions, challenging issues, or intriguing questions. I am considerate of others and oftentimes a leader among my peers.

As you can see, the foundation blocks that indicate probable success in the classroom are present: scientific knowledge, platform/persuasion abilities, organizational capabilities, and personality type.

I thank you in advance for the time you have taken reading this letter and my accompanying resume, and I look forward to meeting with you in person to discuss how I can contribute to the excellence of your school district by making a positive impact on the lives of my students.

Sincerely,

Jerome L. Crown

Enclosure: Resume

The four bold sentences highlight qualities that are found in the best teachers. This candidate makes a strong case for himself by showing that he has these qualities (submitted by Bill Murdock).

Neve Lawrence

July 15, 2005

POSITION REFERRAL CLIENT, ASTD DENVER
POSITION #2569

Dear Hiring Professional:

In response to your posted search through the Denver chapter of the American Society for Training and Development (ASTD) for a quality **Trainer and/or Instructional Designer**, I bring more than 10 years of experience in the training field as well as familiarity with the business environment.

I am an extremely high-energy and innovative professional. I consistently produce strong feedback and lots of spirited interaction in my workshops. My employers and clients have been very pleased with my level of expertise and my enthusiasm for what I do.

More than 9,400 people have been through one or more sessions with me during the last 9 years. I have taught "soft-skills" and management topics (delivering more than 25 different topics and often juggling two or three at a time!). Many of these programs were designed and presented by me, or I researched and radically revised outdated materials and exercises to improve knowledge transfer and participation in the class. I love adding value to my job and to my trainees.

My enclosed resume provides further details of my accomplishments, professional history, and topics taught. I look forward to discussing yet another career opportunity with you and your company. I hope we can arrange a meeting so we may discuss your company's needs in greater detail.

Sincerely,

Neve Lawrence

Enclosure

555 Santa Fe Drive, Littleton, Colorado 80161   (303) 555-8238   nlawrence@hotmail.com

This candidate conveys her depth of experience through numbers. The third paragraph is very powerful (submitted by Gail Frank).

MARISOL RODRIGUEZ

585-586-7718   24 Collingsworth Drive, Rochester, NY 14625   marisolz@frontiernet.net

June 30, 2005

Mr. Jefferson Gottrachs
Vice President of Human Resources
Tellecommex Manufacturing, Ltd.
2000 Commerce Drive
Rochester, New York 14623

Dear Mr. Gottrachs:

Capitalizing on more than 15 years of experience managing employee development and training programs for a 3,000-employee division of a global manufacturing firm, I am seeking a new professional opportunity where these capabilities will contribute to your business success. Having researched a number of local firms, I am convinced that the corporate culture of Tellecommex Manufacturing would be a good match for my professional philosophy and the knowledge and expertise I can contribute. Accordingly, I have enclosed for your review a resume that outlines my career.

Some of my key experiences that may be relevant to a position with your firm include

- *Assessing both the technical and soft-skills training needs of employees through consultation with senior management and supervisors.*

- *Building effective internal teams to develop and deliver training. This includes recruiting and evaluating both internal and external candidates and establishing vision and mission for the training team.*

- *Managing capital projects, including developing specifications, selecting vendors, and supervising implementations for computer labs and other training center facilities.*

- *Designing and implementing training curricula, from developing courses to personally delivering training to employees at a variety of levels within the organization.*

- *Counseling individuals—including retirees and employees in both voluntary and involuntary separation programs—to connect them with outside training and educational opportunities.*

In addition, I am technology proficient, with A+ certifications in Windows and Core Service, plus advanced training in all MS Office applications. I am confident that I will be a valuable asset to your employee development department. I would enjoy meeting with you to discuss how I can best address your current and future needs. I will contact you in a week to arrange an appropriate date and time for an initial conversation.

Thank you for your time and consideration. I look forward to speaking with you soon.

Sincerely,

Marisol Rodriguez

Enclosure

This training professional includes five bullet points that really stand out and describe strong, relevant experience (submitted by Arnold Boldt).

Barbara J. Watson

1624 Blanding Lane   *(209) 653-1722 H*
Turlock, CA 95380   *(209) 698-1624 W*

October 20, 2005

Dr. James Webster
Director, Charter Schools
Bay Valley Office of Education
1305 High Street
Oakland, CA 94601-4409

Dear Dr. Webster:

As promised when we met at your teacher fair yesterday, this letter is my formal application for the position of Instructor of Small Business Marketing and Management at Bay Valley Business High School. Your enthusiasm and excitement about your charter high school are contagious! I believe my unique blend of classroom instruction, educational management, and marketing background is perfect for this new position and the curriculum you are offering to your students.

As my resume and application indicate, I have considerable experience in instruction and in building strong working relationships with business and industry. My qualifications are unusually suited for this position in that I have been successful in creating and delivering business-based curriculum to a wide range of students. It would be my great pleasure to bring that experience to your inventive concept of incorporating business skills with academics.

You mentioned in our brief conversation that the marketing component is a very important aspect of making Bay Valley Business High School a success. I have taught marketing and entrepreneurship classes when presenting employability skills for the Community College's Job Skills Institute, a program for high school students. My students have learned to create Web pages, use PowerPoint for their "corporate" presentations, and use Microsoft Office to develop their personal portfolios. My students create their own small corporation or business in which they develop job descriptions, elect officers, generate budgets, and experience the many facets of starting up a small business. The students love this! And so do I.

Teaching is my passion. I am most effective when I am in the classroom. It brings me great joy to participate as my students connect learning with their future workplace skills. I have heard wonderful things about the quality of the staff and students at Bay Valley Business High School and that your future looks incredibly promising. Your vision of a high school that opens doors for students to achieve both academically and in the business world is innovative and challenging. I believe my passion for education, coupled with my unique background, is a perfect fit with your vision.

I look forward to hearing from your office and the opportunity to meet with the interview committee. Thank you for your consideration.

Sincerely,

Barbara J. Watson

Enclosures: Bay Valley Office of Education application; resume; two letters of reference

This letter was written to follow up after a meeting at a teacher fair. It expands on the points made during that meeting (submitted by Sally Cofer).

SALLY T. HOLMES

March 25, 2005

Adam Bannister, Academic Dean
Connecticut Art Academy
750 Whaley Avenue
New Haven, CT 06510

Dear Dean Bannister:

The opportunity to continue my affiliation with the Connecticut Art Academy as an Assistant Professor is exciting. My experience, expertise, and professional focus are a strong match for the demands of the position, the needs of our students, and the goals of the institution.

Having taught painting and other studio art classes as an adjunct professor at the Academy for nearly 10 years, I have proven my teaching abilities and demonstrated a talent for helping students bring their own unique visions and perceptions to their art. Because I find it exciting and satisfying to teach creative thinking and artistic technique and then see developing artists apply that knowledge to their work, I am committed to continuing my career as a professional art educator.

Of course, it is essential that art educators be artists as well. As a professional painter, I have continued to create and exhibit my work at local and regional galleries and shows, and I have been a driving force behind Nutmeg Arts Showplace, a local gallery that gives exhibition opportunities to widely diverse visual artists.

Enclosed, as requested, are my resume, statement of artistic philosophy, statement of teaching philosophy, list of potential courses, and list of references. I would enjoy meeting with you and members of the selection committee to share my ideas and excitement for this new teaching challenge. I will contact you in two weeks to set up an appointment.

Sincerely,

Sally T. Holmes

enclosures: application materials
                10 slides of artistic production

Even for internal promotions, cover letters are important. This professor was seeking a full-time position at the university where she had been an adjunct faculty member for 10 years (submitted by Louise Kursmark).

Appendix

Internet Career Resources

With the emergence of the Internet as a job search tool has come a huge collection of online resources to help with your search. Here are some of our favorites.

Job Search Sites

You'll find thousands and thousands of current professional employment opportunities on these sites.

Education Career Sites

Academic360.com: Jobs in Higher Education	www.academic360.com
CareerAge (Education)	www.careerage.com/academics/
Chronicle of Higher Education	http://chronicle.com/jobs
Digital Education Network	www.jobs.edunet.com
Education Jobs	www.educationjobs.com
Education Week: Job Search	www.agentk-12.org/
Education World Employment Center	www.education-world.com/jobs
IQ Education	www.iqmedia.co.uk
K–12 Jobs	http://K-12jobs.com
Teacher Jobs	www.teacherjobs.com
Teaching Jobs	www.teachingjobs.com
Teaching Jobs Overseas	www.joyjobs.com
University Job Bank	www.ujobbank.com

GENERAL SITES

6FigureJobs	www.6figurejobs.com
All Star Jobs	www.411jobs.net
America's CareerInfoNet	www.acinet.org/acinet
America's Job Bank	www.ajb.dni.us
BestJobsUSA	www.bestjobsusa.com/index-jsk-ns.asp
BlackWorld Careers	www.blackworld.com/careers.htm
Canada WorkInfo Net	www.workinfonet.ca
CareerBuilder	www.careerbuilder.com
Career.com	www.career.com
CareerExchange.com	www.careerexchange.com
Career Exposure	www.careerexposure.com
Careermag.com	www.careermag.com
CareerShop	www.careershop.com
CareerSite.com	www.careersite.com
Contract Employment Weekly	www.ceweekly.com
Digital City (jobs by location)	home.digitalcity.com
EmploymentGuide.com	www.employmentguide.com
Excite	http://careers.excite.com
FlipDog	www.flipdog.com
Futurestep	www.futurestep.com
GETAJOB!	www.getajob.com
Help Wanted	www.helpwanted.com
HotJobs.com	www.hotjobs.com
It's Your Job Now	www.ItsYourJobNow.com
JobBankUSA	www.jobbankusa.com
JobHuntersBible.com	www.jobhuntersbible.com
Job-Hunt.org	www.job-hunt.org
JOBNET.com	www.jobnet.com/philly
JobsOnline	www.jobsonline.com
JobWeb	www.jobweb.com
Kiwi Careers (New Zealand)	www.careers.co.nz
LatPro	www.latpro.com
Monster.com	www.monster.com

NationJob Network	www.nationjob.com
NCOA MaturityWorks	www.maturityworks.org
Net Temps	www.net-temps.com
Online-Jobs.Com	www.online-jobs.com
The Riley Guide	www.rileyguide.com
Saludos Hispanos	www.saludos.com
SIRC Internet Resume Center	www.inpursuit.com/sirc
TrueCareers	www.careercity.com
Wages.com	www.wages.com.au
WorkTree	www.worktree.com

ENTRY-LEVEL CAREERS

CampusCareerCenter.com	www.campuscareercenter.com
College Grad Job Hunter	www.collegegrad.com
College Job Board	www.collegejobboard.com/?1100
MonsterTRAK	www.jobtrak.com

GOVERNMENT AND MILITARY CAREERS

Federal Jobs Net	www.federaljobs.net
FedWorld	www.fedworld.gov
FRS Federal Jobs Central	www.fedjobs.com
GetaGovJob.com	www.getagovjob.com
GovExec.com	www.govexec.com
HRS Federal Job Search	www.hrsjobs.com
Military Career Guide Online	www.militarycareers.com
PLANETGOV	www.planetgov.com
USAJOBS (United States Office of Personnel Management)	www.usajobs.opm.gov

Company Information

Outstanding resources for researching specific companies.

555-1212.com	www.555-1212.com
Brint.com	www.brint.com
EDGAR Online	www.edgar-online.com

Experience	www.experiencenetwork.com
Fortune Magazine	www.fortune.com
Hoover's Business Profiles	www.hoovers.com
infoUSA (small business information)	www.infousa.com
Intellifact.com	www.igiweb.com/intellifact/
OneSource CorpTech	www.corptech.com
SuperPages.com	www.bigbook.com
U.S. Chamber of Commerce	www.uschamber.com/
Vault Company Research	www.vault.com/companies/ searchcompanies.jsp
Wetfeet.com Company Research	www.wetfeet.com/asp/ companyresource_home.asp

Dictionaries and Glossaries

Outstanding information on keywords and acronyms.

Acronym Finder	www.acronymfinder.com
AltaVista's Babelfish Foreign-Language Translation Service	http://babelfish.altavista.com/
Comprehensive Glossaries of Education Terms	www.glossarist.com/glossaries/ education/
ComputerUser High-Tech Dictionary	www.computeruser.com/ resources/dictionary/dictionary.html
Dave's Truly Canadian Dictionary of Canadian Spelling	www.luther.ca/~dave7cnv/ cdnspelling/cdnspelling.html
Dictionary of Education Terms	www.ascd.org/cms/ index.cfm?TheViewID=1112
Dictionary of Special Education Terms	www.parentpals.com/2.0dictionary/ dictnewsindex.html
Glossary of Education Terms	www.schoolwisepress.com/smart/ dict/dict.html
Merriam-Webster Collegiate Dictionary & Thesaurus	www.m-w.com/home.htm
Refdesk	www.refdesk.com

Technology Terms Dictionary	www.computeruser.com/
TechWeb TechEncyclopedia	www.techweb.com/encyclopedia/
Verizon Glossary of Telecom Terms	www22.verizon.com/wholesale/ glossary/0,2624,0_9,00.html
The Virtual Reference Desk-Dictionaries	http://thorplus.lib.purdue.edu/ rguides/guides.html
Washington Post Business Glossary	www.washingtonpost.com/ wp-srv/business/longterm/ glossary/index.htm
Webopedia: Online Dictionary for Computer and Internet Terms	www.webopedia.com
Whatis?com Technology Terms	whatis.techtarget.com
Wordsmyth: The Educational Dictionary/Thesaurus	www.wordsmyth.net

Interviewing Tips and Techniques

Expert guidance to sharpen and strengthen your interviewing skills.

About.com Interviewing	www.jobsearch.about.com/business/ jobsearch/msubinterv.htm
Bradley CVs Introduction to Job Interviews	www.bradleycvs.demon.co.uk/ interview/index.htm
Dress for Success	www.dressforsuccess.org
Job-Interview.net	www.job-interview.net
Northeastern University Career Services	www.dac.neu.edu/coop.careerservices/ interview.html

Salary and Compensation Information

Learn from the experts to strengthen your negotiating skills and increase your salary.

Abbott, Langer & Associates	www.abbott-langer.com
America's Career InfoNet	www.acinet.org/acinet/select_ occupation.asp?stfips=&next=occ_rep
Bureau of Labor Statistics	www.bls.gov/bls/wages.htm
CareerJournal (the *Wall Street Journal*)	www.careerjournal.com/salaries/ index.html
Clayton Wallis Co.	www.claytonwallis.com
Consultant Salaries	www.cob.ohio-state.edu/~fin/jobs/ mco/salary.htm

Economic Research Institute	www.erieri.com
JobStar	www.jobstar.org/tools/salary/index.htm
Monster.com Salary Info	salary.monster.com/
Salary and Crime Calculator	www.homefair.com/homefair/cmr/salcalc.html
Teacher Salary Survey	www.aft.org/salary/
Teacher Salary Survey	www.payscale.com/salary-survey/vid-8196/fid-6886
Teacher Salary Surveys	http://resource.educationamerica.net/salaries.html
Wageweb	www.wageweb.com
WorldatWork (The Professional Association for Compensation, Benefits, and Total Rewards)	www.worldatwork.org

INDEX OF CONTRIBUTORS

The sample resumes and cover letters in chapters 4 through 14 were written by professional resume and cover letter writers. If you need help with your resume and job search correspondence, you can use the following list to locate a career professional who can help.

You will notice that most of the writers have one or more credentials listed after their names. In fact, some have half a dozen or more! The careers industry offers extensive opportunities for ongoing training, and most career professionals take advantage of these opportunities to build their skills and keep their knowledge current. If you are curious about what any one of these credentials means, we suggest that you contact the resume writer directly. He or she will be glad to discuss certifications and other qualifications as well as information about services that can help you in your career transition.

Lynn P. Andenoro, CPRW, JCTC
President, My Career Resource
1214 Fenway
Salt Lake City, UT 84102
Phone: (801) 883-2011
Fax: (801) 582-8862
E-mail: Lynn@MyCareerResource.com
www.MyCareerResource.com

Bernice Antifonario, M.A.
President, Antion Associates, Inc.
885 Main St. #10A
Tewksbury, MA 01876
Phone: (978) 858-0637
Fax: (978) 851-4528
E-mail: Antion1@aol.com
www.antion-associates.com

Janet L. Beckstrom, CPRW
President, Word Crafter
1717 Montclair Ave.
Flint, MI 48503
Toll-free: (800) 351-9818
Fax: (810) 232-9257
E-mail: wordcrafter@voyager.net

Vivian Belen, NCRW, CPRW, JCTC

Arnold G. Boldt, CPRW, JCTC
Arnold-Smith Associates
625 Panorama Trail, Building One, Ste. 120
Rochester, NY 14625
Phone: (585) 383-0350
Fax: (585) 387-0516
E-mail: Arnie@ResumeSOS.com
www.ResumeSOS.com

Carolyn Braden, CPRW
Braden Resume Solutions
108 La Plaza Dr.
Hendersonville, TN 37075
Phone: (615) 822-3317
Fax: (615) 826-9611
E-mail: bradenresume@comcast.net

Martin P. Buckland, MRW, CPRW, CJSS, JCTC, CEIP
Elite Resumes
1428 Stationmaster Lane
Oakville, ON L6M 3A7
Canada
Phone: (905) 825-0490
Fax: (905) 825-2966
E-mail: martin@aneliteresume.com
www.aneliteresume.com

LeRachel H. Buffkins, CPRW, GCDF, FJST, CFRWC
Writing for You, Inc.
14518 Cambridge Circle
Laurel, MD 20707
Phone: (301) 604-2048
Fax: (301) 604-2100
E-mail: LBuffkins@writingforyouinc.com
www.writingforyouinc.com

Diane Burns, CPRW, CCMC, CCM, CEIP, JCTC
Career Marketing Techniques
Phone: 011-49 (0) 9335-997647
E-mail: diane@polishedresumes.com
www.polishedresumes.com

Nita Busby, CPRW, CAC, JCTC
Owner/General Manager, Resumes, Etc.
438 E. Katella, Ste. G
Orange, CA 92867
Phone: (714) 633-2783
Fax: (714) 633-2745
E-mail: resumes100@aol.com
www.resumesetc.net

Patricia S. Cash, CPRW
President, Resumes For Results
P.O. Box 2806
Prescott, AZ 86302
Phone: (520) 778-1578
Fax: (520) 771-1229
E-mail: pscash@goodnet.com

Sally Shepherd Cofer, CPRW
Career Directions
2401 E. Orangeburg Ave., Ste. 675
Modesto, CA 95355
Phone and fax: (209) 575-4924
E-mail: sallys_c@earthlink.net
www.thecareerlighthouse.com

Kristin Coleman
Career Services
44 Hillcrest Dr.
Poughkeepsie, NY 12603
Phone: (845) 452-8274
Fax: (845) 452-7789
E-mail: kristincoleman44@yahoo.com

Darlene M. Dassy, CRW
Dynamic Resume Solutions
602 Monroe Dr.
Harleysville, PA 19438
Phone and fax: (215) 368-2316
E-mail: darlene@attractiveresumes.com
www.attractiveresumes.com

Laura A. DeCarlo, CCM, CERW, JCTC, CCMC, CECC
President, A Competitive Edge Career Service, LLC
1665 Clover Circle
Melbourne, FL 32935
Toll-free: (800) 715-3442
Fax: (321) 752-7513
E-mail: getanedge@aol.com
www.acompetitiveedge.com

Jewel Bracy DeMaio, CPRW, CEIP
Principal, A Perfect Resume.com
Saratoga, PA
Toll-free: (800) 227-5131
Fax: (610) 327-8014
E-mail: mail@aperfectresume.com
www.aperfectresume.com

Deborah Wile Dib, CCM, CCMC, NCRW, CPRW, CEIP, JCTC
REACH Certified Personal Branding Strategist
President, Advantage Resumes of New York
President, Executive Power Coach
77 Buffalo Ave.
Medford, NY 11763
Phone: (631) 475-8513
Fax: (501) 421-7790
E-mail: deborah.dib@advantageresumes.com
www.advantageresumes.com
www.executivepowercoach.com

Kirsten Dixson, JCTC, CPRW, CEIP
President, New Leaf Career Solutions
P.O. Box 963
Exeter, NH 03833
Phone: (866) 639-5323
E-mail: kirsten@newleafcareer.com
www.newleafcareer.com

Marta L. Driesslein, CPRW, CCM, CECC
Senior Consultant, R.L. Stevens & Associates, Inc.
P.O. Box 5350
Sevierville, TN 37864-5358
Phone: (865) 429-4191
E-mail: mdriesslein@rlstevens.com

Deloris J. Duff, CPRW, IJCTC, CFRWC
President, Document Developers
5030 Guion Rd.
Indianapolis, IN 46254
Phone: (317) 290-0099
Toll-free fax: (877) 463-2034
E-mail: deesdocs@earthlink.net

Michelle Dumas, NCRW, CPRW, CCM
Executive Director, Distinctive Documents
Somersworth, NH 03878
Toll-free: (800) 644-9694
Fax: (603) 947-2954
E-mail: resumes@distinctiveweb.com
www.distinctiveweb.com

George Dutch, CMF, CCM, JCTC
JOBJOY
750–130 Slater St.
Ottawa, ON K1P 6E2
Canada
Phone: (613) 563-0584
Toll-free: (800) 798-2696
Fax: (613) 594-8705
E-mail: jobjoy@sympatico.ca
www.georgedutch.com

Debbie Ellis, MRW, CPRW
Phoenix Career Group
Toll-free: (800) 876-5506
Fax: (859) 236-3900
E-mail: debbie@phoenixcareergroup.com
www.phoenixcareergroup.com

Salome A. Farraro, CPRW
President, Careers TOO
3123 Moyer Rd.
Mount Morris, NY 14510
Phone: (585) 658-2480
Fax: (585) 658-2480
E-mail: sfarraro@careers-too.com
www.careers-too.com

Donna Farrise, JCTC
Dynamic Resumes of Long Island, Inc.
300 Motor Pkwy., Ste. 200
Hauppauge, NY 11788
Phone: (631) 951-4120
Fax: (631) 952-1817
E-mail: donna@dynamicresumes.com
www.dynamicresumes.com

Cindy M. Fass
President, Comprehensive Resume Services
5300 Spring Mountain Rd., 212-D
Las Vegas, NV 89146
Phone: (702) 222-9411
Fax: (702) 222-9411
E-mail: crsinvegas@aol.com

Dayna Feist, CPRW, CEIP, JCTC
Gatehouse Business Services
265 Charlotte St.
Asheville, NC 28801
Phone: (828) 254-7893
Fax: (828) 254-7894
E-mail: gatehouse@aol.com
www.bestjobever.com

Joyce L. Fortier, MBA, CPRW, JCTC, CCM, CCMC
President, Create Your Career
23871 W. Lebost
Novi, MI 48375
Phone: (248) 478-5662
Fax: (248) 426-9974
E-mail: careerist@aol.com
www.careerist.com

Gail Frank, NCRW, CPRW, JCTC, CEIP, MA
Frankly Speaking: Resumes That Work!
10409 Greendale Dr.
Tampa, FL 33626
Phone: (813) 926-1353
Fax: (813) 926-1092
E-mail: gailfrank@post.harvard.edu
www.callfranklyspeaking.com

Roberta Gamza, JCTC, JST, CEIP
Career Ink
Louisville, CO 80027
Phone and fax: (303) 955-3065
E-mail: roberta@careerink.com
www.careerink.com

Louise Garver, JCTC, MCDP, CEIP, CMP
Career Directions, LLC
115 Elm St., Ste. 203
Enfield, CT 06082
Phone: (860) 623-9476
Fax: (860) 623-9473
E-mail: thecareerpro@aol.com
www.resumeimpact.com

Susan Guarneri, NCC, NCCC, CPRW, CCMC, CEIP, MCC
President, Guarneri Associates
6670 Crystal Lake Rd.
Three Lakes, WI 54562
Phone: (866) 881-4055
Fax: (715) 355-1936
E-mail: Resumagic@aol.com
www.resume-magic.com

Michele Haffner, CPRW, JCTC
Advanced Resume Services
1314 W. Paradise Ct.
Glendale, WI 53209
Phone: (414) 247-1677
Fax: (414) 247-1808
E-mail: michele@resumeservices.com
www.resumeservices.com

Beate Hait, CPRW, NCRW
President, Resumes Plus
80 Wingate Rd.
Holliston, MA 01746
Phone: (508) 429-1813
Fax: (508) 429-4299
E-mail: bea@resumesplus.net
www.resumesplus.net

Elona Harkins, MOS
Absolute Jobsearch Services
P.O. Box 2776
Westfield, NJ 07091
Phone: (908) 233-8910
Fax: (908) 301-1234
E-mail: ajs@westfieldnj.com
www.absolutejobsearch.com

Beverly Harvey, CPRW, JCTC, CCM, CCMC
Beverly Harvey Resume and Career Services
P.O. Box 750
Pierson, FL 32180
Phone: (386) 749-3111
Toll-free: (888) 775-0916
Fax: (386) 749-4881
E-mail: beverly@harveycareers.com
www.harveycareers.com

Loretta Heck
President, All Word Services
924 E. Old Willow Rd. #102
Prospect Heights, IL 60070
Phone: (847) 215-7517
Fax: (847) 215-7520
E-mail: siegfried@ameritech.net

Peter Hill, CPRW
Distinctive Resumes
1226 Alexander St. #1205
Honolulu, HI 96826
Phone: (808) 306-3920
E-mail: distinctiveresumes@yahoo.com
www.peterhill.biz

Gayle Howard, CERW, CCM, CPRW, CRW
Top Margin Resumes Online
P.O. Box 74
Chirnside Park 3116
Melbourne, VIC
Australia
Phone: 613 9726 6694
Fax: 613 9726 5316
E-mail: getinterviews@topmargin.com
www.topmargin.com

Deborah S. James, CPRW, CCMC
President, Leading Edge Resume & Career Services
1010 Schreier Rd.
Toledo, OH 43460
Phone: (419) 666-4518
Toll-free: (800) 815-8780
Fax: (419) 791-3567
E-mail: djames@leadingedgeresumes.com
www.leadingedgeresumes.com

Marcy Johnson, NCRW, CPRW, CEIP
President, First Impression Resume & Job Readiness
11805 U.S. Hwy. 69
Story City, IA 50248
Toll-free: (877) 215-6009
Fax: (515) 733-9296
E-mail: firstimpression@iowatelecom.net
www.resume-job-readiness.com

Nancy Karvonen, CPRW, CEIP, IJCTC
Executive Director, A Better Word & Resume
771 Adare Way
Galt, CA 95632
Phone: (209) 744-8203
Fax: (209) 745-7114
E-mail: careers@aresumecoach.com
www.aresumecoach.com

Fran Kelley
President, The Resume Works
71 Highwood Ave.
Waldwick, NJ 07463
Phone: (201) 670-9643
E-mail: TwoFreeSpirits@worldnet.att.net
www.careermuse.com

Myriam-Rose Kohn, CPRW, CEIP, JCTC, CCM, CCMC
JEDA Enterprises
27201 Tourney Rd., Ste. 201
Valencia, CA 91355
Phone: (661) 253-0801
Fax: (661) 253-0744
E-mail: myriam-rose@jedaenterprises.com
www.jedaenterprises.com

Sherry Jean Kolbe, CPRW
President, Resume Consultants
212 Washington Ave.
Towson, MD 21204
Phone: (410) 823-9568
Fax: (410) 494-8434
E-mail: resumeconsult@hotmail.com

Rhoda Kopy, BS, CPRW, JCTC, CEIP
President, A HIRE IMAGE®
26 Main St., Ste. E
Toms River, NJ 08753
Phone: (732) 505-9515
Fax: (732) 505-3125
E-mail: rkopy@earthlink.net
www.jobwinningresumes.com

Louise Kursmark, MRW, CPRW, JCTC, CEIP, CCM
Executive Master Team—Career Masters Institute
President, Best Impression Career Services, Inc.
9847 Catalpa Woods Ct.
Cincinnati, OH 45242
Phone: (513) 792-0030
Toll-free fax: (877) 791-7127
E-mail: LK@yourbestimpression.com
www.yourbestimpression.com

Rolande L. LaPointe, CPC, CIPC, CPRW, IJCTC, CCM, CSS, CRW
President, RO-LAN Associates, Inc.
725 Sabattus St.
Lewiston, ME 04240
Phone: (207) 784-1010
Fax: (207) 782-3446
E-mail: RLapointe@aol.com

Diana C. LeGere
Executive Director, Writing Flair
P.O. Box 634
Colonial Heights, VA 23834
Phone: (804) 720-7236
E-mail: DianaLeGere@aol.com
www.dianalegere.com

Ross Macpherson, MA, CPRW, JCTC, CEIP
President, Career Quest
131 Kirby Crescent
Whitby, ON L1N 7C7
Canada
Phone: (905) 438-8548
Toll Free: (877) 426-8548
Fax: (905) 438-4096
E-mail: ross@yourcareerquest.com
www.yourcareerquest.com

Peter S. Marx, JCTC
3208 Wallace Ave.
Tampa, FL 35611
Phone and fax: (813) 832-5133
E-mail: marxps@aol.com

Linda Matias, CEIP, JCTC
Executive Director, CareerStrides
37 E. Hill Dr.
Smithtown, NY 11787
Phone: (631) 382-2425
Fax: (631) 382-2425
E-mail: linda@careerstrides.com
www.careerstrides.com

Jan Melnik, CPRW, CCM, MRW
President, Absolute Advantage
P.O. Box 718
Durham, CT 06422
Phone: (860) 349-0256
Fax: (860) 349-1343
E-mail: CompSPJan@aol.com
www.janmelnik.com

Nicole Miller, CCM, CRW, CECC, IJCTC
Mil-Roy Consultants
1729 Hunter's Run Dr.
Orleans, ON K1C 6W2
Canada
Phone: (613) 834-4031
E-mail: resumesbymilroy@hotmail.com

Meg Montford, PCCC, CMF, CCM
President, Abilities Enhanced
P.O. Box 9667
Kansas City, MO 64134
Phone: (816) 767-1196
E-mail: meg@abilitiesenhanced.com
www.abilitiesenhanced.com

Doug Morrison, CPRW
President, Career Power
2915 Providence Rd. #250-B
Charlotte, NC 28211
Phone: (704) 365-0773
Fax: (704) 365-3411
E-mail: dmpwresume@aol.com
www.careerpowerresume.com

Eva Mullen, CPRW
A+ Resumes
3000 Pearl St., Ste. 111
Boulder, CO 80301
Phone and fax: (303) 444-3438
E-mail: eva@aplusres.com
www.aplusres.com

Bill Murdock, CPRW
The Employment Coach
7770 Meadow Rd., #109
Dallas, TX 75236
Phone: (214) 750-4781
E-mail: bmurdock@swbell.net

Helen Oliff, CPRW, CFRWC, ECI
Principal, TURNING POINT
2307 Freetown Ct., #12C
Reston, VA 20191
Phone: (703) 716-0077
Fax: (703) 995-0706
E-mail: helen@turningpointnow.com
www.turningpointnow.com

Debra O'Reilly, CPRW, CEIP, IJCTC, CFRWC
A First Impression Resume
Service/ResumeWriter.com
16 Terryville Ave.
Bristol, CT 06010
Phone: (860) 583-7500
Fax: (860) 585-9611
E-mail: debra@resumewriter.com
www.resumewriter.com

Don Orlando, MBA, CPRW, JCTC, CCM, CCMC
The McLean Group
640 S. McDonough
Montgomery, AL 36104
Phone: (334) 264-2020
Fax: (334) 264-9227
E-mail: yourcareercoach@aol.com

Andrea Peak
Envision Resume Services
P.O. Box 7523
Louisville, KY 40257
Toll-free phone and fax: (888) 844-4348
E-mail: amy@envision-resumes.com or
info@envision-resumes.com

Teresa L. Pearson, CPRW, JCTC, FJST, Master in
Human Relations
President, Pearson's Resume Output
Meriden, KS
Fax: (503) 905-1495
E-mail: pearsonresume@earthlink.net

Barbara Poole, CPRW, CRW, CCMC
Hire Imaging
1812 Red Fox Rd.
St. Cloud, MN 56301
Phone: (320) 253-0975
Fax: (320) 253-1790
E-mail: barb@hireimaging.com
www.hireimaging.com

Ross Primack, CPRW, CEIP, GCDF
Connecticut Labor Department
200 Folly Brook Blvd.
Wethersfield, CT 06109
Phone: (860) 263-6041
E-mail: rossprimackcprw@hotmail.com

Anita Radosevich, CPRW, JCTC, CFRW, CEIP
President, Career Ladders
9401 E. Stockton Blvd., Ste. 100B
Elk Grove, CA 95624
E-mail: anita@abcresumes.com
www.federalresumewriter.com

Jane Roqueplot, CPBA, CWDP
Jane D. Rae, Vocational Consultant
JaneCo's Sensible Solutions
194 N. Oakland Ave.
Sharon, PA 16146
Phone: (724) 342-0100
Fax: (724) 346-5263
E-mail: jane@janecos.com
www.janecos.com

Michelle Mastruserio Reitz, CPRW
Printed Pages
3985 Race Rd., Ste. 14
Cincinnati, OH 45211
Phone: (513) 598-9100
Fax: (513) 598-9220
E-mail: michelle@printedpages.com
www.printedpages.com

Teena Rose, CPRW, CEIP, CCM
President, Resume to Referral
1824 Rebert Pike
Springfield, OH 45506
Phone: (937) 325-2149
E-mail: admin@resumetoreferral.com
www.resumebycprw.com

Carol J. Rossi, CPRW
Computerized Documents
4 Baywood Blvd.
Brick, NJ 08723
Phone and fax: (732) 477-5172
E-mail: info@powerfulresumes.com

Jennifer Rushton, CRW
Keraijen—Certified Resume Writer
Level 14, 309 Kent St.
Sydney, NSW 2000
Australia
Phone: (02) 9994 8050
E-mail: info@keraijen.com.au
www.keraijen.com.au

Barbara Safani, MA, CPRW
Career Solvers
980 Madison Ave.
New York, NY 10021
Phone: (212) 579-7230
Toll-free: (866) 333-1800
E-mail: info@careersolvers.com
www.careersolvers.com

Deborah Schuster, CPRW
President, The Lettersmith
P.O. Box 202
Newport, MI 48166
Phone: (734) 586-3335
Fax: (734) 586-2766
E-mail: lettersmith@foxberry.net
www.thelettersmith.com

Janice M. Shepherd, CPRW, JCTC, CEIP
Write On Career Keys
Bellingham, WA 98226
Phone: (360) 738-7958
Fax: (360) 738-1189
E-mail: janice@writeoncareerkeys.com
www.writeoncareerkeys.com

Igor Shpudejko, B.S.I.E., MBA, CPRW, JCTC
Career Focus
23 Parsons Ct.
Mahwah, NJ 07430
Phone: (201) 825-2865
Fax: (201) 825-7711
E-mail: Ishpudejko@aol.com

Kelley Smith, CPRW
President, Advantage Resume Services
P.O. Box 391
Sugar Land, TX 77487
Phone: (281) 494-3330
Fax: (281) 494-0173
E-mail: info@100kresumes.com
www.100kresumes.com

Lisa LeVerrier Stein, MA, MS, CPRW, JCTC
President, Competitive Advantage Resumes & Career Coaching
433 Plaza Real, Ste. 275
Boca Raton, FL 33432
Phone: (954) 571-7236
Toll-free: (800) 750-5690
Fax: (954) 481-2695
Toll-free fax: (800) 656-2712
E-mail: gethired@earthlink.net
www.jobcoaching.com or
www.lawyerresumes.com

Paula Stenberg
Managing Director
CV Style, Ltd.
Auckland Central, New Zealand
Phone: 0064 9 630 6230
E-mail: paula@cvstyle.co.nz
www.cvstyle.com and www.cvstyle.co.nz

Billie Ruth Sucher, MS, CTMS, CTSB
Billie Sucher & Associates
7177 Hickman Rd., Ste. 10
Urbandale, IA 50322
Phone: (515) 276-0061
Fax: (515) 334-8076
E-mail: betwnjobs@aol.com

Linda Wunner, CPRW, IJCTC, CEIP, CCMC
President, A+ Career & Resume Design
E-mail: linda@successfulresumes.com
www.successfulresumes.com

INDEX

V–Z